MW00608885

THE LAWYER'S GUIDE TO
Marketing
ON THE
Internet

Gregory H. Siskind

Deborah McMurray

Richard P. Klau

LAWPRACTICEMANAGEMENTSECTION

FINANCE TECHNOLOGY MANAGEMENT MARKETING

Defending Liberty
Pursuing Justice

Commitment to Quality: The Law Practice Management Section is committed to quality in our publications. Our authors are experienced practitioners in their fields. Prior to publication, the contents of all our books are rigorously reviewed by experts to ensure the highest quality product and presentation. Because we are committed to serving our readers' needs, we welcome your feedback on how we can improve future editions of this book. We invite you to fill out and return the comment card at the back of this book.

Screen shots copyright protected by their respective owners. The following law firms, companies, and individuals provided reprint permission for screen shots of their Web sites in this book: Akin Gump; Alschuler; Arent Fox; Baker Daniels; Ballard Spahr Andrews & Ingersoll; Bartlit Beck; Blue Flag; Bracewell & Paterson; Burnet, Duckworth & Palmer; D'Ancona & Plfaum; Dechert; Duane Morris; EFax; Faegre & Benson; Fredrikson & Byron; Godwin Gruber; Goulston Storrs; Hale & Dorr; Haynes and Boone; Heller Ehrman; Holland and Hart; Hughes & Luce; Jackson Lewis; King & Spalding; Kirkland Ellis; LeBoeuf, Lamb, Greene & McRae; Linklaters; LivePerson; Mayer Brown Rowe & Maw; McDonough, Holland & Allen; Miller Nash; Minter Ellison; Morrison & Foerster; NetIQ Corporation; Orrick; Patterson Belknap; PlaceWare; Pillsbury Winthrop; Saul Ewing; Schulte Roth & Zabel; Sebaly Shillito & Dyer; Siskind, Susser, Haas & Devine; SiteMeter; Sonnenschein Nath & Rosenthal: Sullivan & Cromwell; Venable; Vinson & Elkins; Wilson Sonsini; Winston & Strawn; and Womble Carlyle. All rights reserved.

Sample Web Hosting Proposal and Agreement adapted and reprinted with permission from AZTech Solutions.

The 2002 IMA Awards reprinted with permission from the Internet Marketing Attorney.

Cover design by Jim Colao.

Nothing contained in this book is to be considered as the rendering of legal advice for specific cases, and readers are responsible for obtaining such advice from their own legal counsel. This book and any forms and agreements herein are intended for educational and informational purposes only.

The products and services mentioned in this publication are under or may be under trademark or service mark protection. Product and service names and terms are used throughout only in an editorial fashion, to the benefit of the product manufacturer or service provider, with no intention of infringement. Use of a product or service name or term in this publication should not be regarded as affecting the validity of any trademark or service mark.

The Law Practice Management Section, American Bar Association, offers an educational program for lawyers in practice. Books and other materials are published in furtherance of that program. Authors and editors of publications may express their own legal interpretations and opinions, which are not necessarily those of either the American Bar Association or the Law Practice Management Section unless adopted pursuant to the bylaws of the Association. The opinions expressed do not reflect in any way a position of the Section or the American Bar Association.

© 2002 American Bar Association. All rights reserved.
Printed in the United States of America.

Library of Congress Cataloging-in-Publication Data
Lawyer's Guide to Marketing on the Internet, Second Edition. Gregory H. Siskind, Deborah McMurray, Richard Klau: Library of Congress Cataloging-in-Publication Data is on file.

ISBN 1-59031-118-3

06 05 04 03 02   5 4 3 2 1

Discounts are available for books ordered in bulk. Special consideration is given to state bars, CLE programs, and other bar-related organizations. Inquire at Book Publishing, American Bar Association, 750 N. Lake Shore Drive, Chicago, Illinois 60611.

Contents

Acknowledgments

We have written this book with the direct and indirect support of numerous friends and colleagues.

To our families—Greg's wife, Audrey, and their girls, Eden, Lily and Noa; Rick's wife Robin and their boys, Ricky and Robby; and Deborah's husband, David Guedry, and her Lhasa Apsos, Brio and Fresco. They help us stay focused on life's important things and help us maintain our senses of humor.

To Beverly Loder, Tim Johnson, and Neal Cox of the ABA's Law Practice Management Section Publishing staff. It has been a pleasure to work with them, and their professionalism is consistently outstanding.

To our many industry colleagues who served as resources and sources of inspiration, and who provided many of the examples and exhibits we have included in this book—Burkey Belser, Greenfield/Belser Ltd; Micah Buchdahl, HTMLawyers, Inc.; Tim Corcoran and Chris Fritsch, Martindale-Hubbell; Sara Crocker, Wolf Greenfield; Barbara Finley, Arter & Hadden LLP; Kristen Gunlock, Lewis and Roca LLP; David Hambourger, Winston & Strawn; Erik Heels, Law Offices of Erik J. Heels; William Hornsby, the ABA's resident authority on legal marketing/advertising and ethics; Chad King, Hughes & Luce LLP; Nancy Roberts Linder, Nancy Roberts Linder Consulting; Roberta Montafia, 2002 LMA President and CMO, Baker & McKenzie; Drew Naukam, AzTech Solutions; Pam M. Ringquist, Locke Reynolds; Ken Vernon, Halogen Consulting; and Nicole Wyman, Fulbright & Jaworski LLP. Thanks, too, to our colleagues at Siskind, Susser, Haas & Devine and Interface Software for their friendship and support throughout this project.

To the trusted volunteer book-draft reviewers, including Susan Ross, Jim Keane, and Dan Coolidge, who improved our book with their challenging and thoughtful suggestions.

Thanks to the Law Practice Management Section Publishing Board, who had the faith to commission a twenty-something Greg Siskind for the first edition of this book in 1996. And thanks to them again for believing that this second edition could be even more relevant and successful.

And finally, to the three authors of this book—we learned a great deal from each other and we know that this Internet marketing journey is just beginning.

Greg Siskind
Deborah McMurray
Rick Klau

About the Authors

Gregory H. Siskind is a partner at Siskind, Susser, Haas & Devine, an immigration law firm with a number of offices around the world. He practices in the firm's Memphis, Tennessee, headquarters. He is the publisher of one of the nation's largest immigration law publications, *Siskind's Immigration Bulletin*, and is also the author of several books including the *J-1 Visa Guidebook*, published by Lexis-Nexis.

When his home page debuted in 1994, Greg was one of the first lawyers to establish a World Wide Web site for his law firm. *Siskind's Immigration Bulletin* was one of the first online legal publications and now is electronically distributed to more than 30,000 subscribers every week. The firm's Internet success story has earned Greg numerous awards, and he has been profiled in a number of publications and media outlets, including the *Wall Street Journal, USA Today, Law Practice Management, American Lawyer, Lawyer's Weekly,* and NPR's *All Things Considered.*

Greg earned his Bachelor's Degree from Vanderbilt University and his law degree from the University of Chicago. He has been an active member of the American Bar Association's Law Practice Management Section and is the Chair of its Publishing Board. He has also held various appointments with the American Immigration Lawyers Association, the Memphis Bar Association, and the Tennessee Bar Association. Greg also currently serves as a board member for the Hebrew Immigrant Aid Society, the nation's oldest refugee resettlement organization.

Greg welcomes your email at **gsiskind@visalaw.com** and invites you to visit **www.visalaw.com**.

Deborah McMurray is a Principal of Deborah McMurray Associates, a strategic marketing consulting firm to the legal industry. She advises law firms on marketing initiatives that focus a firm's strategy and its investments. She develops targeted positioning and branding strategies for firms throughout the U.S., including the creation of collateral, advertising campaigns, Web sites, and other print and electronic materials.

She is an industry leader in law firm marketing metrics, helping firms measure and track return on investment. Deborah created Couch Money®, a law firm cost recovery program and marketing budgeting system that finds "lost" money and helps firms reallocate their dollars more strategically. She works with marketing departments and firm leadership to help firms find typical amounts of at least $1,000 per lawyer.

Deborah trains lawyers and other professionals in the areas of client relationship management and communications. She created "Leveraging your Business . . ." interactive communications training programs that have been used nationally by Merrill Lynch, as well as law firms, accounting firms, and legal departments.

She has nineteen years of experience in strategic marketing, positioning and communications, seventeen years in professional services marketing, and served for eleven years (1987–1998) as the first in-house marketing director at Texas-based Johnson & Swanson/Gibbs and Hughes & Luce, LLP.

Deborah has served on the Legal Marketing Association's national board of directors, and is a frequent speaker at national programs. She has written articles for the *National Law Journal, New York Law Journal, Legal Times, Law Practice Management, Of Counsel, Texas Lawyer, STRATEGIES: The Journal of Legal Marketing,* and various local and state bar publications.

Please visit **www.deborahmcmurray.com** or contact her at **mcmurray@couchmoney.com**.

Rick Klau is Vice President of Vertical Markets at Interface Software, Inc., the leading provider of CRM software and services to professional services firms. He is the co-author of several books about law and technology, and co-authors a column about technology in the legal profession that has run continuously since 1994.

While attending the University of Richmond School of Law, Rick founded the first law journal in the world to publish exclusively online, *The Richmond Journal of Law & Technology.* Along with fellow editors on the journal, Rick established a standard format for citing to online publications, a standard ultimately adopted by the editors of *The Bluebook.*

Rick is a frequent speaker at law, technology, and marketing conferences in North America and Europe. His articles have appeared in dozens of publications nationwide, and interviews with Rick have run in *The Wall Street Journal, USA Today, American Lawyer, National Law Journal, The Lawyer, eWeek,* and *IT Week.*

Rick earned dual degrees with honors in International Affairs and French from Lafayette College in Easton, Pennsylvania, and his Baccalaureate Degree from L'Université de Bourgogne in Dijon, France. He received his J.D. from the T.C. Williams School of Law at the University of Richmond in Richmond, Virginia, where he was awarded the T.C. Williams Award by the faculty for the member of the graduating class who made the largest contribution to legal scholarship. He is a member of the ABA Law Practice Management Section.

Rick's professional Web site is at www.rklau.com/tins/ and he can be reached at rick@rklau.com.

Introduction

IF YOU BUILD IT, will they come? The answer is a qualified "Yes." Let's assume that "they" includes your target audiences—corporate counsel seeking the best lawyer in West Virginia or Illinois, referring lawyers in big, prestigious law firms in all fifty states, individuals and small businesses hunting the Web for the right law firm, and hungry law students starved for the mental and financial stimulation your firm can provide. "They" won't come if your Web site is bad.

Well, that's not entirely accurate. They might visit once, but they won't come back. Moreover, you have spent all this money and time for just one visit.

Think of the Web site as your firm's face to the world. If, in designing your site, you try to look and feel like the law firm down the street, you aren't telling your firm's unique story. Why *should* the corporate counsel hire your firm? Why *are* you the best choice for the law student? It's imperative you know the answers to these questions and design your site accordingly.

There is a popular axiom that tells us we shouldn't judge a book by its cover. The fact is we can all admit to buying books for countless reasons that had nothing to do with their content. Your marketing strategy is critical. Web design—the look and feel—is important.

The first edition of *The Lawyer's Guide to Marketing on the Internet,* written by Gregory H. Siskind and Timothy J. Moses, was published by the American Bar Association (ABA) in 1996. Some things haven't changed. Providing extraordinary client service and being highly ethical are top ingredients for running a successful law practice. Marketing for lawyers was important in 1996—but it is even more important today.

To be a successful Internet marketer, you don't have to be fluent in geek-speak and whiz around with the latest gadgets and technology toys. However, you must have some facility and understanding of what technology can do for your practice and your client relationships. This book doesn't require you to be an early adopter, but it does insist that you adopt if you want to succeed.

There are several differences between this book and the first one. First, we assume that all readers will either know Internet fundamentals (what is the Internet, how did it start, etc.) or know where they can find this information. We also eliminated the plusses and minuses discussion of marketing on the Internet. We believe there are only plusses and that the Internet is a critical component of *every* law firm marketing strategy—no matter where you are, how large your firm is, or the areas in which you practice.

The level of Web strategy, design, and development talent available to you today is far more broad and sophisticated today than it was in 1996. This is partly because the technology itself is exponentially better, but it's also because we all have a half a dozen more years under our belts. We're just smarter.

In this book we help you identify the resources that will fit best with your firm, and give you sample Web site RFPs, a hosting proposal, and a hosting agreement that you might use. Resist the temptation to hire your ninth-grade daughter to build your Web site—even if she's incredibly gifted. Compare the building of your Web site to engaging a medical specialist—an orthopedist or cardiologist. It's simply wiser for you to hire experts.

Creating a Web marketing plan is a critical step for your firm. We help you understand the elements to consider and the options that are available to you.

In the 1996 book, it was critical to cover email—while common, it was still an evolving technology and a new application in the law firm. As familiar as email is to everyone today, we have two chapters dedicated to email marketing and "netiquette," because sometimes email has become *too* familiar. Employed thoughtfully, it can revolutionize client relationship management. Used haphazardly, it can damage or destroy relationships up and down your organization.

Content was king in 1996 and it still is. Current, relevant content will make your site compelling to visitors—they'll be eager to return. Outdated, dusty content suggests that your law firm is just that. It takes a huge intellectual commitment to continually refresh your online offerings. We help you identify the types of content possible, ways to maximize the impact you have, and how you can leverage your time by recycling firm material and adding third-party content.

We cover the latest Web technology that you can use to market your firm, including Webinars, extranets, wireless devices, and other tools. With the "latest and greatest," there is also the risk of "tacky and inappropriate." We also help you sift through what's new and worthwhile versus what's simply new.

How will you know if your Web site is bringing you a return on your investment? There are ways to qualify and measure your visitors and their traffic patterns on your site. There are also ways to measure how people found you in the first place. Don't take this lightly. For many firms, the Web investment may be the single greatest marketing expenditure they make. You should expect a return, and don't let anyone tell you otherwise.

Finally, the ethics of online marketing are important to know. Our book covers the basics, but we recommend that you purchase the ABA's *Marketing and Legal Ethics, Third Edition*, by William E. Hornsby, Jr., for more information. Consult your state bar association before you develop your site. It's easy to comply with most state's rules—and it is imperative that you know what they are so you can avoid any missteps.

We have our contact information listed at the end of each of our bios so you can reach us easily if you have questions about the material contained in this book, or about things that you don't see here. In addition, we have created an accompanying Web site that is designed to ensure that information in the book will be updated (see below). The 1996 book was a great start—this book gives you countless more Internet marketing possibilities. We wish you continued success and curiosity as you map out strategy for the future generations of your law firm Web sites.

Using This Book's Web Site

Like the book? Then be sure to visit the blog!

Make sure to drop by **bookblogs.com/lawmarketing**, where we continue the conversation online. You'll stay current on the latest trends in law firm marketing on the Internet, learn what's working and what's not, and get information about the newest products and services to better market your firm. You'll also get an opportunity to join the conversation by commenting on anything we post—as well as anything your fellow readers have said. If you're interested in staying current with law firm marketing on the Internet, visit **www.bookblogs.com/lawmarketing/** and add it to your Favorites.

CHAPTER ONE

Choosing Your
Web Consultants

IN THE EARLY DAYS of law firm Web sites, it was enough for a firm to choose an Internet Service Provider (ISP) and a savvy 16-year-old to build the site. Since these first-generation static sites were no more than an electronic firm brochure, this amount of sophistication was just fine.

With strategy now driving Web site launches, overhauls, and face-lifts, the band of consultants you assemble today is critically important. For a larger firm, your Web site planning team could include many of the members described in this chapter. (Note that the external team members may wear more than one hat—the copywriter might be inside the design firm, or the design and development groups might be in the same firm).

Remember—your Web site is first and foremost a marketing and communications tool. It just happens to be powered by technical applications. Hiring a "geek" firm gets you a back end that works (presumably), but it doesn't get you closer to your business strategy, clients, targets, and so on.

Large-Firm Web Site Team

Internal

- ◆ Firm marketing partner (or other senior, well-respected partner);
- ◆ Firm chief marketing officer or marketing director;
- ◆ Firm Web master or other staff person responsible for day-to-day upkeep (who is also the content manager);

- ♦ Firm information technology director; and
- ♦ Firm human resources director (for the intranet pieces only).

External

- ♦ Strategy and branding consultant (focuses on firm's long-term positioning and branding goals);
- ♦ Copywriter or copy editor;
- ♦ Design firm (focuses on look and feel);
- ♦ Web development firm (builds infrastructure, navigation, functionality, and back-end content management);
- ♦ Host (site may be hosted on firm servers or by a third party);
- ♦ Tracking service (typically offered by third-party host companies); and
- ♦ Search engine optimization company.

Your team for a smaller firm is diminished in size, but the functional responsibilities should be in place regardless of firm size. It's imperative that a senior, well-respected partner "own" the Web site project, regardless of firm size—and that this lawyer works with the marketing department or designated personnel to delegate portions of the project to others in the firm.

Small-Firm Web Site Team

Internal

- ♦ Firm marketing partner (or other senior, well-respected partner);
- ♦ Firm marketing staffer;
- ♦ A staff person responsible for day-to-day upkeep (also content manager);
- ♦ Person in charge of information technology; and
- ♦ Person responsible for HR matters (if the firm plans to create an intranet).

If your firm doesn't have professional staff, assign interested lawyers to the following key areas:

- ♦ Oversight of the Web project from start to finish (the buck stops here);
- ♦ Content building; and
- ♦ Day-to-day upkeep (an out-of-date site does almost nothing for your firm).

External

- ♦ Strategy consultant (focuses on firm's long-term positioning/ branding goals—may lead Web team);
- ♦ Web design and development firm;
- ♦ Host (most likely hosted by a third party);
- ♦ Tracking service (typically offered by third-party host companies); and
- ♦ Search engine optimization company.

Whom Should You Choose? How Should You Choose?

Rules that apply to print media don't universally apply to an electronic format. However, many of the same guidelines *should* apply to the Web.

Above all, remember that your Web site is your most visible first impression. It also has a chance of being your best second and third impression, if it is compelling enough to draw visitors back. Think of it as a marketing, communications and recruiting tool—not as a piece of technology.

One-Stop Shop Option

There are several one-stop shop choices—companies that can help you create, design, develop content, build, and host your Web site. Other companies provide design and development, but no strategy or content. These companies typically are geared to a segment of the market, such as small firms or large firms.

One-stop shops aren't always the least expensive option, nor are they always the most convenient. Interview these companies with your firm's goals in mind, just as you would interview any other strategic vendor partner. In working with these companies, be diligent in insisting that design decisions are consistent with your firm's key messages and watch that they don't recommend an off-the-shelf or template look and feel that won't appeal to your client audience and key target markets, and doesn't differentiate you.

Web Designer or Developer

You have an infinite number of choices here, which makes the choosing both easy and difficult. Here are the questions to ask:

1. Do we have an existing, trusted relationship with this studio or firm? (A shared history isn't imperative, but we think it can be helpful.)

2. Who are the Web designer or developer's clients? A commercial law firm should ask, "What do their other business-to-business sites look like? How do they navigate? Who are the target audiences of their clients' sites? Does the designer or developer understand e-commerce?" Personal injury and other consumer-oriented firms should ask how intuitive and user-friendly the sites are that they've created. Will the everyday Joe and Jane needing a lawyer be able to find you and the information they want?

3. How do they staff Web design or development projects (all in-house, or do they outsource pieces of it—one is not necessarily better than the other)?

4. What is their track record for bringing projects in on time and within budget? (You'll want to talk to their clients.)

5. Do they know the legal industry inside and out? Can they help you with marketing strategy and enhance your marketing vision, or are they best described as highly capable geeks?

6. What is their philosophy about using the Web site as a positioning and branding tool? How have they demonstrated this?

7. Are their prices competitive with the market? If not, is there a good reason?

8. Does it make sense to have one firm handle your identity creation, advertising, and brochures, and another firm handle your Web site?

Caution: Law firms often do the very thing they wish their clients wouldn't do—they spread marketing and design work around. The marketing initiatives that involve producing brochures, Web sites, advertising, and other visual elements should be centralized and coordinated to ensure strategic and visual consistency. Regardless of medium, the law firm's positioning strategy should remain constant. This process and the result are harder to control if several design firms are involved. Leverage of concepts, copy, and design (i.e., saving time and money) is harder to come by if messages and images are being created by several firms.

Choose a Web design or development team that understands how far law firms have come (remember law firms have been advertising since 1977). Say "no!" to any design firm that suggests a home page with a collage of a Mont Blanc pen, the *Wall Street Journal*, and a gavel. This means they don't really understand the business you're going after.

Strategy Consultant: Positioning and Branding
This is a new breed of marketing strategist that is common in corporate America, but is less so in the legal industry. It's someone who is current

with legal industry trends and is familiar with your clients' industries. It's someone who won't let you go to market as "full service" because everyone else does, or allow you to be solely internally focused. It's also someone who will fall on a sword before allowing you to compromise the integrity of your firm identity, position, and brand (see sidebars).

Why is it ineffective for a law firm to focus inwardly instead of gearing messages to their outward audiences? We'll give you two examples.

1. Imagine a lawyer resume for Tom Jones that lists "commercial litigation" as his primary area of practice. It also details all bar activity, articles written, and speeches presented. A prospect reading this is given no clue about specific cases Tom has handled, or the experience he has in certain industries and substantive areas of the law, such as IP or products liability. Tom has focused on credential building only, *not* what he's specifically done for past clients and what he can do for future ones. He's not making it easy to hire him.

2. Another example is how firms present practice capabilities. Many firms organize their Web sites the way they are organized internally. Corporate and real estate might be combined in a "business" or "transactional" section, while labor and employment are part of the "litigation" section. If you present your practice capabilities this way, a real estate developer needing representation in your region will have no idea that your firm represents develop-

WHAT IS POSITIONING?

▼▼▼▼▼

What is positioning strategy, and how does it fit with branding? Embarking on a branding campaign without positioning strategy analysis is akin to a lawyer giving a closing argument to the jury before developing case strategy or doing any discovery. Positioning strategy analysis gets to the heart and soul of what makes your firm different and better than your competitors.

If every lawyer and most employees in your firm can't answer the question "Why should I hire you?" with a uniform and relevant response, you have failed to focus your key messages. You have not positioned your firm. There is nothing to brand.

Full service is a bad market position. Do you really believe that your firm can do everything—much less everything profitably and equally well? Besides, how does this distinguish you from the full service firms on the fifth through the forty-fifth floors of your building? Having no stated market position also makes it harder for your clients to refer you to others—they may like you, but you aren't making it easy for them to sell you to others.

ers—because the information isn't organized so that interested visitors can easily find it.

Do you need a consultant who can help you avoid these mistakes? It might make your job easier and your end product better. Many firms do not have the luxury of having a senior marketing strategist in their employ—someone whose job it is to maintain the thirty-thousand-foot view of your firm. If your firm is lucky enough to have a chief marketing officer, oftentimes that person is involved in broader firm initiatives; she doesn't have the time to be the firm's brand manager and Web project manager. It is very helpful to have one person oversee the development of all the visual elements of a firm's go-to-market strategy, whether online or off-line—and often that person doesn't need to be a full-time employee.

Copywriter or Copy Editor

It's best that you hire a copywriter or copy editor. Remember that the goal of your Web site is to communicate with your target audience in a language they understand. Many design firms employ copywriters and editors who can become a part of your Web development team.

It is critical that the copywriter has a working knowledge of the law. This will save you considerable time (you won't have to explain Hart-Scott-Rodino or FMLA), money, and possible embarrassment in the event the copywriter incorrectly uses legal or business terminology. Besides knowing the difference between a tort and a torte, a copywriter also needs the ability to distill complex subject matter so that it "speaks" to your visitors.

The tone of practice descriptions, lawyer resumes, firm history, etc., should be

---

WHAT IS BRANDING?

▼▼▼▼▼

Branding is not advertising, a logo, or a tagline. It is the sum total of everything you print, publish, and do—it reflects your personality. It is an opportunity for you to guide and control the market perception about your firm. What is included in a brand? Everything—especially client service. And your walk must match your talk. Branding must truly differentiate your firm and be constant, consistent, and honest.

A successful brand tells the marketplace about your firm and the way you do business. If prospects don't know your firm, it's the name recognition or unique brand that will frequently get you on the short list. You want prospects to say, "Yes, I've heard that ABC law firm is known for their work in public finance," as opposed to, "XYZ firm—never heard of them."

conversational. Tell stories about what you do. Simple, short, engaging copy will keep your visitors coming back to learn more. Don't be afraid to inject personality into your Web site copy—don't be afraid to come across as "human."

Hosting

Don't think of your host as being human. Rather, it's more like Hal from *2001: A Space Odyssey*. Your host is actually a computer that functions as the end point of data transfer on the Internet. Your options are to host your Web site on your law firm server. or to outsource the hosting to a third-party company.

Hosting is a key decision that must take into account your firm's technical capabilities. If you have a strong information technology team, then hosting may not be a daunting task. If, however, your IT staff is challenged by keeping your email system running, then consider outsourcing.

Drew Naukam, President of AzTech Solutions, a Texas-based company, identifies the following key questions to ask when deciding whether to host or not to host:

1. Do we have excess bandwidth coming into our offices?
2. Does our firm have firewall security in place?
3. How critical is it for the site to be up 24/7?
4. How stressed and stretched are our technical resources? Are they keeping up with their current responsibilities?
5. What is the purpose of the site? Is it going to be used for marketing and communication purposes only, or will we grant access to password-protected information on a select basis?
6. What level of traffic do we expect?

AzTech also identifies the following advantages and disadvantages of hosting:

Advantages of Self-hosting

♦ You have greater control over your site and its contents;
♦ You can save money by leveraging your internal technology infrastructure (assuming you already have the bandwidth and server capacity).

Disadvantages of Self-hosting

- ◆ You must dedicate network and human resources to hosting;
- ◆ You open up a portion of your internal network to outsiders whose intentions could be less than honorable.

Advantages of External Hosting

- ◆ You can "outsource it and forget about it";
- ◆ This is the hosting company's core business, not yours, and many of these companies have now been in business for several years;
- ◆ If your server crashes, your number-one sales and recruiting tool doesn't crash with it; and
- ◆ Unlimited bandwidth, frequent backups, and power redundancy means the site should be available 24/7. Some companies also automatically mirror sites on remote backup servers, in case of a disaster.

Disadvantages of External Hosting

- ◆ The expense can range from $50 to $1,000 per month, or more;
- ◆ Customer service isn't always the best in the hosting business (think of telephone companies); and
- ◆ Financial stability may be a concern. There has been some high-profile bankruptcies in the hosting market in recent months.

Sample third-party hosting agreements and proposals are included as Exhibit One at the end of the book.

Web Tracking

If you want to ensure that your site is doing what you intended (solidifying client relationships, generating new business, offering legal and business reference information, or recruiting new lawyers), you must track your visitors. According to Chicago consultant Nancy Roberts Linder, there are only three critical pieces of information you need on a monthly basis:

1. **What is the number of visitors?** A hit is the number of total accesses to a Web site's pages measured over a period of time. This means that if Johnny visited your home page, then went to lawyer bios, then headed back home, then checked out your real estate section, then back home, this would count as five hits. Hits don't

accurately measure the number of people on your Web site—
although they can measure traffic patterns.

2. **Who is looking?** Tracking will not tell you the identity of individual visitors, but will tell you how many visitors came from a
   particular domain or IP address. This information is useful
   because it tells you if a visitor is from a commercial entity (.com,
   .net, .biz and others), an academic entity (.edu), a government
   body (.gov), or from a non-profit (.org). If you want to attract
   more first-year law students, reviewing the activity by the .edu visitors will help you evaluate if your site is meeting its intended purpose. You should organize this report by domain name so that all
   .com addresses are together, .edu are together, and so on. The new
   domains (.biz, etc.) will also fall into the major categories of commercial, government, and so on.

3. **What are your visitors visiting?** Tracking where your visitors
   go on your Web site (the specific pages they visit) helps you analyze the usefulness of material you have posted on your site.
   Merger and acquisition or venture capital project hype was very
   popular in 2000; now the interest in those topics has waned given
   slower market conditions. Are your visitors telling you something
   by the pages they are visiting? Some pages on your site might not
   receive any traffic. Ultimately, you should evaluate the usefulness
   of the material you post and eliminate material that, over several
   months, doesn't attract or hold your visitors' interest.

There is much more information about Web tracking in Chapter
Fourteen, "Measuring the Results of Your Internet Efforts."

Web Site RFPs

Many firms prepare and distribute formal RFPs to Web designers and
developers. We have included two representative samples of RFPs that
firms have used in creating their third-generation dynamic Web sites. See
Exhibit Two at the end of the book.

Web Site Maintenance

Do you need a Web master—someone who updates the site when lawyers
leave or join the firm, and keeps the content fresh? Larger firms have the

luxury of a marketing team that might include a Web master or database manager. Others utilize an interested lawyer, paralegal, or another firm employee to keep the content relevant and current.

Some static sites require basic knowledge of HTML. Others are created using programs that enable you to convert Microsoft Word documents, for example, into HTML. If your site is static, a third-party host or administrator should do your updates, unless you have an employee who is comfortable with Web-development tools.

Firms on a tight budget often opt for a static site since the associated costs are typically much less. In some cases, if there is no money to pay someone to update the site regularly, you can have your site developer create templates for the site and then train you to maintain and update it yourself.

If your site is database driven, changes can be made by an administrative person inside the firm. Making these changes is easy and instantaneous. Content-management systems vary greatly from Web developer to Web developer—some are far more intuitive than others. Some development companies have designed off-the-shelf products that you can demo before you buy. Others custom-develop the back end so that you buy only what you want and need. Off-the-shelf doesn't mean cheap, and custom development doesn't always mean more expensive.

What does a Web master do? According to the March 2001 Institute of Management and Administration (IOMA) *Salary Zone*, "The Web master is the creative force behind a Web site. This position is responsible for the content and consistent look of the overall site. The Web master maps the flow of the site, creates general graphics, provides specifications to the Web author, the Web developer and the outside vendors for the development of databases, interactive applets and custom graphics." See **www.ioma.com** for a more comprehensive description.

*CHAPTER***TWO**

Developing an Internet Marketing Plan

SPENDING ANY AMOUNT OF money designing and building a Web site without a written marketing plan that defines goals is akin to building a house without any architectural blueprints. And it can cost about the same amount of money!

Use the suggestions in this chapter to develop a marketing plan before you spend one dollar on a new or improved site.

Analyze Your Firm

Analyze Your Practice

1. Analyze your practice—be specific. Who are your clients today, and whom do you want as clients in the future? What are their industries? Who are your clients' customers?
2. How will your practice change over the next five years?
3. How will your clients' companies and industries change over the next five years (regulation, deregulation, consolidation, globalization)?
4. What are the important problems your clients face? What keeps them awake at night?
5. How does your firm help them solve these problems?

Analyze How You Market Your Practice

The following questions should be answered by key practice leaders in your firm:

1. How do you market your practice?
2. Do you participate in "beauty contests"? What do you say or bring? Do you ever use PowerPoint for these presentations?
3. Why do clients hire your firm?
4. Who is your competition?
5. Why is your firm different and better?
6. What are your goals for a Web site?
7. Do your lawyers publish regularly?
8. Do you have a knowledge-management system that enables you to easily harness the expertise of your lawyers?

Note: Firms create a wealth of legal research memos that they don't leverage. These memoranda are fodder for great content, but too often they're forgotten and end up as dust catchers.

Analyze the Perception of the Firm

1. How is the firm perceived—by clients, prospects, other law firms, law students?
2. How should these perceptions be changed?
3. How would you *like* to have the firm perceived?

Identify the Firm's Qualities

1. How would you characterize the firm's atmosphere, attitude, and style?
2. What is unique about this firm?
3. If your firm was a car, what car would it be today?
4. What car do you want it to be five years from now?

The answers to these questions will help you formulate your market position, and identify differentiating features and key messages. This information will help you choose one course of action over another and will prevent you from going to market with a "one size fits all" Web site. It also serves as the foundation for all design decisions.

Analyze Your Business Approach

The next questions relate more specifically to your approach to the business of law:

1. Are you comfortable listing client names under representative matters and on lawyer resumes? Consider ordering client information by practice area and by lawyer. It speaks to both camps of clients—those who hire law firms and those who hire lawyers. (Note: Always get client permission before doing this and verify that it's permissible under your state bar's rules. See Chapter Fifteen, "Web Ethics and Ethical Issues of Online Marketing.")

2. Are you comfortable giving content away to visitors at no charge?

3. Are you comfortable charging clients and prospects for white papers and other substantive industry information?

4. Are you committed to keeping your site current and relevant? Whose responsibility is it?

5. Do you want to have password-protected areas for clients only, so they can see and retrieve proprietary information?

Survey Your Clients

Many lawyers are still shy about asking their clients' opinions about their delivery of services, marketing offerings, etc. In our experience, clients are delighted to be asked! We have included a sample client Web survey at the end of this chapter.

In addition to your own client investigation, there is current research that tells you what corporate counsel and visitors want from law firm Web sites. "Finding and Working with Lawyers on the Web," a report published by Greenfield/Belser Ltd and FGI Market Research in 2001, is a summary of corporate counsel and executive telephone interviews about how they connect law firms and the Web (the report can be viewed at **www.gbltd.com**):

The study answers the following questions:

1. Do buyers of legal services search online? How often? For what?

2. Where do they start? What are they thinking?

3. Do Web sites replace familiar methods of law firm marketing— ads, newsletters, and brochures?

4. Once buyers find your site, which features are preferred? Which are disdained?

5. Once they choose you, how do they want to use the site to work together?

Domain Names

In the early days of law firm Web sites, firms abbreviated the firm name. For example, Hanson Johnson Thompson and Swanson LLP became **www.hjts.com** and Pony Smith Thatcher LLP became **www.pstlawfirm.com**. Today, visitors (especially law students) search intuitively—we type in "hansonjohnson" and "ponysmith" and hope the firms' Web sites will appear. Your domain name is part of your firm's positioning and branding strategy—it should advance your firm's name in the marketplace. Initials don't do that.

Avoid being a victim of cyber-squatting. If you are currently using initials for your domain name, reregister a more complete firm name, plus all its derivations. Don't make people have to remember more than your firm name.

Also register all .net, .info, .pro, .biz, .us, and .org versions—the price of name and reputation protection is worth the few hundred dollars this will cost. Get clever with your domain name. The State Bar of Texas and other state bar associations say that you can't use names like **www.thebestlawyerintx.com** or **winyourlawsuitinflorida.com**. However, most, if not all state bar associations enable you to create vertical sites and call them **antitrustlitigation.com**, **visalaw.com**, or **deregulation.com**. Read more about these "killer category" sites in Chapter Six, Informational Content. Remember: your domain names aren't merely locating devices—they have the capacity to convey a very important positioning and branding message.

Trademark and register all derivations of your domain name and firm name, including misspellings. Bieser Greer & Landis, a Dayton, Ohio law firm (**www.biesergreer.com**) has also registered "**beisergreer.com**." Think of your domain names as firm assets and intellectual property that should be protected.

Traditional Marketing Tools

A Web marketing plan will include tactics to keep your Web site top-of-mind in your target audiences. According to "Finding and Working with Lawyers on the Web," traditional marketing materials are what draw the buyers of legal services online. Survey respondents stated, "Law firm Web sites depend on tried-and-true print media to drive site traffic." Nearly half the buyers surveyed had visited a law firm Web site because of a promotional mailing. Almost as significantly, just under half went to one after seeing a law firm's print ad. Note, however, that the study found that law-firm Internet banner ads brought very few people to a firm's Web site.

Consider the following ideas to promote your Web site:

♦ A signature toy or mouse pad with the firm's URL on it;

♦ A brochure that gives readers a tour of site highlights;

♦ A postcard mailer announcing the new or upgraded site. Think ahead, however. Don't be content driving traffic just this once. When you design your postcard, think of ways to get them to return a second and third time.

♦ A CD-ROM mailer that takes your audience on a tour of the site and has links to various sections. (Note: Before investing in a CD, know your audience. Anecdotal evidence suggests that a very small number of people who receive such CD mailers ever open them.)

Online Marketing Tools

The best online tool is having all lawyers and staff email the site link to their closest clients, referral sources, and friends of the firm. Don't send to everyone you know—you want to avoid any hint of spam. Tell them you want their candid opinions, and keep track of these for future updates and upgrades. (Be prepared to accept both praise and criticism.) Share these responses with your Web development team.

According to the research study, other online promotions fall flat. A miniscule number of buyers of legal services want to download lawyer announcements, notices of other new developments, or press releases.

If your firm pays to be listed in *The Martindale-Hubbell Law Directory*, check your online listing at **www.martindale.com**. Add your URL to your listing, as well as email links to your lawyers' listings. Pay a little extra each year to be able to link to your Web site—as of publication, the cost is $225. It's well worth it.

According to Tim Corcoran, a senior executive with Martindale-Hubbell, "An average of fifteen percent of visitors to **Martindale.com** click through to the law firm Web site. However, an analysis of literally hundreds of WebTrends reports and other statistical reports shows that this traffic is still the third- or fourth-highest referring domain to those law firm sites." Generic search engines may precede Martindale on the referring domain ranked list, but it's arguable that visitors who click through to your site from **Martindale.com** are "more qualified" than visitors from generic search engines.

Positioning Your Firm

Take a lateral step left and think of untraditional sites that can market your firm's capability in a particular area. The Outsourcing and Technology section at Hughes & Luce LLP created **www.commercebynet.com** (see figure 2-1). This is a site that digs deep into e-commerce trends, companies, laws, and news. It pulls content from major news sources (with the appropriate arrangements in place), and includes articles from firm lawyers on relevant topics, such as Internet technology, the ABCs of bankruptcy, and international e-commerce. The site also has video-stream seminars. There is a small reference and a link to Hughes & Luce at the top, but it has the appearance of being an independent, third-party site.

These sites must follow the same ethics rules as your primary firm site.

Search Engines

Keep current with search-engine registries and register key words from your practice areas. This is a highly specialized area and requires someone with experience in providing this service. Your Web developers may not have this in their shop, but make sure they recommend someone to do it.

As mentioned above, law-firm banner ads on other Web sites aren't yet driving traffic to law firm Web sites. Perhaps it's still early—but for now, your money would be spent better elsewhere.

Growing Your Site

Remember that building a Web site is an evolving process, not an event. Don't forget about it and assume it will continue to work for you. Your marketing plan should outline how you might expand the scope and reach of your Web site over the next twelve to twenty-four months. For example, will you:

1. Translate it into a foreign language (see **www.pillsburywinthrop.com** or **www.goulstonstorrs.com**)?
2. Add an intranet or extranet?
3. Add a "quick guide" giving visitors one-click access to their favorite information (practice and industry areas, lawyers, offices)?

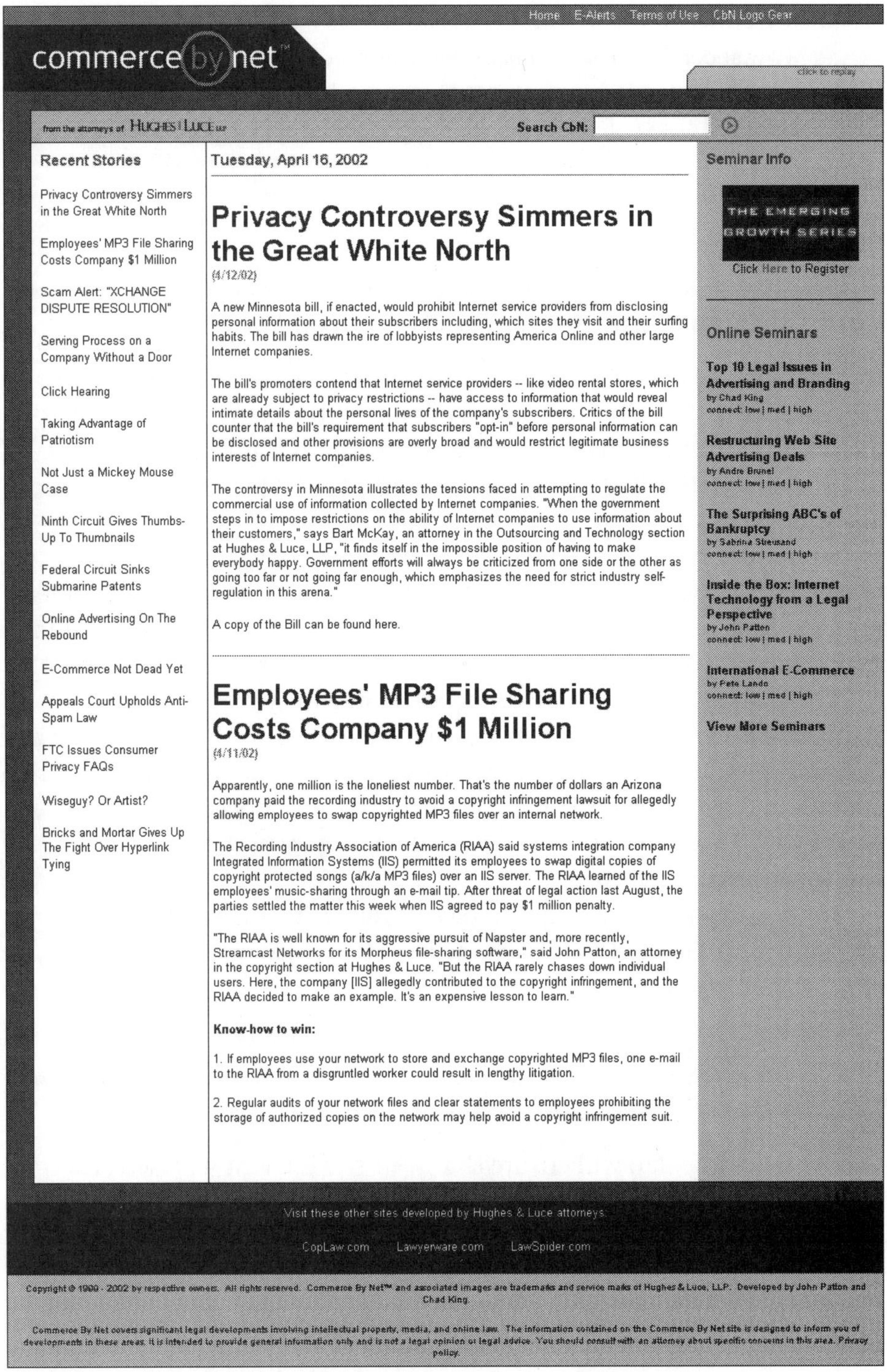

commerce by net™

Home   E-Alerts   Terms of Use   CbN Logo Gear

click to replay

from the attorneys of HUGHES LUCE LLP   Search CbN: [   ]

Recent Stories

Privacy Controversy Simmers in the Great White North

Employees' MP3 File Sharing Costs Company $1 Million

Scam Alert: "XCHANGE DISPUTE RESOLUTION"

Serving Process on a Company Without a Door

Click Hearing

Taking Advantage of Patriotism

Not Just a Mickey Mouse Case

Ninth Circuit Gives Thumbs-Up To Thumbnails

Federal Circuit Sinks Submarine Patents

Online Advertising On The Rebound

E-Commerce Not Dead Yet

Appeals Court Upholds Anti-Spam Law

FTC Issues Consumer Privacy FAQs

Wiseguy? Or Artist?

Bricks and Mortar Gives Up The Fight Over Hyperlink Tying

Tuesday, April 16, 2002

Privacy Controversy Simmers in the Great White North
{4/12/02}

A new Minnesota bill, if enacted, would prohibit Internet service providers from disclosing personal information about their subscribers including, which sites they visit and their surfing habits. The bill has drawn the ire of lobbyists representing America Online and other large Internet companies.

The bill's promoters contend that Internet service providers -- like video rental stores, which are already subject to privacy restrictions -- have access to information that would reveal intimate details about the personal lives of the company's subscribers. Critics of the bill counter that the bill's requirement that subscribers "opt-in" before personal information can be disclosed and other provisions are overly broad and would restrict legitimate business interests of Internet companies.

The controversy in Minnesota illustrates the tensions faced in attempting to regulate the commercial use of information collected by Internet companies. "When the government steps in to impose restrictions on the ability of Internet companies to use information about their customers," says Bart McKay, an attorney in the Outsourcing and Technology section at Hughes & Luce, LLP, "it finds itself in the impossible position of having to make everybody happy. Government efforts will always be criticized from one side or the other as going too far or not going far enough, which emphasizes the need for strict industry self-regulation in this arena."

A copy of the Bill can be found here.

Employees' MP3 File Sharing Costs Company $1 Million
{4/11/02}

Apparently, one million is the loneliest number. That's the number of dollars an Arizona company paid the recording industry to avoid a copyright infringement lawsuit for allegedly allowing employees to swap copyrighted MP3 files over an internal network.

The Recording Industry Association of America (RIAA) said systems integration company Integrated Information Systems (IIS) permitted its employees to swap digital copies of copyright protected songs (a/k/a MP3 files) over an IIS server. The RIAA learned of the IIS employees' music-sharing through an e-mail tip. After threat of legal action last August, the parties settled the matter this week when IIS agreed to pay $1 million penalty.

"The RIAA is well known for its aggressive pursuit of Napster and, more recently, Streamcast Networks for its Morpheus file-sharing software," said John Patton, an attorney in the copyright section at Hughes & Luce. "But the RIAA rarely chases down individual users. Here, the company [IIS] allegedly contributed to the copyright infringement, and the RIAA decided to make an example. It's an expensive lesson to learn."

Know-how to win:

1. If employees use your network to store and exchange copyrighted MP3 files, one e-mail to the RIAA from a disgruntled worker could result in lengthy litigation.

2. Regular audits of your network files and clear statements to employees prohibiting the storage of authorized copies on the network may help avoid a copyright infringement suit.

Seminar Info

THE EMERGING GROWTH SERIES

Click Here to Register

Online Seminars

Top 10 Legal Issues in Advertising and Branding
by Chad King
connect: low | med | high

Restructuring Web Site Advertising Deals
by Andre Brunel
connect: low | med | high

The Surprising ABC's of Bankruptcy
by Sabrina Streusand
connect: low | med | high

Inside the Box: Internet Technology from a Legal Perspective
by John Patton
connect: low | med | high

International E-Commerce
by Pete Lando
connect: low | med | high

View More Seminars

Visit these other sites developed by Hughes & Luce attorneys.

CopLaw.com   Lawyerware.com   LawSpider.com

Copyright © 1999 - 2002 by respective owners. All rights reserved. Commerce By Net™ and associated images are trademarks and service marks of Hughes & Luce, LLP. Developed by John Patton and Chad King.

Commerce By Net covers significant legal developments involving intellectual property, media, and online law. The information contained on the Commerce By Net site is designed to inform you of developments in these areas. It is intended to provide general information only and is not a legal opinion or legal advice. You should consult with an attorney about specific concerns in this area. Privacy policy.

FIGURE 2-1. A subsidiary site for e-business topics

4. Introduce new vertical, single-issue sites (see **www.deregulation.com, www.securitizationlaw.com,** or **www.mbpprojectfinance.com**)?
5. Create multiple home pages to drive clients and prospects to your targeted sites?
6. Add a virtual tour of your firm that will bring your offices to life (see **www.goulstonstorrs.com/virtual_frame.htm**)?

What Do Clients and Prospects Want from Your Site?

According to the respondents included in "Finding and Working with Lawyers on the Web," on-point experience matters. On a scale of one to ten, seventy-one percent of the survey respondents ranked "experience with specific matters" as one of the most important pieces of information on a site.

Equally significant is what is *not* important to respondents. News releases, diversity, and recruiting were all low on the list of important features. *Pro bono* ranked next-to-last. Does this mean you shouldn't include these items on your Web site? Certainly not—just don't lead with them.

Recruiting is an important aspect of a law firm's Web site, but your clients and future clients probably care very little about it. Why not create a separate recruiting site? It should look and feel similar to your main site, and link to your home page, but the recruiting site should help you go to market with a contemporary or fresh personality (your URL might be **www.firmnamerecruiting.com**).

To view unique approaches to recruiting, visit **www.sonnenschein.com**, (see figure 2-2), **www.hellerehrman.com, www.foley.com, www.dancona.com,** or **www.womblecarlyle.com**.

Practice Descriptions and Industry Strength

A Web marketing plan will ensure that your site is client–focused and that you are offering current and relevant information. "Finding and Working with Lawyers on the Web" states that "along with legal skills and experience, sophisticated buyers expect outside counsel to offer in-depth industry knowledge." More than sixty-nine percent consider industry knowledge to be a critical feature of online practice descriptions.

Industry overviews, white papers, and other industry briefings establish your mastery of a particular business sector. As a large firm, Mayer Brown Rowe & Maw has created numerous industry- and topic-specific sites that all link to the firm's home page (**www.mayerbrown.com**). A mid-

FIGURE 2-2. Recruiting approach

sized firm that has organized its expertise and experience first by industry, then by practice area, is the Texas-based litigation firm Godwin Gruber PC (**www.godwingruber.com**). Know your audiences, and know how they search for information. It is more common for business executives to search first by industry, and for corporate counsel to search first by practice area.

Lawyer Resumes

Your marketing plan should include a template for your online lawyer biographies. Keep the bios short, current, and focused. Buyers of legal services want to know what you can do for them—and what you have done lately. List specific industry experience, specific matters, and outcomes (but watch the various state bar association rules and restrictions). Do list alma maters; don't list every civic or charitable activity, or other personal or family information. It's better to include community and *pro bono* information in a specific section of the site, rather than going on too long in a resume.

The best lawyer bios are one page. If lawyers in your firm are noted experts in an area and require more space, their bios can include a link to additional information. Also use a link to list numerous speeches and publications, rather than forcing visitors to scroll through multiple pages.

Include a current photo. Consider a full-body shot like Sebaly, Shillito & Dyer in Dayton, Ohio (see figure 2-3), **www.ssd.com/member**. Or try more informal shots like Bieser Greer, also in Dayton, (**www.biesergreer.com/lawyers.asp**). See Chapter Five, "Promotional Content," for more detailed information and examples of content.

THE FIRM   THE PRACTICE   PROFILES   OPPORTUNITIES   CONTACT

SEBALY SHILLITO + DYER
A LEGAL PROFESSIONAL ASSOCIATION

+ MEMBERS OF THE FIRM

ss+d

Martin A. Beyer
E: mbeyer@ssdlaw.com
P: 937.222.2514

Marty is a litigator. He handles a wide variety of disputes, commercial and personal, at both the trial and appellate levels. In addition to jury trials, Marty has experience with bench trials, arbitration hearings, and mediations. Marty handles cases involving clients of various types and sizes, including individuals, small businesses, and Fortune 500 corporations. He has extensive experience in banking law, property disputes, trust and estate litigation, contract disputes, employment litigation, non-compete agreements, and business torts of all kinds.

Marty's style is a combination of substantive aggressiveness and civility. He takes pride in adhering to the client's budgetary constraints without compromising effectiveness. He always tries to move cases as quickly as the courts will permit.

Marty is a member of the Dayton Bar Association, and serves on its ethics committee. He also is a member of the Inn of Court, an organization that strives to enhance advocacy skills among members of the bar. He sometimes sits as an arbitrator for the Montgomery County Common Pleas Court. Marty's non-legal activities include serving in his local Rotary club and on his church's foundation board.

When not in the office, Marty likes to spend time with his wife and two young daughters. On weekends he can be found cooking dinner on his grill. A former football player, Marty stays in shape running road races with Team SS+D and lifting weights.

Marty was admitted to the Ohio bar and the U.S. District Court for the Southern District of Ohio in 1992. He received his B.A., *cum laude*, in 1988 from Hillsdale College and his J.D. in 1992 from the University of Dayton. He is a member of the Dayton, Ohio State, and American Bar Associations. His areas of concentration are Business and Commercial Litigation.

the firm | the practice | profiles | opportunities | contact

© 2000 Sebaly Shillito + Dyer.

DISCLAIMER

Shareholders
MARTIN BEYER
MICHAEL BOOTH
DANIEL BROWN
JAMES DYER
GALE FINLEY
JOHN GLANKLER
DEBORAH HUNT
MICHAEL MOLONEY
JON SEBALY
BEVERLY SHILLITO
JEFFREY SHULMAN
KARL ULRICH
LAWRENCE WALTER
NITA YATES

Associates

Of Counsel

FIGURE 2-3. Lawyer resume

SAMPLE CLIENT WEB SURVEY

NAME/DEPT._____

COMPANY_____

1. How often do you use the Internet during your *business* day?
   A. Daily
   B. Weekly
   C. Several times per month
   D. Occasionally
   E. Never
2. Do you rely on email during the business day for (check all that apply):
   A. Routine business correspondence
   B. Routine personal correspondence
   C. A substitute for telephone conversations
   D. All business correspondence
   E. To receive important documents
   F. To "talk" to my lawyers about ongoing matters
3. If you use the Internet for business, please rank the following choices in order of importance. *Place a 1 by your top priority, 2 by your second priority, etc.*
   A. Research about my markets
   B. Research about my competition
   C. Current news stories—*Wall Street Journal, New York Times,* etc.
   D. Government agencies, bureaus, etc.
   E. Research about law firms
   F. Corporate, product, service information on companies
   G. Industry data
   H. Other (please list) _____
4. If you use the Internet for business, please describe the sites or types of sites you find most useful.

   _____
   _____
   _____

5. Have you ever visited the following Web sites?
   A. Law firms: Yes _____ No _____
   B. Major or regional accounting firms: Yes _____ No _____
6. If yes, what was the last law firm site you visited?

   _____

What was the last accounting firm site you visited?

_____

7 Do you participate in online educational programs?
Yes _____ No _____
If yes, what topics?

_____

If not, is this something you'd consider and find beneficial?

_____

8. Rank the following features/benefits of a <u>law firm Web site</u> in order of importance. *Place a 1 by the most important, 2 by the next most important, etc.*
    A. Online education relevant to my industry and company
    B. Document sharing with my lawyers
    C. Links to government sites (such as SEC, agencies and state legislature)
    D. Links to industry sites
    E. Industry white papers and newsletters on the site
    F. Access to bills and work in progress statements
    G. Resumes of a firm's lawyers
    H. Practice group descriptions—with cases and deals
    I. Client testimonials
    J. Current news/events that flash or pop up on the home page and change frequently
    K. Other (please specify) _____

9. How many law firms do you use? _____
    How many of these firms' Web sites have you visited? _____

10. Please tell us your favorite Web site of all Web sites and why.

    _____

    _____

    _____

11. What favorite sites have you bookmarked?

    _____

    _____

12. Do you have a portal or page of entry you always use?

    _____

CHAPTER THREE

Email Marketing: Leveraging the Mass Appeal of Email

THERE IS A DIFFERENCE between individual email messages (one-to-one) and mailing lists. Rather than sending individual email messages to promote your firm, you can leverage technology that will distribute your messages to hundreds, if not thousands, of people. Using this one-to-many model, you can get your message out to a large audience quickly and efficiently.

This chapter explores the options you have with email, recommends ways to fully exploit the technology, and gives you tips and tricks to help you benefit from the medium.

Mass Mailings and Spam

So you've heard of Spam®, the lunchmeat. And you've also probably heard of spam, the unwanted email. Are the two related? Yes and no.

Thirty years ago, the British comedy troupe Monty Python did a sketch about a group of Vikings who ate at a restaurant that only served Spam. Almost every item on the menu was Spam. "Spam, Spam, Spam, baked beans and Spam" was one entrée. In the sketch, any time the word Spam was repeated more than four or five times, a chorus of Vikings would chant "Spam" over and over again.

Pretty goofy. But the mindless repeating of the word Spam came to symbolize unwanted repetition. And when unsolicited email messages started showing up on the Internet, someone on the net equated the end-less stream of email with the endless stream of Spams being sung by the Vikings in the Monty Python sketch. Unfortunately for the Hormel Cor-poration (the trademark holder for Spam), the term stuck. Today, spam (with a lowercase *s*) is synonymous with unwanted email.

For more on this, see the rather amusing Spam Web site at http://www.spam.com/ and the FAQ about Spam and spam at http://www.spam.com/ci/ci_in.htm.

Distinguishing your broadcast email messages from spam is not hard. As a general rule, if you have a relationship with the email recipient—either she requested to receive the email, or you have a business relation-ship with her—then you can't really be accused of spamming anyone.

If, on the other hand, you add email addresses to your list without permission, you're at risk of being accused of sending unsolicited com-mercial email (also known by the acronym UCE). For more on keeping up good relations with your email recipients, see the Tips and Tricks section at the end of this chapter.

Remember, the first rule in client relationship management is to honor your clients' wishes. If they ask *not* to be included in email newsletters and broadcasts, ensure that everyone in the firm knows not to include them.

Should You Use Your Email Program?

If you are a "power user" of an email program such as Microsoft Outlook, Qualcomm's Eudora, Lotus Notes, or Novell Groupwise, then you know it's possible to use the mail merge function to send email messages out to a number of people. We'll look at Outlook as an example, but the general premise is common across all platforms.

The idea behind a mail merge is to allow you to personalize your email and still broadcast it to a large group. This is similar to using a mail-ing list (discussed below), but it is implemented using your email pro-gram.

If you're familiar with the mail merge functionality built into Microsoft Word, the basic idea behind an Outlook email merge is very similar. You can draft the text of the email in Word, and use Outlook for the list of names and email addresses. You can insert merge fields (such as first name, last name, company name, etc.) that make the email appear to be an individual message to the recipient (see figure 3-1).

While it is entirely possible to use your email program to send a lot of messages, you will find that you are faced with a number of limitations:

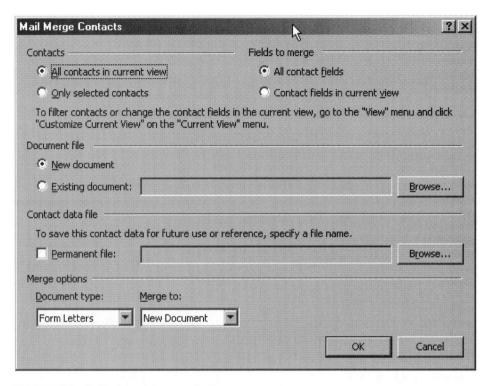

FIGURE 3-1. Outlook mail merge window

- **Bounces.** When you send out a large number of email messages, a certain number will be returned (because the recipient's mail server is down, the recipient's email address is no longer valid, etc.). If you are sending the email from your program, those bounced messages will be returned to your inbox. Just filtering these out—and then updating your own list of names and addresses—can take hours.
- **ISP limits.** Make sure you check with your firm's ISP. Many ISPs place hard limits on the number of email messages you can send out—this is a direct reaction to the explosion of spam. If you send too many messages, you may have your account disabled, or messages delayed or deleted.
- **Server limits.** Be aware that some mail servers restrict mass email and will shut down if the number exceeds the capacity of your firm's server.
- ***To: v. Bcc:*** If you are sending individual email messages, be careful about how you send the message. Mark Cuban, the billionaire founder of **Broadcast.com** and owner of the Dallas Mavericks NBA basketball team, sent a broadcast email to all Mavericks fans— several thousand people. One problem: he included all of the

addressees in the *To:* field, meaning that every recipient saw *all* of the other recipients. And a few of the irked recipients decided to hit "reply all" in their email programs to complain. The result? A few weeks' worth of angry Mavericks fans' email messages flying back and forth—with absolutely no way to stop them. To prevent this from happening, use the *Bcc:* (blind carbon copy) field and each recipient will see only one address. A reply will come back to the sender personally, but not to everyone else who received the email.

Discussion Lists and Distribution Lists

Email, more than any other Internet technology, is what feeds community. And firms that can foster a community online will go a long way in reaping the benefits of Internet marketing.

Two different manifestations of email marketing are discussion lists and distribution lists. While their names are fairly descriptive, the ways in which they are used and their benefits to your firm are very different.

Discussion Lists

Discussion lists are exactly what they sound like: lists of individuals who are interested in participating in a discussion. Often grouped by topic ("Elvis lovers," "Grassy Knoll Theorists," "Frank Sinatra Fan Club"), the lists may be high-traffic (many messages per day) or they may produce just a few messages per month.

Your law firm can try to foster a community among your clients by creating discussion lists. The firm creates a group of similar individuals who are interested in asking questions, providing answers, and discussing a certain topic.

But there is a risk. By allowing anyone to participate in the discussion list, the firm cedes control to whomever is subscribed. Some people with email accounts aren't always the most concise, focused communicators. Messages could reflect poorly on the firm, discussions could quickly veer off-topic, and it could become difficult to exercise any control.

With risk, however, comes the possibility of reward. If your firm is viewed as the facilitator of an engaging discussion with useful information, participants in the list will come to view the firm as a valuable resource. The more positive the perception of the firm, the more likely it is that participants will come to you for help.

If the firm is interested in building a community, but doesn't necessarily want to abandon all control, it is possible to moderate the discussion. This allows participants to send posts, but someone at the firm must approve the posts before they go out to the list. While this can be a significant commitment of time for any one lawyer, several interested and capable colleagues could co-moderate.

Distribution Lists

As opposed to discussion lists, distribution lists are a one-way broadcast medium that allows the firm to communicate with any number of recipients. Typically, firms will use distribution lists for topic-specific news (i.e., *Intellectual Property Newsletter, Labor & Employment Update,* etc.). The model is simple: the firm can post to the distribution lists, but recipients are not able to post.

Distribution lists should be used regularly—if someone receives email only once a year, he is not likely to think of the firm when the time is right. Sending regular information via the distribution list will keep the firm's name and expertise in each recipient's mind.

The advantage to this medium is that you're the authority, providing the content. You have control over what gets distributed, and you can shape the message. The disadvantage? You're providing the content. If you're the only one writing the news, you'll find that the burden of coming up with new information can be too much to bear.

How do you address this? Recruit others from the firm to provide new content. It doesn't have to be long—just fresh. If more people are contributing, it will be easier to keep up with reasonably frequent mailings.

Be aware of the ethical issues associated with discussion and distribution lists and ensure that you are complying with the various bar regulations. See Chapter Fifteen, "Web Ethics and Ethical Issues of Online Marketing," for more information.

Why Use Email for Marketing?

Why use email for marketing? It's a fair question. With the popularity of the Web, it's reasonable to conclude that email would be a less popular option. However, the reality is that email remains the most widely available and adopted Internet technology. And, according to Forrester Research, email newsletters have an eighteen percent response rate, compared to single-digit response rates for Web-based marketing techniques.

Email is what's known as "push technology"—that is, users don't have to seek it out. Instead, the email finds them. When you send it, it finds its way into their inboxes. In this way, you can ensure that anyone who has expressed an interest in hearing from you will hear from you as often as you want.

Implementing an Email Marketing Strategy

On a Shoestring

So you've decided it's worth using email to market your firm. You have persuaded your colleagues to write the content (or you are the writer), and you're ready to go. But you are operating on a shoestring and don't want to spend a lot of money on the project until you can demonstrate that it is actually providing value.

Fair enough. Luckily, you have a number of options. Your best bet is to go with a Web-based solution. A generation or two ago (in Internet years; that's more like a year or two), "application service provider" (ASP) was a popular buzzphrase. The idea behind an ASP was that companies would provide applications to customers through the Web, saving the customers the need to actually install anything.

The model made sense, except that many of these applications were "mission critical" and firms did not want to take the risk of hosting critical information on someone else's server.

Though the ASP fad has faded, there are a few ASPs that make a lot of sense. One example is a Web-hosted email group. You don't have any installation or setup concerns, and you can get a discussion or distribution list up and running in less than an hour. (Really!)

Ongoing administration of Web-based email groups is exceedingly simple. Often you don't have to do anything except send and receive messages. Best of all, these services are free to use.

Summary of Key Web-based Mail Services		
Web-based Mail Services	*Comments*	*Price*
Yahoo! Groups	Formerly known as eGroups (Yahoo! acquired the company in 2000), this is probably the most popular free Web-based group service. You can create distribution or discussion lists, control subscriptions, and automatically handle bounces. It includes ads on all messages. See http://groups.yahoo.com.	Free

Summary of Key Web-based Mail Services (*continued*)		
Web-based Mail Services	***Comments***	***Price***
Topica	The biggest alternative to Yahoo! Groups, home to hundreds of thousands of groups. Groups include more than thirteen million subscribers and the service sends out more than four billion email messages per year. See http://www.topica.com.	Free (premium options can be purchased, from $15 to $500 per month). (Note: this price is current as of publication, but inevitably will change.)

Depending on your preferences, you have a number of alternatives when using Web-based mail services. Some examples of sites providing similar functionality are listed in the above table.

One downside to these Web-based services is that in order to remain free, they are ad-supported. The result is that when your messages are sent out to your subscribers, they have ads at the bottom. This may not be a big deal, but you should bear in mind that you will be sending email that advertises someone else's services. In addition, the return email address of the messages is "**yourfirm-news@yahoogroups.com**" instead of "**news@yourfirm.com**."

With a Budget

If you're with a larger firm, or you have committed to using email for marketing purposes and want the system under your control, you may wish to explore setting up your own mailing list system.

There are two options in implementing your own system: you can either pay a service provider to host your list (the **LawMarketing.com** listserv, for example, is hosted by First Step Internet) or you can buy the software and install it on your own server. In order to use your own server, you should have a dedicated connection to the Internet and a dedicated mail server. (Setting these up is beyond the scope of this book; if you don't have someone in-house who understands it, consult with a local systems integrator or consultant who does.)

Mailing-List Software

In order to use this software, you'll need to do some customization so that the system knows where your mail server is located, how to access your Internet connection, who has rights to send mail to the lists, and so on.

Once configured, you'll have complete control over the lists: how they operate, whether they are moderated, how they accept subscribers, and whether the messages are archived. The advantages to this choice is that you won't be including any outside advertising, and the email messages will come from your firm's domain name rather than from a third party's domain.

By owning your own system, you will not be subject to any limitations on the number of email messages you can send, or how many recipients you can have. Mailing-list software systems can include other features—like intelligent bounce handling (outdated email addresses are automatically removed from the list) and filtering of duplicate messages—that result in a better overall list experience for you and for your subscribers.

The most popular mailing-list software packages are listed below. Be sure to distinguish between applications that run on a typical stand-alone computer, and list-service software that requires more powerful hardware. (Note: prices listed below are current as of publication, but inevitably will change.)

Summary of Key Mailing-list Software Packages		
Mailing-list Software	*Comments*	*Price*
Arrow Mailing List	Popular "personal" mailing list application that will run on most versions of Windows (does not need to be on a server). Supports distribution lists but not discussion lists. See www.jadebox.com/arrow.	$50 to register the software.
L-Soft Listserv	The oldest and most high-end option, a true email list server. Has been around for years and powers some of the world's largest and busiest lists. See www.lsoft.com/listserv.htm.	Prices vary depending on the number of lists and the number of subscribers. Expect cost to start in the thousands. (There is also a Listserv Lite product that is lower-cost and appropriate for smaller customers.)

Summary of Key Mailing-list Software Packages (*continued*)		
Mailing-list Software	*Comments*	*Price*
LetterRip Pro	A Mac-based email distribution list program. Has received high marks from the Mac press. See **www.fogcity.com/letter-rip.html**.	$395 to register.
Lyris	An established competitor to L-Soft. Has been around nearly as long and has grown in popularity in that time. Server supports both distribution and discussion lists. See **www.lyris.com**.	Free download for lists with fewer than 200 subscribers. Prices start at $500 for 200+ subscribers, and can go as high as $30,000 for unlimited usage.
MailKing	Windows-based personal bulk email program. Will support mass mail merges with data sources from a database, Excel spreadsheet, or contact manager. Supports Office 2000 and is customizable. Distribution lists only. See **www.mailking.com**.	$199 for download; $229 for CD and "media kit" (documentation).

Mailing-List Services

The middle road between free services like Yahoo! Groups and software packages like L-Soft's Listserv is to buy a service.

The idea behind these services is to provide the convenience of a Web-based service and the features of a software solution without requiring you to own a server. In some cases (see the chart below), you can even pay a company to host a Lyris or Listserv server on their equipment, saving you the administrative burden while giving you access to the full power and flexibility of those systems.

For as little as $100 per month, you can have subscriber management, statistical reporting on list distributions (see more on this below), unlimited subscribers, and ad-free mailings. The chart below shows some popular Web-based hosting services. (Note: prices listed below are current as of publication, but inevitably will change.)

Summary of Web-based Hosting Services		
Web-based Hosting Services	*Comments*	*Price*
iMakeNews.com	Popular newsletter distribution service. Basic service includes HTML-formatted email messages and sophisticated tracking of readership and click-throughs. See **www.imakenews.com**.	Monthly costs start at $200 and go up based on the number of lists and the number of recipients.
SparkLIST	Offers customers the choice between hosted lists and dedicated servers (where you have your own Lyris server to run as many lists as you want). Fully configurable. They can assist with HTML formatting for email messages and can provide training, list backups, and other value-added services. See **www.sparklist.com**.	Basic service starts at $50/month and goes up; dedicated servers are at least $1500 per month.
ListHost.net	Less sophisticated service than SparkLIST, but also more aggressively priced. Offers Web-based mailing list management and numerous reporting capabilities. See **www.listhost.net**.	From $25/month.

What Goes in Your Email Messages?

What you put in your email messages will depend on what you're trying to accomplish with your email marketing effort. If you're using the distribution list to send out firm news, consider making the email focus on a particular practice group. You could talk about new developments in the law, updates about your own practice (has someone joined the firm with particular experience?), or more general news of interest to your clients relating to your practice area. You could link back to content on your Web site as a way to encourage visitors to return to your site.

The Benefits of Email Marketing

By regularly communicating with individuals via email, you can accomplish a number of goals:

1. **Cross-selling.** Very often, individuals are aware of the expertise that *you* provide them, but they aren't aware of the other services the firm could provide them. By including this kind of information in your email messages, you can effectively cross-sell other services in the firm. By expanding your relationship with these individuals, you'll ensure that you have deeper relationships with your clients.

2. **Education.** If you are the one to explain a concept to a person or to enlighten him about a particular legal risk, you have a greater chance of being the lawyer he will want to help with that issue. By using your email messages to educate your audiences, you are helping them better understand the issues that affect them. You also become a more trusted advisor, which can only lead to more business for the firm.

3. **Traffic.** You can use your email messages to encourage repeat traffic to your Web site. (Always include links to your Web site(s) in your emails.) No matter how effective your Web site is, people won't necessarily remember to come back and visit often. By sending email out periodically, you can remind people that there is valuable content at the Web site.

4. **Attendance.** If your firm hosts a number of events, email is a good, non-threatening way to ensure higher attendance. You can remind invitees, enable them to RSVP online, and give directions to registrants.

A Word about Newsgroups

Before the Web gained popularity, most of the information that was exchanged on the Internet was exchanged through a system called

Usenet. Usenet is a collection of "newsgroups"—topic-specific groups that allow people to send and receive email focused on a particular subject. Newsgroups are functionally similar to mailing lists, though newsgroups are archived and do not run on a single server. (The difference in technology isn't particularly important, but if you're interested in learning more, you can do so by visiting **http://www.faqs.org/faqs/usenet/faq/part1**).

Today, Usenet is mostly a niche application used by technically sophisticated users and individuals interested in particularly esoteric topics. While legal-specific newsgroups exist today, much of the traffic on the groups is of the "I need a lawyer to sue my doctor" variety. If you have a consumer-oriented practice, you may find some merit in marketing your firm on Usenet newsgroups. If you don't, you can probably afford to avoid them entirely.

We should add one potential exception: Google, the popular Internet search engine, acquired Deja News, the original Web archive of Usenet newsgroup postings. Google added functionality and content, as well as a superior search engine, and released "Google Groups." You can now search a complete archive of every posting to Usenet since 1981. (For fun, search for the first mention of Microsoft, or Marc Andreesen's announcement of Mosaic [precursor to Netscape], or Linus Torvalds' announcement of Linux.) Because of Google Groups, you may see some advantage in posting newsletters, firm announcements, etc., on a relevant newsgroup. With Google's archive, users are able to search for content in which they're interested, and could easily find your postings. (See **http://groups.google.com.**)

Tips and Tricks for Email Marketing

- ♦ **Keep it brief.** Be respectful of the recipients' time. Even if you have a wealth of content to share, include just a headline and synopsis, with a link to the full text of the article on your Web site. In this way, people can get a quick update if they're in a hurry. If they want more information, you're giving them access to it.
- ♦ **Use other people's content.** There's no rule that says that the content in a newsletter must be your own. As long as you include attribution, you can link to other news items on the Web. The benefit? You can include timely content and point your readers to a variety of sources. They will appreciate the inclusion of relevant information, and you benefit by periodically getting your name and firm information in front of these readers. (Note: be mindful of copyrights.)

- **Track click-throughs.** Without customization, you won't have any way to track when people click on links in your email messages. (If the links are back to your Web site, you'll be able to track traffic to those URLs. But you will not be able to know which visitors came from email, and which came from links within the Web site.) The value of tracking click-throughs is that you get a better idea of how many people are actually reading your email. There are a variety of ways to accomplish this. Check with your Web site programmer or see an HTML reference site like CNET's **Builder.com** for more information.

- **Track readership.** While email can be a powerful marketing tool, it's not worth doing if nobody is reading. You can use sophisticated tools to find out if anyone is reading your email messages; these may be offered through the software or the services you use (if you're not sure, be sure to ask). With tracking, you'll be able to tell if you have enough readers to justify your efforts.

- **Use HTML.** Traditional email messages are sent in plain text. There is no formatting (underline, bold, font size increases, etc.). HTML, the language of Web pages, is increasingly common for email as well. Many email programs are capable of reading HTML, which means your recipients will see a message that stands out from the other email they receive. You can include images and colors. Dressing up email can make it far more attractive, as well as easier to read.

  Be aware that images require more bandwidth and will delay downloads if your readers have slower connections.

- **Let people unsubscribe.** Be a good Internet citizen. If people who receive your email ask to be removed from your list, remove them immediately. If you don't, you run the risk of (at best) annoying them or (at worst) violating a variety of Coalition Against Unsolicited Commercial Email (CAUCE) policies (see **www.cauce.com**). There are no federal UCE laws in place right now, although several proposals are pending. The UCE laws that have passed are state-by-state, and fewer than half the states have passed UCE-specific laws. Of those that have, fewer than half require an opt-out. For more information, see **www.spamlaws.com**.

*CHAPTER***FOUR**

Email Netiquette

Email HAS REVOLUTIONIZED COMMUNICATION. What began as a convenient business tool has turned into a conduit for the sharing of family stories, jokes, and restaurant recommendations. Formality and caution have been thrown to the wind, and it's unfortunate. Civility has suffered. Good grammar and eloquent expression are often no more than a fleeting afterthought, long after a message has been sent.

You only have one chance to make a first impression, so it had better be good. In hard-copy correspondence, lawyers scour the page thoroughly—for content, to ensure their messages are clear and concise, to avoid slang or vernacular that may be inappropriately familiar, and for grammatical and spelling correctness. Why then is email not subject to the same careful scrutiny?

Business email should always follow certain guidelines or protocol, regardless of how friendly the parties to the email have become. Lawyers, when using email to communicate with clients and to transmit documents, should be especially careful to follow the basic rules of "netiquette."

1. **Use a business conversational tone.** While the advantages of email are informality and speed, don't take this to mean "haphazard" or "no-need-to-proof." Spelling errors, catchy phrases, incomplete sentences, and highly personal inferences or references are inappropriate in business correspondence—electronic or otherwise. Your test of appropriateness should be: how would I feel if my message was forwarded to the company CEO, or to my managing partner?

2. **Change the subject line to reflect the body of your email.** It's common to have five and six rounds of replies to an

original email. The information contained in the last two or three may not have anything to do with the original subject header. As your information and focus changes in your email exchange, change the subject, too. You can track it more easily and will be able to search for references to specific matters or issues later on.

3. **Never use profanity.** It doesn't matter how angry you are, how irritating the other side of a negotiation is, or how thrilled you are with a result. Profanity is never appropriate in any business communication—oral or written. This includes racist remarks (often included in jokes), and sexual innuendoes as well.

There is a lot of humorous material circulating via email. Before you forward limericks to your client or referral list, remember that some might find this entertainment questionable, or their employers may have policies against receiving this kind of material at work. Know your audience and respond accordingly.

4. **Use a memo or modified letter format.** Even though you have an email address, you should begin your business correspondence with *To, From, Re,* or *Dear Harry* and type your name at the end. If there are *cc*'s, use the full name of the recipients.

Never use all capital letters—IT'S LIKE SHOUTING. Avoid cute smiley faces and other "emoticons" in business correspondence, unless your client has taken the lead in this regard. While emotions work with your mother in Milwaukee or your freshman daughter at the University of Virginia, they might appear silly if your message is ever forwarded upstream in the company.

5. **The need for speed.** Since an advantage of email is speed, know that your clients and others expect quick response and turnaround when sending you messages or requests for information. Read your incoming mail several times a day and respond promptly. If you don't have an immediate answer to a question, say that you are seeking a response and will get back in a designated period of time. Never leave your clients and others hanging, waiting and wondering if you received the email and when they will next hear from you.

6. **Confidential information takes great care.** We have all heard horror stories about confidential documents being emailed to the wrong distribution list. This is a completely avoidable mistake. Choose your addressees, attach documents, prepare a cover memorandum or letter, and double-check *all* addresses on your distribution list before transmitting.

7. **Speaking of confidential.** Double-check the *To:* field before sending a reply to ensure that your comments are *only* going to your colleague or client, and not to the other side. Also double-check the chain of messages in the subsequent rounds of replies to ensure that there isn't anything that should not be forwarded to someone who was not a party to the original conversation. There are unfortunate but true stories about email messages that disparaged opposing counsel in early replies, but by five or six rounds those comments had been forgotten, and the message seemed "safe" to send.

8. **A word about discussion groups and mailing lists.** Participating in a casual discussion group or on a mailing list about a substantive area of law or business doesn't give you permission to throw online caution to the wind. Every word of your dialogue should be as carefully chosen as if you were speaking to an audience of a thousand CEOs or corporate counsel.

   Choose your discussion group or mailing list carefully. Select forums that focus on your areas of expertise, so you can demonstrate your insight and problem-solving skills. **Caution:** Everyone is pressed for time. Do not ramble on and on in your posts. Be clear, concise, and make your point quickly. Offer your phone number and email address to interested parties who may want additional information from you.

   Don't forget that anything you post to a group or mailing list is likely to be archived somewhere online—*forever*. While you may be interested in participating in an online forum today, keep in mind that ten years from now, someone could find your off-the-cuff remark in an online archive. Will that remark reflect positively on you and your firm? If not, consider the *ESC* key instead of the *SEND* key.

9. **Cool off and count to ten.** Everyone gets angry and many of us express ourselves in vivid detail. Typing a fierce and pointed response may console you for the moment, but sending a foot-stomping, door-slamming retort may accelerate the debate or controversy in an unintended way. You will appear as if you've lost control.

   Type the message you wish, but wait to transmit until you've cooled down and regained your perspective. If the response still seems appropriate, send it. If not, you've saved yourself the embarrassment of being caught in a tantrum. Write a neutral, more-controlled message that will, undoubtedly, be better received.

10. **Email policies.** If you don't have an email policy, create one—
    or better yet, an Internet use policy. Your policy should inform
    firm employees that their email isn't private and that "deleted"
    messages don't really disappear and can be found later on. In
    addition, the policy should state the firm's tolerance of employ-
    ees receiving and directing personal email. You might suggest
    that if employees need to receive personal email at work, they
    should create a separate, free account (such as one from MSN
    Hotmail—see **www.hotmail.com**), but that they should limit this
    to pressing family matters.

    To enforce firm policies, it may be a good idea to include a for-
    mal "acceptable use policy" (AUP) governing use of all the firm's
    electronic resources. An AUP gives employees a solid understand-
    ing of how and when it's appropriate to use firm resources, and
    gives guidance with regard to employees' rights concerning per-
    sonal matters. If you want more information about AUPs, visit
    Yahoo! or other Internet directories.

11. **Email hyperlinks on your Web site.** Many law firm sites
    have several ways in which visitors can contact firm lawyers. The
    email address is hyperlinked on lawyer resumes, in the broader
    directory, and in practice-area descriptions. This establishes an
    expectation that these lawyers will respond to queries by visitors.
    If you have no intention of answering visitors' email questions
    or comments, do not hyperlink your email addresses on your
    Web site. This also goes for email hyperlinks on your listing at
    Martindale.com.

    Most law firm sites have a "contact us" section. The email
    address often goes to a site administrator or Webmaster. Who is
    this person? Is the person qualified to route email messages to
    the appropriate parties in your firm? Ensure that this individual
    understands the urgency of a rapid response, and will follow up
    with the lawyers to see that they are handling the queries.

12. **"My secretary prints out emails and I read them that
    way."** Call us sticklers, but why bother? We aren't suggesting
    that you should be an early adopter, but we *do* believe that any
    lawyer not using email to regularly communicate with clients is
    missing out completely. Show us a business decision-maker who
    doesn't depend on email during the business day, and we'll show
    you a company whose stock price is declining.

13. **Who sent this email?** Insist that everyone in your firm
    include a signature block that automatically appears at the end

of every email they create. The block should include the writer's name, firm name, mailing address, phone, fax, and email address. It can also include a positioning tag line that your firm uses in its advertising. Most email programs enable you to set up an automatic signature. (In Microsoft Outlook under the Tools menu, click on Auto Signature and follow the instructions.)

Some programs allow users to create and attach digital business cards. Users of Microsoft Outlook and other email programs (such as Goldmine) can automatically transfer the card into their contact files. This is useful for the first correspondence with someone, but over time it clutters up the mailbox with duplicate attachments.

14. **Disclaimers.** Most law firms include a disclaimer on every email. Read yours carefully. Are twelve lines of warnings really necessary? Shorten your disclaimer so that it satisfies the basic concerns, but doesn't go overboard.

Communication between a lawyer and a client or prospect should be comfortable, but always professional. It should be consistent from one medium to the next. Focus on how you are perceived electronically and follow these guidelines. This should give you and your colleagues the flexibility and speed you want without sacrificing your firm's message and reputation in the process.

*CHAPTER***FIVE**

Promotional Content

An Introduction to Web Site Content

The formula for a successful Web site is not complicated. The site should be marketed well, and when visitors get there, they should find a great-looking site with superb content. This sounds simple, but executing it is another story. In the next five chapters, we will focus on content strategies. We will review content-strategy basics, and look at some of the creative offerings on many of the Web's best law firm sites.

Determining what content you will have on your Web site largely depends on whom you want to attract to your site. Prospects, law-school recruits, reporters, and current clients all want different kinds of information. Once you have clearly defined your target market or markets, the task of determining your site's content will be simplified.

While your target markets will determine the specific types of content you have on your site, there are some common denominators. A good law firm Web site will typically be strong in the following four content areas:

+ Promotional content;
+ Informational content;
+ Interactive content; and
+ Navigational content.

Promotional Content

In the early days of the Web, the legal profession's Internet gurus preached that the only type of content that mattered was informational content. It is true that a site with rich information can pay off handsomely. But it was probably never true that a site's promotional content lacked importance. A good Web site will have the same effect as a polished brochure—plus the potential for much more. A site should enhance a firm's image and help clients, referral sources, reporters, and others determine if the firm has the appropriate expertise and credentials. And the site should readily communicate the most basic contact information—a firm's email addresses, phone numbers, office directions, and so on.

The first law firm Web sites in the mid-90s were modest in their promotional-content offerings. Lawyer biographies, descriptions of the firm's practice areas, information on contacting the firm, and perhaps a mission or philosophy statement were the staples of these sites; little more was offered. These are still the most common features on law firm Web sites. But firms have invented numerous variations on the old formula and added new types of promotional content.

Introduction to the Firm

Firm Mission Statement or Introduction

Most law firm Web sites contain basic introductory information about the firm. This often starts with a well-crafted mission or positioning statement or introduction included on the site's home page (see figure 5-1). While the statement might be brief—a few words in a tag line or a sentence or two—the impact of these words may be as important as anything else on the site. The introduction can describe the firm's main practice focus and its philosophy about the practice of law, as well as the firm's unique selling point. Avoid platitudes and descriptions that hundreds of other law firms use, such as "We are client-centered, cost-effective, and responsive. We partner with our clients, whether Fortune 500 or small business owners."

Firm Profile

Within the site itself, a firm should consider a separate section of the site for a more detailed firm profile (see figure 5-2). The section might include a detailed practice overview that provides a quick synopsis of the firm's capabilities and personality. How firms label this section varies. Some use terms like "Welcome," "Firm Overview," "The Firm," "Our Firm," "Firm Info," and "About Us" as the page title. On some sites, the content is minimal—just a short description of the firm. Others will write much more extensively about the firm, linking to pages describing the markets served, the firm's practice focus, size, etc.

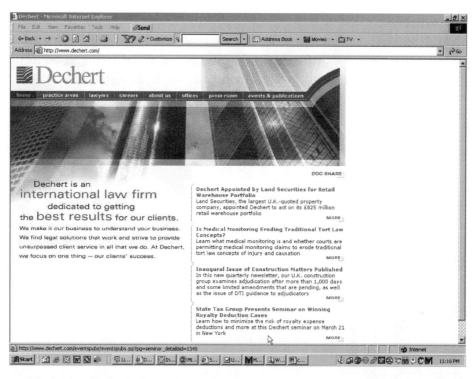

FIGURE 5-1. Dechert's introductory message

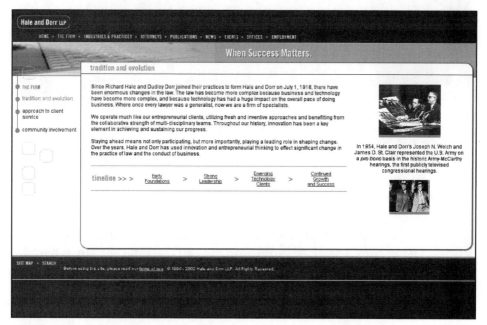

FIGURE 5-2. Hale and Dorr's firm profile page

Firm History

Most firms have a story to tell. Including a section of the site for the history of the firm (see figure 5-3) can be interesting, if it doesn't go on too long. Of course, this assumes that there is an impressive story about which to write. Some firms have gone so far as to produce entire books about their history. An advantage of the Web is that you can add hundreds of pages of additional text for virtually no extra cost. Publishing a book on a Web site is not a difficult task.

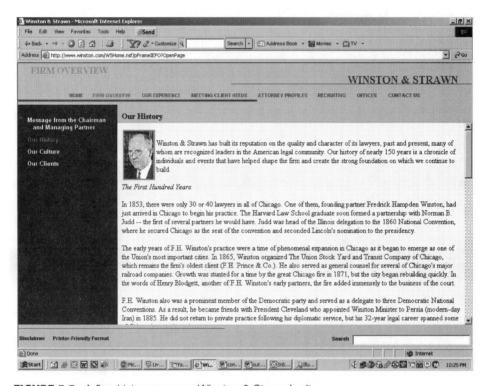

FIGURE 5-3. A firm history page on Winston & Strawn's site

Firms often view their history as more critical to new client relationships than clients do. Most clients don't really care. If your history is rich, however, breathe life into your firm's ancestors by telling stories, rather than merely regurgitating details. A Dayton, Ohio-based firm, Bieser, Greer & Landis, dates back before the Civil War. The firm has some colorful and unusual stories, including the firm founder making it into *Ripley's Believe It or Not!* twice! So they created a "Firm History" Flash timeline at **www.biesergreer.com**.

Practice Areas and Industry Areas

Most midsize and larger law firms organize themselves in traditional practice groupings—litigation, corporate, tax, trusts and estates, etc. There are numerous multidisciplinary practice areas as well. The challenge in designing the site is the same challenge firms face when organizing themselves. How many lawyers should you have to form a department? Is it better to go with just a few departments and bring lawyers together with a range of experience? Or is it a better business and marketing move to have many departments?

Most law firm Web sites include links to major practice groups. But how much emphasis should be placed on small practice groups? With limited time and financial resources, many firms have opted to focus on developing content for their primary practice areas, rather than including everything.

Still, other firms promote unusual practice areas on their sites. While most midsize and large-sized firms have real estate practices, how many have, for example, a golf practice? Saul Ewing, LLP, one of the first law firms to have a Web site, is a large Philadelphia firm with this niche practice (see figure 5-4).

Practice areas don't have to be divided along traditional lines (see figure 5-5). Forward-thinking firms realize that most non-lawyers don't distinguish lawyers this way. These firms focus first on the industries in which their clients are engaged. Many firms are now organizing themselves by industry, grouping lawyers delivering a variety of legal services around a particular group of clients. Technology and health care are two prominent examples. Others have gone with a hybrid approach where lawyers are grouped in traditional practices as well as industry areas.

Prospects want to know three things: 1) what you've done, 2) for whom you've done it, and 3) what you can do for them. The industry and/or practice area section of a Web site should:

   ♦ List the specific cases and matters that each group handles;
   ♦ Link to the resumes of each member of the practice group;
   ♦ Link to substantive content on the site (and perhaps on other sites) that would be of interest to visitors; and
   ♦ Name the clients or the types of clients the group serves (such as Fortune 500 energy and pharmaceutical companies or small cap and midmarket technology companies). Check your state bar's

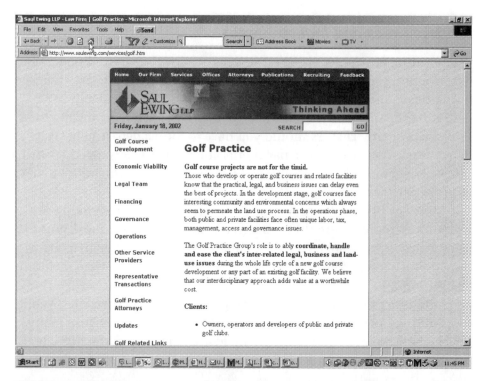

FIGURE 5-4. An example of a page marketing a niche practice area

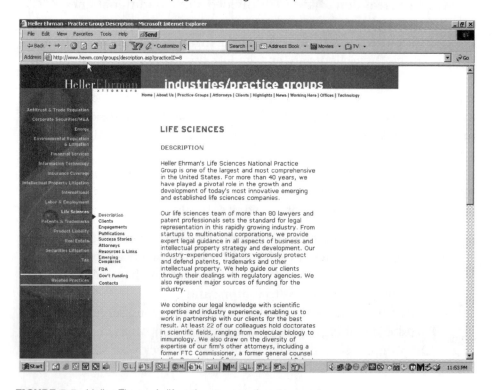

FIGURE 5-5. Heller Ehrman's life sciences practice group page

ethics rules before naming clients, then obtain your clients' permission. See Chapter Fifteen, "Web Ethics and Ethical Issues of Online Marketing," for more information.

Lawyer Resumes

We briefly discussed lawyer resumes in Chapter Two, "Developing an Internet Marketing Plan," but they deserve more attention. Virtually every law firm Web site includes biographies of the firm's lawyers. This isn't surprising since resumes are a primary target for people visiting law firm Web sites. A basic biography is a must, but firms vary significantly in how they present biographical information.

Many firms provide just the bare facts in lawyer biographies—*á lá* Martindale-Hubbell listings—but we think they are missing out. Many, like Vinson & Elkins (**www.velaw.com/our_lawyers/our_lawyers.cfm**) write extensively about their lawyers (see figure 5-6). Calgary's Burnet, Duckworth & Palmer (**www.bdplaw.com**) jazzes up their resumes by telling a little about the personal lives of each of the lawyers, with a photo to match (see figure 5-7). To put your best foot forward, the resume should include the following information:

- Lawyer contact information (phone numbers, email address, etc.);
- The lawyer's position in the firm (associate, partner, etc.);
- The city where the lawyer practices (if a firm has multiple offices);
- Department or practice area(s) in the firm where the lawyer spends the majority of time;
- Photograph;
- Description of areas of experience, and specific matters handled;
- Other professional experience (CPA, banker, executive, etc.);
- Bar memberships and bar leadership;
- *Recent* publications;
- Honors and awards received;
- Schools and degrees;
- Board memberships (civic, professional, trade); and perhaps
- Video or voice introduction (this is becoming more popular).

But having excellent lawyer biography pages is only part of the job. Making it easy to find the *right* lawyer is the other part. There are simple ways to handle this. You can simply include a list of lawyers, divided alphabetically or by practice area, and hyperlink to each lawyer's biographical page. The list might be in the form of a table that contains contact information for each of the lawyers as well.

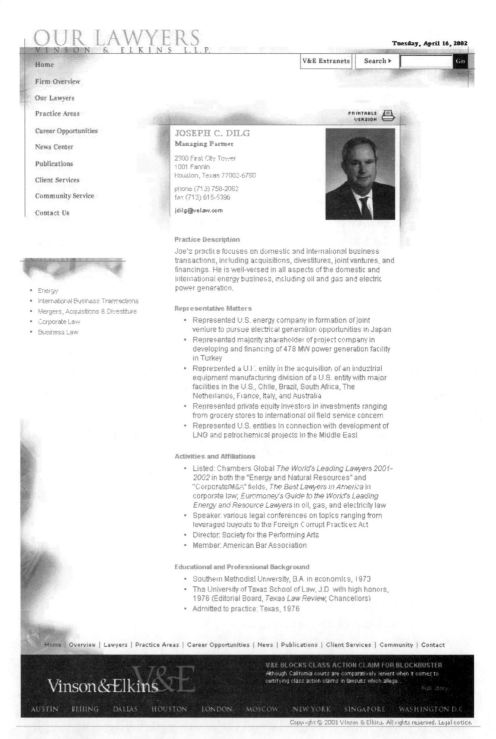

FIGURE 5-6. An extensive lawyer biography

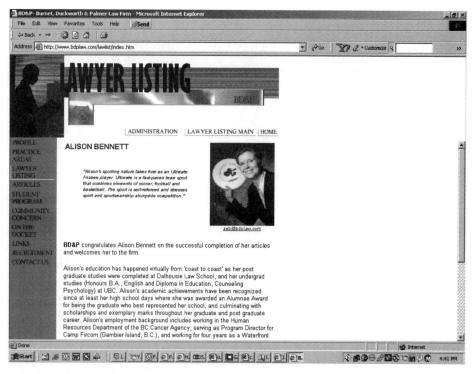

FIGURE 5-7. A lawyer bio with personal information

But for firms with hundreds or even thousands of lawyers, finding a specific lawyer is more of a challenge. Minnesota's Faegre & Benson LLP (**www.faegre.com**) addressed this by developing lawyer search engines that allow readers to scan the list of lawyers and search by various categories or by key words (see figure 5-8). Other sites allow searching based on categories that include the following:

◆ Name;

◆ Title (associate, partner, of counsel, etc.);

◆ Law school;

◆ Practice group;

◆ Industries and practices;

◆ Professional and trade association or organization memberships;

◆ Languages spoken;

◆ Bar and court admissions;

◆ Office location; and

◆ Links to Martindale and West biographies.

Another excellent example of a site that makes it easy to search for lawyers based on multiple search categories is Squire Sanders (**www.ssd.com/who**), a firm with more than 750 lawyers (see figure 5-9).

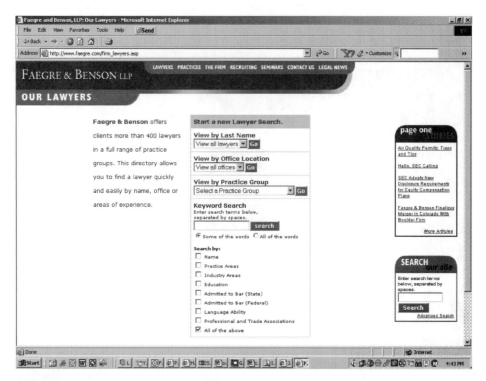

FIGURE 5-8. Faegre & Benson's attorney search engine

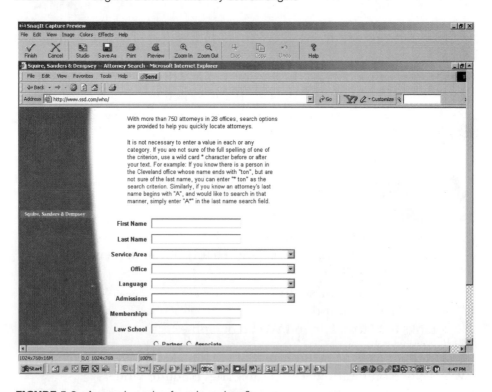

FIGURE 5-9. A search engine for a large law firm

You can do your clients a favor and boost morale among your professional staff by including information on the firm's professional and support staff, particularly their contact information.

Awards

What better place to promote the firm's accolades than on a Web site? The public-relations shelf life of a mention in the media is brief. On a Web site, a major honor can be announced and the notice left up indefinitely. Some firms have developed "trophy cases" on their sites that link to information about the various awards and honors the firm and its members have received.

Pro Bono *and Community Service*

Deserved or not, lawyers have a lousy reputation. People are often pleasantly surprised when they learn how much time lawyers give away to worthy causes. Even if as a profession we fail to publicize this "secret," your law firm should not repeat this mistake.

Promoting the firm's *pro bono* activities gives welcome recognition to the lawyers and staff who are doing this work. A Web site is not just targeted at people outside the firm. In midsize and larger law firms, the firm's Web site tells people *inside* the firm what is going on. And getting recognition from one's colleagues is rewarding for nearly everyone.

Pro bono work can be important to a firm's recruiting efforts. While many lawyers think the only thing that matters to new graduates is money, the truth is that law students care a lot about what type of life they are accepting when they join a firm. A firm's commitment to *pro bono* and community service work shows that the firm's priorities are in order.

Reporters also care about *pro bono* projects. Although a case may not produce revenue for a firm, it may raise interesting and important legal principles that catch the attention of a journalist.

Finally, *pro bono* work may not pay off in fees received, but writing about your *pro bono* cases does demonstrate experience in handling a particular type of matter. When a lawyer is trying to establish herself in a particular practice area, accepting a *pro bono* case is a way to get her feet wet. Prospects will care that she has the experience, and won't care if she was paid.

The firm's *pro bono* and community service pages should provide brief descriptions of the projects or issues. And, where possible, provide links to the email addresses and Web sites of the organizations assisted. As a matter of courtesy, be sure to contact the organization to request their permission to include the link. Remember to create a new pop-up window inside your site to open any links, rather than sending visitors away from your site.

One of the best examples of a firm promoting its *pro bono* activities online is Fredrikson & Byron (**www.fredlaw.com/probono/**). The firm includes its annual *pro bono* report, as well as information on each of its departments' *pro bono* activities (see figure 5-10).

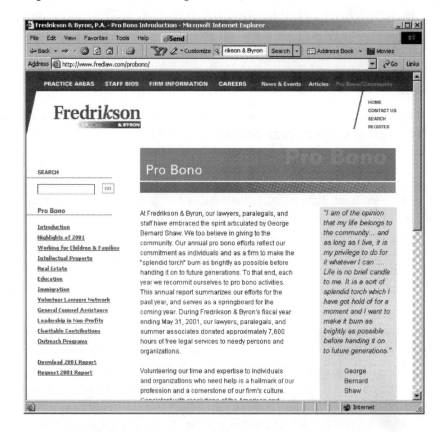

FIGURE 5-10. A page featuring *pro bono* work

Office Tours

A number of law firms have taken advantage of the Web's unique attributes and included virtual office tours on their sites. Some are slide shows and (see figure 5-12) some incorporate technology from a company called iPix that allows a viewer to get a 360-degree view of a room (see figures 5-11 and 5-13). Who really wants to tour a law firm? Anyone being recruited to work at a firm will probably be interested.

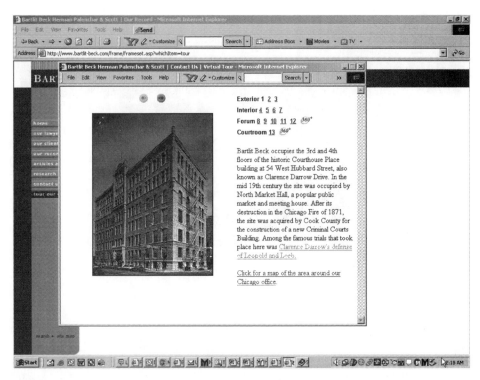

FIGURE 5-11. A virtual tour of Bartlit Beck, featuring a slide show and iPix view

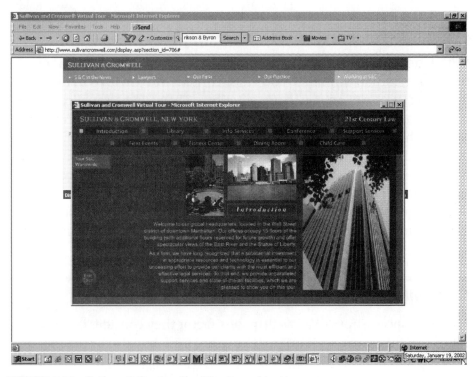

FIGURE 5-12. Sullivan & Cromwell's slide-show virtual tour

FIGURE 5-13. iPix virtual tour of Schulte Roth & Zabel

Audio, Video, and Animated Presentations

With faster Internet connections becoming the norm, more and more firms are incorporating audio and video content into their Web sites, including the use of animated presentations. They add personality to your site and can draw visitors into your site in a way that simple text cannot.

But there are downsides to consider. First, this type of content uses a lot of bandwidth and it is dangerous to assume that all of your visitors will have high-speed Internet connections. Second, producing top-quality audio and video frequently requires expertise that is beyond your typical Web designer—you might need an advertising agency or production company. Third, the price tag for a Web site with this content rises significantly.

Client Information

When prospects shop for a law firm, one factor they consider is a firm's list of current clients—not just for the entire firm, but also by practice area and by lawyer. A Web site is one place to showcase your clients, but don't just list them. The Maryland law firm Linowes & Blocher LLP (**http://www.linowes-law.com**) lists their representative clients and then includes a description of the client and a link to the client's Web site. Not only are they giving prospects a better idea of the types of clients and matters the firm can handle, but also they are helping to promote their existing clients. If you do include references to clients, get permission before mentioning their names.

Client testimonials are compelling and provide useful information to prospects. Silicon Valley's Wilson Sonsini (**www.wsgr.com**) has presented client testimonials stylishly. It includes short quotes from major clients, followed by information on the clients and links to the clients' Web sites (see figure 5-14). Before even discussing the benefits of this, a firm will want to check their state's ethics rules, since a number of jurisdictions restrict this. But assuming that testimonials are permitted, these pages add great depth to a law firm's service descriptions. See Chapter Fifteen, "Web Ethics and Ethical Issues of Online Marketing," for more information.

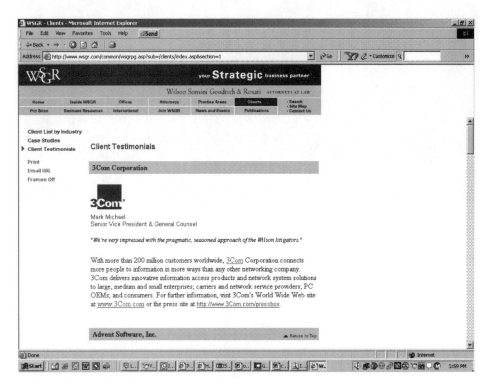

FIGURE 5-14. Client testimonials

Contact Information and Guest Services

Many people visit a law firm's Web site with nothing more in mind than getting basic contact information on the firm. Yet some firms that spend a fortune on their Web sites seem to be ignoring these users. Fortunately, this is one of the easiest features to include on your Web site. Include the most basic contact information on every Web page—a phone number, email address, and postal address on each Web page or a link to a page that includes all of this information. If your firm has multiple offices, have one central page that includes contact information for each of these offices. You can then link to separate, smaller sites for each of your branch offices. See the Winston & Strawn Web site (**www.winston.com**) for a good example of this (see figure 5-15).

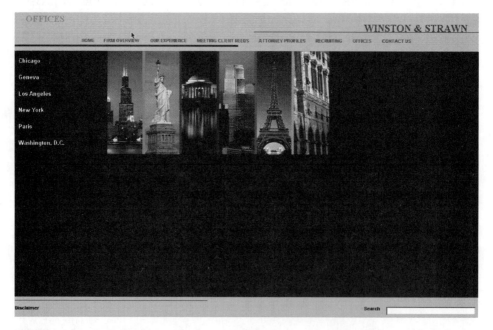

FIGURE 5-15. This site has a page for each of the firm's offices (Viewable on Netscape 4.7 and above.)

If your state bar requires a statement saying which lawyer in the firm is responsible for the site, this is a good place for it.

What type of contact information should you include? Consider the following:

- ♦ **Phone numbers:** The main numbers, plus direct-dial numbers for lawyers and support staff. Smaller firms might consider including lawyers' cell phone and pager numbers.

- **Fax numbers:** A firm's main number. Consider getting direct fax numbers for each lawyer by using eFax. EFax (**www.efax.com**) provides a free fax number and delivers faxes as email attachments (see figure 5-16).

- **Directions:** A map and driving directions so clients can easily get to your offices. Want to do it inexpensively? Mapquest (**www.mapquest.com**) can create a map that is designed to be integrated right into your Web page. It is not a bad idea to also include links to nearby hotels, as in the Web site for Patterson, Belknap, Webb & Tyler (see figure 5-17), **www.pbwt.com**. Double check to ensure that Mapquest doesn't require formal permission to include their name.

- **Email:** A general email address for inquiries from people who may not have a specific contact at your firm. Then provide a link to your lawyer resume section for visitors seeking the email address of a specific lawyer.

- **Postal address:** Addresses for each of your offices. Include P.O. Box numbers and street addresses, for packages and overnight deliveries.

FIGURE 5-16. Using **eFax.com's** services

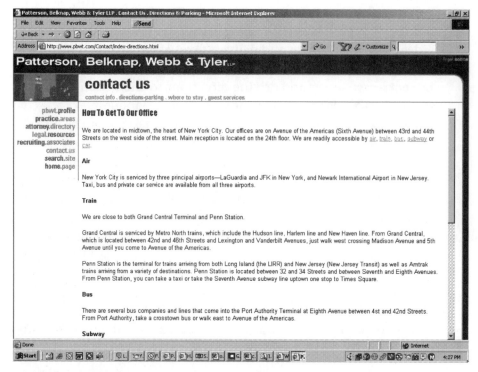

FIGURE 5-17. A guest services page

♦ **Instant Messaging:** Sometimes a prospect is hesitant to telephone the firm blindly and would prefer email. A few clever firms, such as Washington's Miller Nash, have incorporated an instant chat feature into their Web pages, making it possible for a visitor to have a real-time chat with a member of the client-services department (see figure 5-18). Just be cautious about making sure you address ethics issues such as inadvertently creating an attorney-client relationship when you pursue this strategy.

This tool can be incorporated inexpensively into your site using a service like LivePerson (**www.liveperson.com**). LivePerson's software tells you when someone is on your site, what pages he is viewing, and from where he linked to your site. You can invite a visitor to chat with you and, for example, answer a query about your firm's telecommunications experience by pushing the visitor to that industry description. For more information about these services, see Chapter Twelve, "Using Web Technology to Market Your Firm."

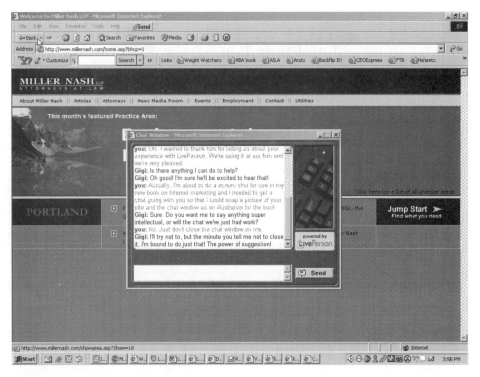

FIGURE 5-18. Real-time chat feature

News Clips

Legal marketers have long known that a well-placed story in the news can be as valuable (or more so) than any form of paid advertising. But the shelf life of the public-relations benefit is limited, since the story typically runs just once. A law firm Web site can help extend the benefit by including a link to the story. The Siskind, Susser, Haas & Devine Web site's news clipping page (**www.visalaw.com/news**), for example, includes links to more than a hundred news articles about the firm, as well as to the Real Audio files of radio interviews (see figure 5-19).

Announcements and Firm News

Your Web site can be a useful vehicle for making announcements about your law firm. These might include announcing new lawyers, success stories, new offices, etc. Also consider including a public calendar of events to

VISALAW.COM AND SSHD IN THE NEWS

APRIL 2002

The Washington Times quotes Greg Siskind in a recent article on amnesty, April 9, 2002.

JANUARY 2002

Lawyers.com praises Visalaw.com in a recent article, January 4, 2002.

The Law Marketing Portal talks about Siskind's Immigration Bulletin, January 22, 2002.

DECEMBER 2001

Memphis Business Journal quotes Greg Siskind and Lynn Susser in an article about the INS and student visas, December 14, 2001.

ABA's Law Practice Management Magazine talks about SSHD when discussing contact and relationship management technology, Nov/Dec 2001

ABA's Law Practice Management Magazine discusses Visalaw.com in its latest article titled SEND-ONLY AND DISCUSSION LISTS TO GET OUT THE NEWS, Nov/Dec 2001.

FIGURE 5-19. A news clipping page

announce seminars and social events, and to enable online registration and RSVPs (see figure 5-20). When lawyers are speaking at events hosted by other organizations, you can include links to that organization's Web site, or a phone number and email address for the event sponsor.

Press Room

Law firms are recognizing that members of the media frequently visit their Web sites for firm information. Now it is more common to see Web sites with online "press kits" to give journalists easy access to the information they are seeking. North Carolina-based Womble Carlyle provides a useful pressroom on its Web site (see figure 5-21). The site offers journalists the following:

- ◆ Recent press releases;
- ◆ List of experts and contact information;
- ◆ Registration page for journalists to receive firm email announcements;
- ◆ A contact page for the firm's communications specialist;
- ◆ A fact sheet on the law firm;
- ◆ Images of ads run by the firm; and
- ◆ History of the firm.

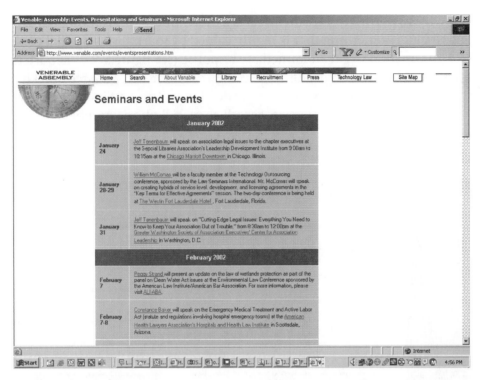

FIGURE 5-20. Venable's announcements page, with links to additional information

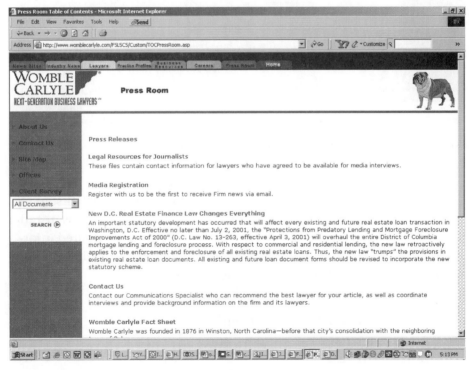

FIGURE 5-21. An extensive Press Room page

Orrick, Herrington & Sutcliffe has a more modest press room, but it does include something that is highly valued by journalists—special contact information to get an immediate response (see figure 5-22). Reporters usually are working on deadline, so if they cannot reach a source quickly, they will move on to someone else. Orrick knows this and includes an email address for urgent matters, as well as special phone numbers to reach someone quickly.

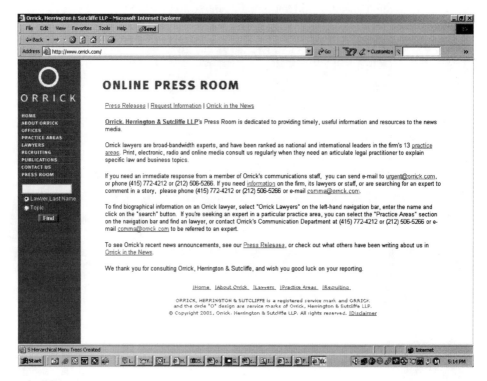

FIGURE 5-22. A press room with links for immediate response

Seattle's Miller Nash has a press room that requires a journalist to register before logging in (see figure 5-23). The registration process is instantaneous so the journalist will not be delayed in getting the desired information. Once in, the journalist can get into several areas in addition to some of the ones mentioned above. They include:

◆ Story ideas;
◆ Downloadable logos for the firm;
◆ A link to a "chat now" window; and
◆ Noteworthy cases.

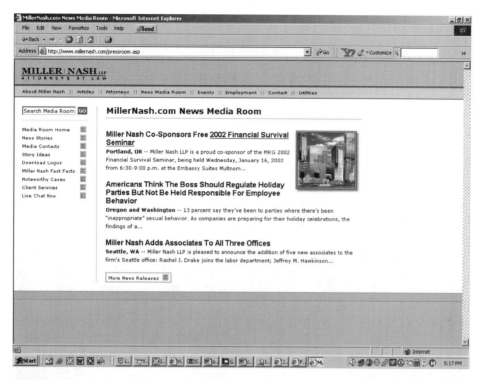

FIGURE 5-23. A site News Media Room

Recruiting

If you analyze the traffic of the typical large law firm Web site, you will discover something very interesting. The majority of visitors may not be prospects, journalists, existing clients, or competitors. The majority of visitors are coming from law schools. More specifically, they are coming from law students hunting for jobs and researching possible future employers.

Law firms invest millions of dollars in recruiting top talent. So it is not surprising that many of these firms are focusing on developing Web content that is specifically geared to recruiting law students as well as lateral hires. Many firms include "Recruiting" or "Careers" sections on their sites, and more ambitious firms have developed separate Web sites just for recruiting. Firms frequently design their recruiting sites or sections differently so they are more edgy, contemporary, and fun. They may avoid bandwidth-consuming Flash in other sections of the site, but they often include it here.

One of the better recruiting sites belongs to Chicago-based Kirkland & Ellis. Kirkland & Ellis builds a customized Web page for each law school (see figure 5-24). For example, on the University of Chicago page, the firm lists interview dates on campus, members of the firm who lecture or have lectured at the school, scholarships sponsored at the school by the firm, links to alumni of the school who work at the firm, as well as testimonials from some of the alumni. The site also provides more general information, including a class profile for the summer associates in each of the firm's offices, information on the summer associate program, video testimonials from members of the firm, and a copy of the National Association of Law Placement (NALP) form.

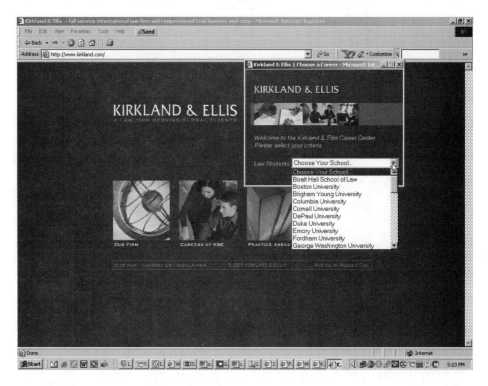

FIGURE 5-24. A customized recruiting page

Kirkland also has a section of its Web site devoted to recruiting other professionals and staff at the firm, something that many firms forget.

Atlanta's King & Spalding has developed an elaborate training program for new lawyers, called K & S University, which they showcase on their Web site (see figure 5-25). (For fun, on its "Recruiting" page, King & Spalding also includes an outtakes video—those moments captured on film that show the lawyers at their most humble. See **www.kingandspalding.com**. The outtakes video is not viewable with Netscape 4 and Windows 98. With Windows XP and Netscape 4, the video has to be downloaded and saved to disk before viewing.)

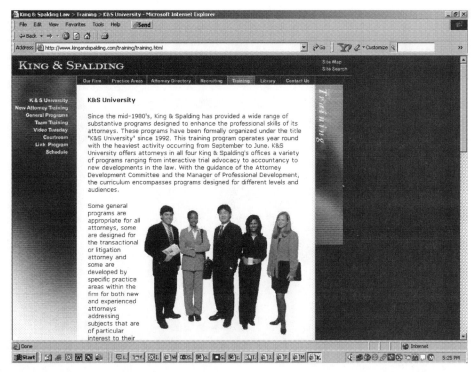

FIGURE 5-25. K&S University

Alumni

Short-sighted law firms look at a lawyer leaving the firm as a sort of betrayal. Smarter firms realize that lawyers who leave are potential referral sources and their future success reflects well on the firm. For example, Texas' Bracewell & Patterson has an entire section of its Web site devoted to its alumni program (see figure 5-26). Articles from the firm's alumni magazine are included, and alumni can update their profiles on the Web site.

Firm Personality

Many law firm Web sites look the same. But a few firms manage to let their hair down and have the courage to let personality shine through. An example is Sacramento's McDonough, Holland & Allen (www.mhalaw.com). The firm includes a section called "After Hours" and describes its art collection (see figure 5-27), as well as a section called "The Fridge," where it chats about the extracurricular activities of the firm's lawyers. It also has a "Community Chest"—a section that showcases its community service projects.

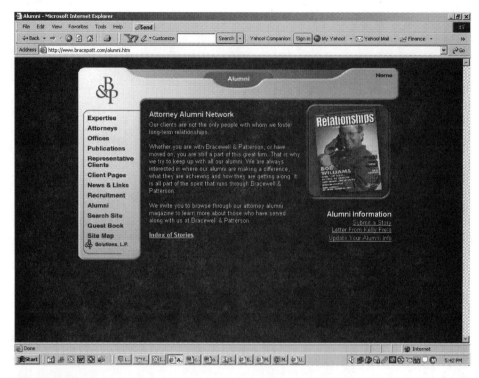

FIGURE 5-26. Alumni page

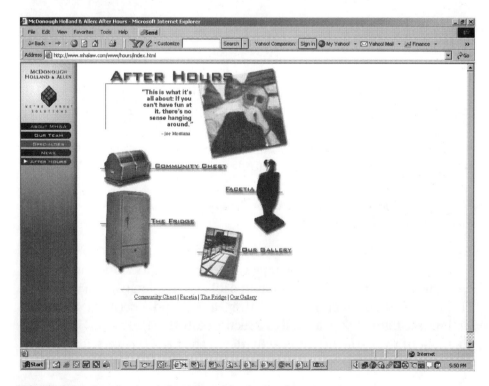

FIGURE 5-27. A page showing another side of a law firm

Another firm that has used its recruiting section to show personality is D'Ancona & Plfaum, a Chicago-based firm (**www.dancona.com**). Click on the recruiting link to learn about the "Buzz on D'Ancona" and see a good but simple use of animation (see figure 5-28).

Many firms also include humor sections that typically take the form of lawyer jokes. Unfortunately, most of the jokes are stale and create a lasting, but unfortunate, impression of the firm. If you want to incorporate humor into the Web site, preview it with people outside your firm and outside the legal profession. You may find that what you think is funny isn't appreciated by everyone. If you have a question about it, avoid it.

Other firms have managed to get creative in different ways. Baltimore's Venable law firm has a law quiz on its site (see figure 5-29), Orrick has a recruiting game (see figure 5-30), and Houston-based Baker Botts has a section on its recruiting page that includes video games.

FIGURE 5-28. A creative recruiting section

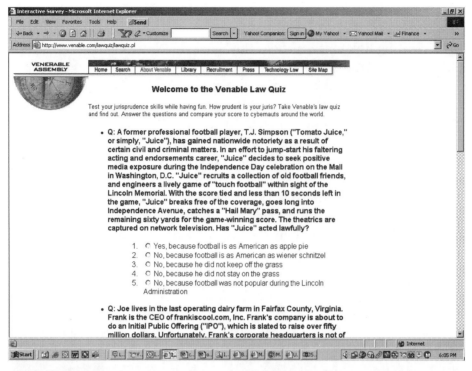

FIGURE 5-29. Law quiz

FIGURE 5-30. Recruiting game

Proposal Center

A new use of the Web is to generate and publish proposals for prospects. Miller Nash has designed a system that pulls content from its Web site, combines it with custom information for a particular client or prospect, and then generates a proposal that is viewable over the Web and easily printable (see figure 5-31). The typical Miller Nash Web-based proposal includes the following:

- Cover page;
- Introduction letter;
- Practice area descriptions with hyperlinks;
- Lawyer biographies;
- Custom text-only pages;
- Standard page about the firm;
- Fee information;
- Client lists; and
- Index.

Cover page to a hypothetical
proposal to Chad Summers International

FIGURE 5-31. Proposal Center

*CHAPTER***SIX**

Informational Content

EFFECTIVELY PUBLICIZING AN ATTRACTIVE, well-organized site with lots of promotional information may initially attract a visitor to your home page, but getting repeat visitors and building name recognition and reputation through your Web site requires much more.

Sophisticated legal marketers have long realized that being published is one of the more effective means of promoting your practice. A timely article on a hot topic can bring considerable recognition, and writing a book is even better. The Internet now offers a new opportunity for lawyers to be published since Web sites are, at their essence, a form of self-publishing. Publishing on relevant topics can make your Web site, and your firm, stand out in the crowd.

Traditional publishing, in many respects, is less effective than Internet publishing. Traditional publishing usually requires a publisher to help disseminate information. It may take a long time for an article or book to get into print, and space is often at a premium. On a Web site, information can be published almost as soon as it is written. You can write as much as you want with no additional cost.

Some law firm Web sites now have such strong content that they rival traditional legal publishers in their usefulness. These sites are helping the firms position themselves as leading experts in their fields, and bringing new clients to the firms.

When developing an information product for your Web site, consider several points:

- ♦ What written information does your firm currently produce?
- ♦ Do you already produce client newsletters or bulletins?
- ♦ Do you disseminate memoranda to clients, updating them on important developments in the law?

♦ Do you have access to information that people can't easily find else-where?

♦ Have you recently prepared written material for a seminar? Train your lawyers to make any written material intended for outside audiences available on the firm's Web site.

Newsletters

Firm and practice-group newsletters are popular items to post on a firm's Web site. Some of these publications are produced in hard copy and republished on the Web as text or Adobe PDF. (PDF is a popular format for publishing on the Web.) Others are now being produced exclusively for the Web. Online newsletters can be accessed by Web site visitors who follow a hyperlink, or can be sent as text pasted into email. If you post your newsletter on your Web site, you can send email that includes the newsletter table of contents, short teasers about the stories, and a hyperlink to the newsletter that will pull readers back to your site.

Baker Daniels has a comprehensive collection of online newsletters on its Web site. Publishing as many as fifty different weekly, biweekly, or monthly newsletters, Baker Daniels has an off-line distribution strategy to complement the online one (see figure 6-1). See "Newsstand" at **www.bakerdaniels.com**.

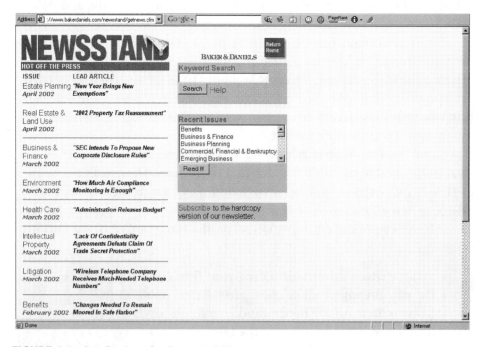

FIGURE 6-1. A collection of online newsletters

Some firms' newsletters are also produced in a format that can be read on handheld computing devices or Personal Digital Assistants (PDAs). Users of Palm and Microsoft PocketPC devices can view newsletters with the popular AvantGo reader software.

A firm that produces an interesting online newsletter using articles written for print publications is Seattle's Betts, Patterson & Mines (**www.bpmlaw.com**). Its *Surf & Turf* newsletter is a compilation of articles written for various publications in the transportation and logistics industry, and is produced in PDF (see figure 6-2).

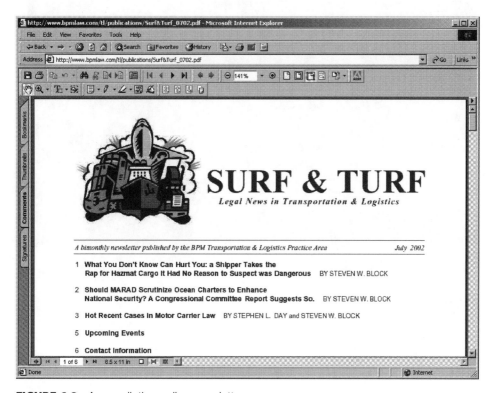

FIGURE 6-2. A compilation online newsletter

For more information on newsletters, see Chapter Three, "Email Marketing."

Case Studies

Case studies are useful alternatives to the deadline-driven newsletter. One of the best examples of case studies as Web site content is found at Texas-headquartered Akin Gump's site. The firm has created a subsidiary site called **www.akingumpcases.com** to highlight recent cases of note (see figure 6-3). Currently the firm is using this site to profile its defense of a New Hampshire Supreme Court justice who was being impeached. The site features include:

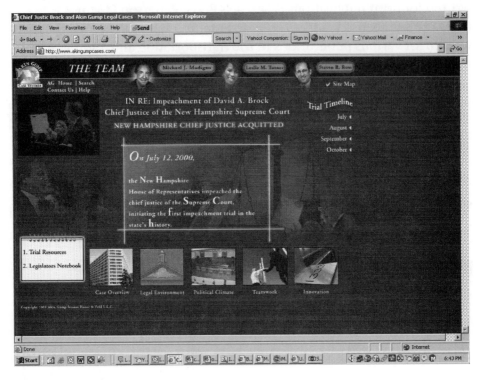

FIGURE 6-3. A subsidiary site for case studies

- A case overview;
- Profiles of the lead lawyers;
- Videos of interviews with the lawyers;
- Links to the state legislature as well as the New Hampshire statutes;
- Discussions of the legal and political climate;
- Links to a variety of trial documents, including transcripts and discovery documents;
- Links to various legislative documents, including legislative committee reports and attorney general reports; and
- A multi-month calendar showing a timeline for the case, and links to documents associated with events.

The site is well executed, and is an outstanding resource for anyone researching this case. A site like this will attract journalists interested in a high-profile case, and may allow a firm to influence coverage in the media by being a primary source of facts about the case.

Discussion Boards

Discussion boards are popular with Web site visitors. These are threaded email discussions that allow readers to post questions on the Web site, and receive answers on the site and by email. Discussion boards have been part of law firm Web sites for years, but only a few firms use them. The boards can be very successful, but they are effective only if lawyers actively participate. The "granddaddy" of law firm discussion boards belongs to Washington, D.C.'s Arent Fox. The firm hosts discussions on four topics: advertising law, consumer product safety, contests and sweep-stakes, and online privacy law (see figure 6-4).

FIGURE 6-4. Discussion board

Discussion boards offer several plusses. They allow the content on a site to be shaped by what readers actually *want* to know, not what the lawyers *think* readers want to know. They require less creativity and planning than more formal traditional or online publishing. They can be much more timely than sites where all the content must be pre-planned.

Caution: There are downsides to discussion boards. The firm cannot easily control the content. Discussions about controversial subjects can get heated, and lawyers may find themselves playing censors or bouncers, "firing" people from the discussion. Disclaimer language should be included in every message posted, or readers should at least be required to click on and read a disclaimer before entering the discussion. Disclaimers alone may not be enough to inoculate you from liability, though in over ten years of lawyer participation on discussion boards, no one has successfully sued a lawyer for providing bad advice in a board, even when there was no disclaimer.

One way to control the board is to moderate the discussion and pre-screen postings for relevance. As noted earlier, adequately staffing a discussion board is important, and failure to monitor the discussion is a wasted opportunity to develop relationships. A discussion board is an excellent way to develop rapport with a community of self-selected readers. A reader who might hesitate to telephone a law firm may feel more comfortable addressing the lawyer on a discussion board. After the conversation is initiated on the board, the reader might be ready to take the conversation offline, particularly if the discussion begins to include the specifics of a case.

Note: Participants who are not lawyers may view the discussion as receiving legal advice. The issues surrounding this are complex, so it's important to note any ethical landmines. The disclaimer must be careful to address these issues and comply with your state's bar rules.

Audio and Video Content

In 1996, when the first edition of this book was published, virtually everyone on the Internet used slow, dial-up modem connections. Now that many users have high-speed connections, having video and audio content on Web sites makes sense. Lawyers are often great writers. But video and audio communication is a new area for lawyers, and most firms have not yet successfully migrated in this direction. A few have made creative efforts in this area. Morrison & Foerster created Mofo Talk Radio (see figure 6-5), an online show where lawyers discuss legal issues with guests (www.mofotalkradio.com). On Mayer Brown Rowe & Maw's **www.appellate.net** site, audio files of lawyers' oral arguments are posted (see figure 6-6).

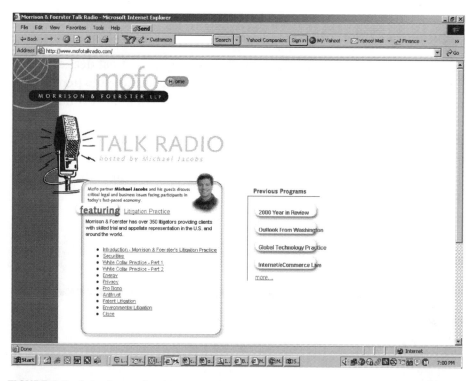

FIGURE 6-5. An online audio show

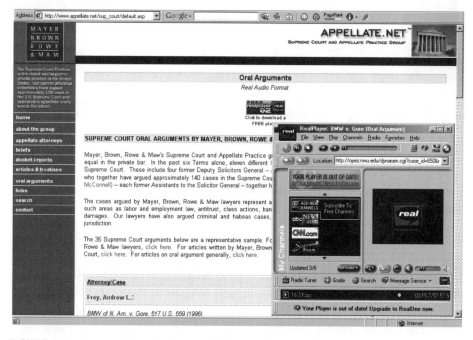

FIGURE 6-6. A page with audio files containing oral arguments

Documents Collections

Other information-rich content that doesn't require a great deal of effort is a collection of documents that cannot easily be found elsewhere. This can be as simple as combing the Web for publicly available, primary-source documents and reposting them or linking to them from your site. Or it may involve creating electronic versions of traditional documents and posting them on the site. An example of an online document collection can be found at Mayer Brown's **www.appellate.net** site (see figure 6-7).

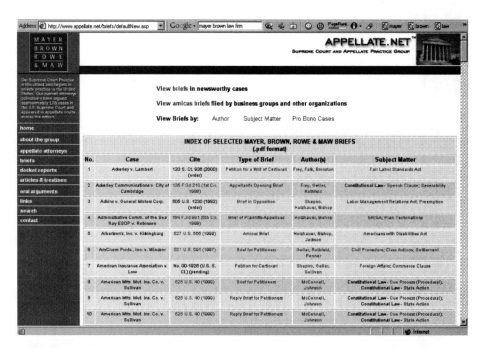

FIGURE 6-7. Online documents collection

News Feeds

Providing fresh and original content on a regular basis is often a tough challenge for firms. Why not buy the content? Companies like West Group and LEXISNEXIS sell content that enables firms to turn their sites into news distribution centers. If the goal of a site is to get important information to clients and prospects, it may not matter that the firm did not originate the articles. Instead, the firm's site becomes known as a place to find critical information.

Ancillary Businesses

Do you think the legal business is just about practicing law? Today, law firms are diversifying the services they offer and creating ancillary businesses as new sources of revenue generation. Many firms have created Web sites just for these businesses, linking them to their main sites. Labor firm Jackson Lewis markets its HR Comply human resource training publishing business at **www.hrcomply.com** (see figure 6-8). Denver's Holland and Hart spun off CaseSHARE Systems (see figure 6-9), a litigation management software system, and markets the product at **www.caseshare.com.** Siskind, Susser, Haas & Devine created an online jobs database at **www.visajobs.com** for immigrants seeking jobs in the United States (see figure 6-10).

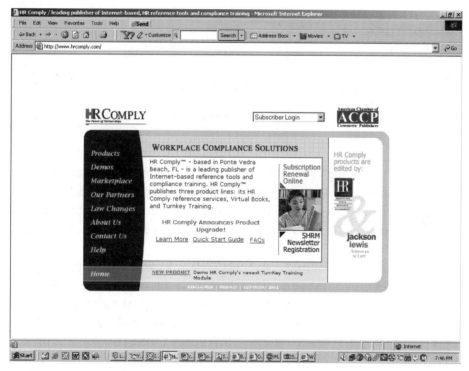

FIGURE 6-8. HRComply.com, an ancillary site for Jackson Lewis's publishing business

Links Pages

Many of the first law firm Web sites contained pages of links to resources on the Internet, primarily because these resources weren't known by or accessible to the everyday visitor. This is still a popular feature on many

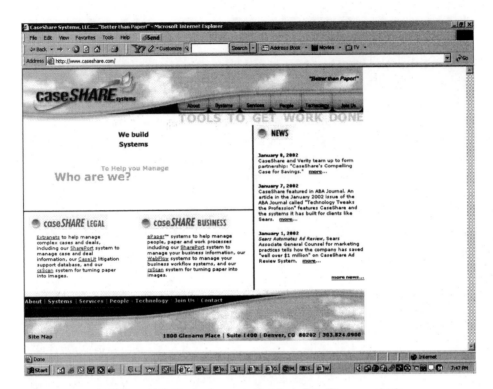

FIGURE 6-9. Holland and Hart's site for marketing their CaseShare product

law firm sites, although it is now included for different reasons. A links page is relatively easy to create and can be presented as a "work in progress," growing over time. Also, many lawyers and professional staffers can contribute to it, instead of it being handled by one or two Web-content administrators.

Everyone saves bookmarks in their Web browsers, and a links page is simply a collection of those bookmarks. The secret of a successful links page is to offer something unique. Too many firms post a general list of "legal resources on the Web" that does not give the reader anything he can't readily find elsewhere. The best links page is one that focuses on a particular niche area, or that is so in-depth or well organized that it can compare with the top general legal Web sites. We suggest including a links page *only* if you are prepared to keep the links up-to-the-minute, and compete at the highest level.

Caution: Remember that your goal is to keep visitors on your site as long as possible. Linking to outside resources gives your visitors reasons to exit your site and they may not return. Consider putting these pages in pop-up windows.

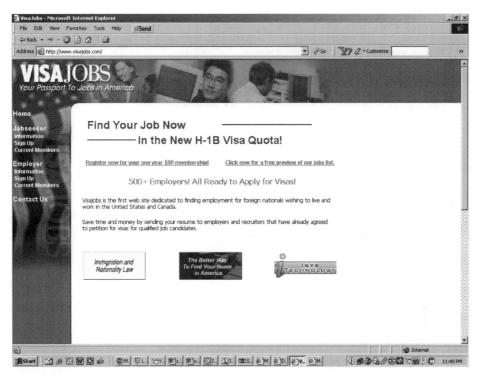

FIGURE 6-10. Visajobs.com, an online jobs database created by Siskind, Susser, Haas & Devine

A well-organized links page can be found on Australia's Minter Ellison site at **www.minterellison.com** (see figure 6-11). An excellent legal-research links page has been created by Philadelphia's Ballard Spahr at **www.virtualchase.com** (see figure 6-12).

Subsidiary or Vertical Sites

Law firms that want to showcase particular practice areas have created stand-alone "vertical" Web sites devoted to practice or industry specialties. Perkins Coie has created a vertical site for its Washington, D.C., office's political law group (**www.perkinscoie.com/politicallaw/index.htm**). The site includes the expected information on the practice group, as well as extensive analysis on legislative activities in Washington. LeBoeuf, Lamb, Greene & MacRae has created a Web site for its iBusiness Survival Guide (**www.llgm.com/survival.asp**) that contains a number of articles on legal issues affecting high-tech clients (see figure 6-13). Mayer Brown Rowe & Maw (**www.mayerbrown.com**) has several vertical sites, including sites related to securitization, international arbitration, project finance, and numerous others (see figure 6-14).

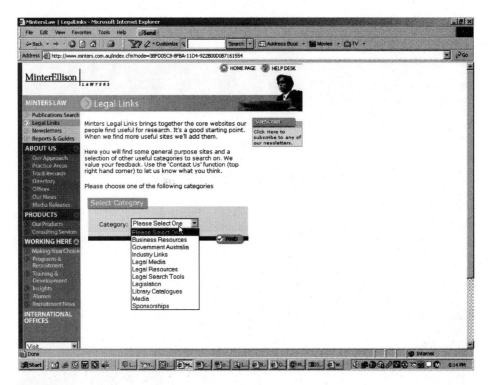

FIGURE 6-11. Legal links page

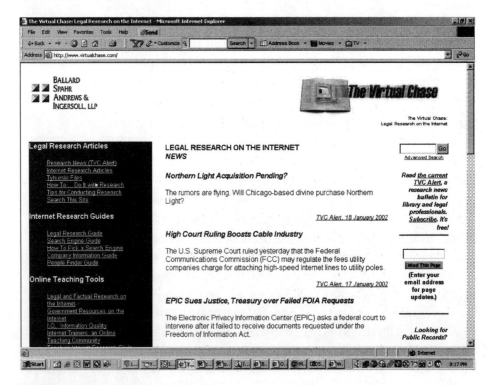

FIGURE 6-12. Legal research links site

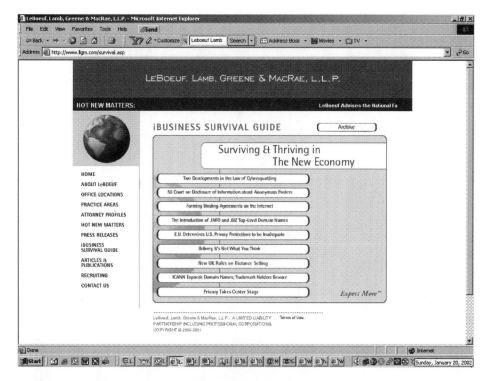

FIGURE 6-13. A vertical site for an iBusiness Survival Guide

FIGURE 6-14. A page with links to numerous vertical sites

CHAPTER SEVEN

Interactive Content

ONE OF THE MOST revolutionary aspects of marketing on the World Wide Web is the ability to interact with your Web site visitors. Some of the more innovative law firm Web sites use interactive tools to improve the appeal and usefulness of their home pages. For example, after a visitor completes an online form, the information is sent back to the firm as an email and the data is added to a database.

Consider the following uses for interactive content on your Web site:

- ♦ Welcome your visitors with a guest book;
- ♦ Invite clients to request a consultation with a questionnaire or intake form;
- ♦ Use marketing information requests;
- ♦ Include client feedback surveys;
- ♦ Provide newsletter and mailing list subscription forms;
- ♦ Incorporate an instant message feature into your site;
- ♦ Provide email links for all lawyers and professional staff; and
- ♦ Place seminar and event registration materials on your site.

Registration Forms

An important goal of Web site marketing is developing a relationship with your visitor. We know that a visitor is more likely to become a future client if she returns to the site on a regular basis. You will also stand a greater chance of retaining a potential client if you can profile her and can instantly shape your content to meet her needs. One of the ways to profile your visitor is a registration form.

Probably the most common registration form is a newsletter subscription page. Readers can view the newsletter on the Web site, but through the use of a mailing list, they can also receive future newsletters by email.

The only piece of information that is absolutely necessary in the registration form is the reader's email address. Everything else can be viewed as "nice to know" market research. Don't require or expect your visitors to provide all the information you request.

In the early days of law firm Web sites, a number of firms posted online "guest books." These were simple feedback pages that asked visitors their opinions about the site, how they got there, and some basic demographic information. We rarely see these pages today because, to be frank, people don't want to supply this information unless there is something in it for them. Having a Web site is no longer a novelty and visitors don't want to spend more time on a Web site than is necessary. The newsletter subscription form is one way to get the information that guest books used to supply.

What Information Should You Request?

What information would be useful to receive? Consider the following:

♦ Basic contact information (name, address, email, phone number, etc.);
♦ Demographic information—age range, sex, income;
♦ Occupation;
♦ Employer's industry and name, if they'll give it;
♦ Suggestions for articles, updates, or alerts;
♦ Questions for the firm;
♦ Asking if they would like to receive email alerts in relevant areas;
♦ Asking if they would like to be contacted by the firm regarding a particular legal matter; and
♦ Asking how they found the site. Consider including a drop-down menu providing a list of major link sources. Always have an "other" option with an area for typing in text.

You can control which of the fields are optional and which are mandatory. Making most of the fields optional may make a reader more comfortable subscribing to your publication, but many people will still volunteer much of the information you desire, particularly if you offer something of value in return.

Respond to each visitor who completes the registration form. Personalize a thank-you email to each person who subscribes. Subscription forms should be reviewed by as many lawyers in the firm as possible. Why? First, it lets lawyers know that interested people are visiting the site and reading the newsletter. This is a natural motivator in the constant struggle to develop content, particularly if you can show that important clients and prospects are subscribing. Second, you never know when someone in the firm will have an existing connection with a subscriber. If there is a connection, then that lawyer can also dash off a "welcome" email message. This personalized response is often enough to generate a conversation that, in turn, may evolve into an engagement.

If you use the registration-form information to regularly deliver content-rich email to your site's visitors, you have possibly achieved one of your main marketing goals—getting people to return to your site on a regular basis.

Presentations

Long before the Internet, lawyers marketed their services by delivering speeches and presentations to showcase what they knew. The Web can be utilized to make these presentations more lasting. A PowerPoint presentation can be converted to a Web format and posted on your firm's site (see figure 7-1). A speech can be recorded in audio or video format and made available on your Web site; the presenter can then create a discussion board enabling attendees to discuss the speech online in the days and weeks following the talk. If the presenter collects the email addresses of those attending the speech, he can send periodic updates on the topic to those who were interested. Course materials can also easily be posted on the site. Assuming the presenter collects the email addresses of those attending the speech, periodic updates on the topic can be sent to those who have expressed interest.

Client Surveys

One of the most important marketing initiatives a firm can pursue is surveying clients to determine how happy they are with the firm. Many firms don't survey clients at all; perhaps they are afraid of hearing bad news. Or maybe it's because of the potential effort involved—"If I survey, I

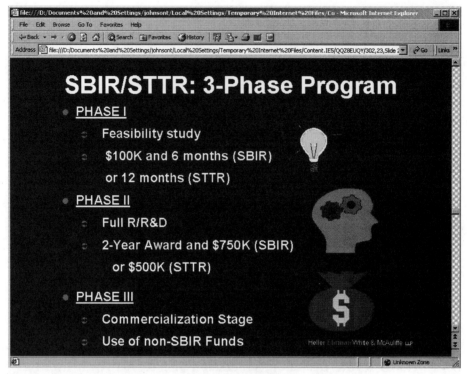

FIGURE 7-1. Heller Ehrman's online PowerPoint presentation

have to change." Or it could be because no one has thought of it. In any case, if you are not surveying your clients, you are ignoring a critical client-relationship management tool and a potential source of information. Firms need to know if clients are unhappy, so they can address concerns before they lose the clients. The greatest source of new business is recommendations from existing clients; it is important to make clients believe that their opinions and feelings matter.

Fortunately, the Web can help in this process. At least one firm, Womble Carlyle, uses its Web site to survey its clients on their satisfaction with the firm. Its survey is designed for ease-of-use (see figure 7-2).

To ensure that a sizable portion of clients participates and that the measurement is ongoing, surveys should be emailed to clients when projects are completed or cases concluded. Some clients, particularly the firm's most important, should also be interviewed in person. But with many clients, the online survey can be very enlightening.

To ensure that the data you are collecting is meaningful and that it is as valid as possible, hire a professional who can assist you in crafting your survey and analyzing the data. Remember that if your clients are completing an online survey, they are volunteering to do so. What does it say

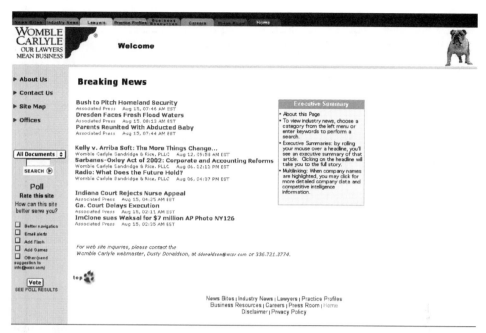

FIGURE 7-2. Online client survey

about those clients who don't complete a survey? Are they mad? Are they defecting? Are they busy, or on vacation? You can't know. Respondents are self-selecting—you can't extrapolate that your nonresponding clients feel the same as your responding ones. Don't fall into the trap of believing that "seventy percent of our clients are very satisfied" and get lazy about client service. All this means is that on those days, when those people responded, seventy percent of them were very satisfied. And what satisfied them might not be what satisfies others. When you consider your entire client base, seventy percent could be a pretty low number.

Request Information Buttons

The point of providing informative content on your Web site is to add value to existing clients and attract future ones. Yet some sites make it difficult to translate someone's interest in an article into a conversation with the firm. Washington, D.C., intellectual-property firm Staas & Halsey includes a link with each article that says "Find out more." When a reader clicks on the link, a pre-addressed email window pops up, with a subject header referring to the topic of the article, such as "Request Information about U.S. Patent Statistics for 2000" (see figure 7-3).

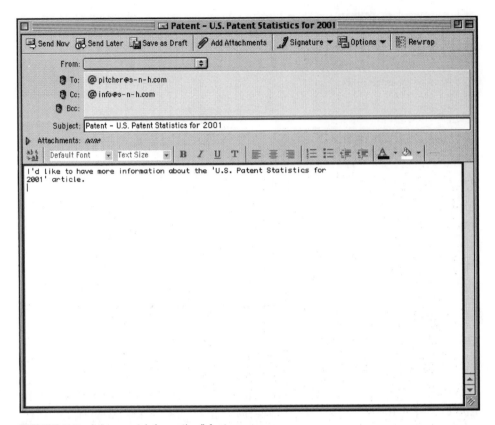

FIGURE 7-3. A "request-information" feature

Sending Articles to Other Parties

Many of the best general-news sites include links with their articles that allow readers to email articles to other people. What could be better than getting your readers to do your marketing for you? For a good example of a site that has this feature, see **www.duanemorris.com** (see figure 7-4).

Duane Morris

News
& Events

About
the Firm

Services

People

Recruiting

Publications

Additional
Resources

Search

Site Map

Home

Press Releases

Duane Morris in the News

For the Press

Seminars & Speaking Engagements

News & Events
Duane Morris LLP and Affiliates

Making
News and
Offering Insights

Email Link to Colleague   Print Friendly Version

Duane Morris Partner Named to American Bar Association Post
July 25, 2002

Paulette Brown Appointed A Division Director of the Litigation Section

July 24, 2002 - Philadelphia - The Litigation Section of the American Bar Association has appointed Paulette Brown, a partner at the international law firm of Duane Morris, as a Division Director. The Litigation Section is the largest of the American Bar Association's divisions.

Ms. Brown's term will begin in August, 2002. She will be responsible for overseeing, directing and supporting the Committees and Task Force Chairs and ensuring their compliance with Section goals, policies and procedures. As a Division Director, she will also serve as the principal liaison between Committee Chairs and the Council of the Section.

Ms. Brown practices in the area of civil defense litigation, with an emphasis on product liability and employment matters pertaining to sexual harassment and race and gender discrimination. Prior to joining Duane Morris, she was a founding partner with the law firm of Brown & Childress, LLC for 15 years. Ms. Brown served as judge of the municipal court of the City of Plainfield, New Jersey and was corporate counsel for several Fortune 500 companies.

A former president of the National Bar Association and the Association of Black Women Lawyers of New Jersey, Ms. Brown served as chair of the American Bar Association's Council on Racial and Ethnic Justice, and she is currently a member of the House of Delegates and co-chair of the Woman Advocate committee for the Section of Litigation of the American Bar Association. She is a frequent lecturer and panelist for national and international legal education programs and has received numerous awards in recognition of her commitment and contributions to the legal community, including the Equal Justice Award from the National Bar Association and the New Jersey State Bar Foundation's Medal of Honor. Ms. Brown is a 1976 graduate of Seton Hall University School of Law and a graduate of Howard University.

About Duane Morris

Duane Morris LLP, among the 100 largest law firms in the country, is a full-service firm of approximately 500 lawyers. In addition, Duane Morris has approximately 35 professionals engaged in its non-legal service businesses. The firm represents major companies throughout the United States and Europe. Its offices include: New York; London; Chicago; Houston; Philadelphia; San Francisco; Boston; Washington, D.C.; Atlanta; Miami; Newark, NJ; Wilmington, DE; Harrisburg, PA; Princeton, NJ; Palm Beach, FL; and Westchester, NY. For more information, visit the firm's Web site at: www.duanemorris.com

FIGURE 7-4. Duane Morris's site allows readers to forward (Email link) articles to other people

*CHAPTER***EIGHT**

Navigational Content

PROVIDING EASY AND INTUITIVE navigation on a Web site is critical, yet too often navigational content is poorly executed. You can spend a lot of money and countless hours developing superb content for your site, but what good does that do if your readers can't find it? There are a number of tools your firm can integrate into your site to make it easy for readers to find what they need.

The easiest navigation tool is the all-purpose hyperlink. This can be just a simple link, multiple links embedded in a table, or a more elaborate, expandable menu of links. Using small linked icons is another useful technique to help readers move through the site. Maintain consistency from link to link—use the same font and same colors throughout the site.

Several firms use image or site maps as a navigation tool. These are graphics or text with clickable areas that link to various sections of the site. If a site opens with a large graphic, a smaller image map with navigational features can be incorporated into the interior pages. A similar tool is the site map, which is especially helpful on large sites (see figure 8-1). This is a page that provides a structural overview of the site and links to all of the site's sections.

For sites with extensive content, consider adding a subject-matter index. This can be a simple list of links to pages on the site. It is easier to maintain a subject-matter index on a database-driven site where articles and pages can be marked with key words. The key words can then be used to create an automatically generated subject-matter index.

Another tool that is useful on larger sites is a search engine. Search engines can be built into the site itself or a search field for a third-party search engine can be built into the page. The third-party search engine combs the site, limiting the search to the site.

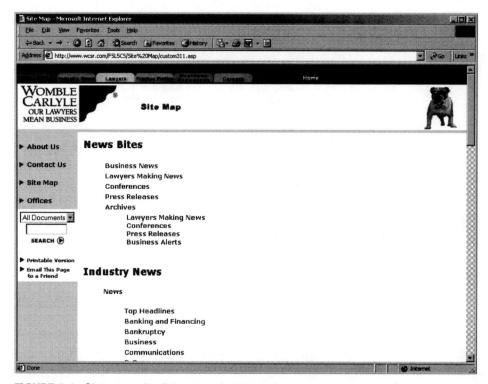

FIGURE 8-1. Site map using links as navigation tools

An updates section is a helpful resource on sites with content that changes regularly. This can be a simple page that includes links to new features on the site, or it can be done with streaming text on the front page of the site. You can also add a service like NetMind's MindIt, which allows readers to sign up to be notified by email when a site changes.

Whatever techniques and tools you use for navigation, there is one common denominator: it must be intuitive and easy for your readers to access every page on your site. Make sure your navigation tools look consistent and are simple to use, and consider placing them on every page.

*CHAPTER***NINE**

More Possibilities and Leveraging Your Content

Extranets

Extranets are an exciting client-relationship management trend available to law firms. Clients can log in to a "clients only" section on the firm's Web site and see important, up-to-the-minute information on their own matters. The clients can view documents and case status, interact with their lawyers, and so on. The purpose of this book is to discuss how the Internet can be used to effectively market a law firm; law firm extranets, while important, are largely outside the scope of this book. (See Chapter Eleven, Wireless, Extranets, and Other Tools, for additional information.)

Indeed, the subject of extranets could very well fill its own book. (Stay tuned for the ABA Law Practice Management Section's upcoming book on extranets, scheduled to be published in early 2003.) But a critical aspect to mention here is that if a law firm has invested in a client extranet, this is important information to share with potential clients. The best way to advertise that something special is available to firm clients is to have a "client login" feature on the Web site home page.

We suggest placing a "clients only" button on the home page, and then leading to a second page with actual login fields, as well as information for prospective clients on what is available on the firm's extranet. A lot of firms are missing the boat on this last point. Having an extranet is a major selling point for a firm, but this value-added service is rarely communicated to prospects.

Ethics Content

The question is not whether your Web site is subject to advertising rules—it is. But how should you deal with this on your site? Disclaimers are one way to comply, and nearly every law firm Web site is required to have one (see figure 9-1). Some firms include disclaimers on their home pages, and others make readers click through a disclaimer before they can even enter the page. Still others make the disclaimer pop up in a small window the

FIGURE 9-1. Disclaimer page

first time a reader visits the site. Some go so far as to post the disclaimer on every page. For a more extensive discussion of Internet ethics, see Chapter Fifteen, "Web Ethics and Ethical Issues of Online Marketing."

Multilingual Sites

If your firm targets an international or immigrant audience, consider including foreign-language versions of the content on your site (see figures 9-2 and 9-3). If the point of a Web site is to communicate, and translating your content will help you better reach your audience—then this is a winning strategy. Don't rely on your high-school Spanish or German. Have native speakers check the translations for accuracy and readability.

Content for Handheld Devices

If you don't own a Palm or other handheld device, you might be feeling like a late adopter in your business meetings. More and more lawyers rely on these mini-PCs for part of their daily computing—whether inside or outside the office. Some of these handheld devices contain Web browsing software so content can be delivered directly to the device. A few firms are now producing content for handheld devices (see figure 9-4). The most popular software for accessing content on handheld computers is from AvantGo (**www.avantgo.com**).

Syndicated Content

Developing excellent content for your Web site is a great way to generate traffic and form relationships with new clients. But why limit access to your material to just your own Web site? Good content is in demand all over the Web; it is possible to find high-traffic sites that are interested in publishing high-quality material from lawyers.

The key is to identify the sites where your target audiences search for information. Then become the legal expert at a site that targets the profile of your ideal client. This could mean writing articles for a site, or moderating a discussion board. It might mean being the host of an online chat. For example, Greg Siskind "appears" weekly as the immigration expert on **Monster.com's** online chat, and **Monster.com** has republished dozens of his articles.

当事務所紹介｜弁護士紹介｜業務分野｜オフィス一覧｜ニュース｜出版物｜イベント｜就職情報｜意見・感想

ピルズベリー・ウィンスロップ　　　　　　　　　　　　　サイト・サーチ

発見

経歴｜ジャパン・プラクティス｜業務分野｜グローバル・プラクティス弁護士｜グローバル・オフィス

ピルズベリー・ウィンスロップ法律事務所：グローバル・プラクティス
誇り高き伝統
2001年1月、カリフォルニアを拠点とするピルズベリー・マディソン・アンド・スートロ法律事務所（「ピルズベリー」）とニューヨークを拠点とするウィンスロップ・スティムソン・パットナム・アンド・ロバーツ法律事務所（「ウィンスロップ」）が合併しました。新たにピルズベリー・ウィンスロップと改名されたこの事務所はまさに世界で最も卓越したサービスを提供できる多様性ある弁護士事務所のひとつとなりました。当事務所は、ロンドン、東京、香港、シンガポールおよびシドニーを含めた16のロケーションにオフィスを構え860名以上の弁護士を擁しています。

ウィンスロップが世界に飛躍するウォール街の弁護士事務所となるその土台づくりに逸早く貢献したのはその創設者のひとりエリヒュ・ルートでした。ルートはテオドア・ルーズベルト大統領の政権の下で国務長官を務めました。1912年には政治家かつ外交官として果たした世界平和への貢献が認められノーベル平和賞を受賞しました。ルートの培った公共奉仕と世界平和の精神はブロンソン・ウィンスロップとヘンリー・スティムソンに受け継がれました。後年、ヘンリー・スティムソンは歴代4人の大統領の下であらゆる官僚ポストに就任しました。ウィンスロップは世界各地に向けて大規模な取引やインフラストラクチャーの開発に係わる高質な法務サービスの拡張に専念する米国弁護士事務所の先頭に立ってきました。

後にピルズベリーとなる法律事務所を創設したパートナーのひとりクラレンスR.グレートハウスは1886年に駐日米国総領事に指名されました。その後、同氏は朝鮮国王の信任顧問として活躍しました。同氏は同国王の信任のもと、朝鮮で郵便制度および司法行政機関の設立に従事しました。また、ピルズベリーの創設者のひとりオスカー・スートロは1901年フィリピンに駐在事務所を設け同国法典の草稿に従事しました。

1930年、（1991年にピルズベリーと合併するに至る）リリック＆マックホースの創設者のひとりアイラ・リリックは日本の船会社をクライアントに迎えました。もうひとりの創設者ジョンC.マックホースも日本政府高官や事業家の私的顧問として活躍する傍ら、多数の大手日本企業を代理し米国進出を支援しました。また、リリック＆マックホースは、日本企業と培ってきた絆を大切にし、第二次世界大戦後いち早く日本企業の代理を開始した法律事務所のひとつとしてもよく知られています。

1996年9月、ピルズベリーは知的財産の分野での卓越したサービスで有名なクッシュマン・ダービー・クッシュマン法律事務所（「クッシュマン」）と合併しました。クッシュマンは米国国際取引委員会（ITC）の特許訴訟において日本、韓国、スイス、カナダを始めとする外国の法人を代理し国際的な賞賛を受けました。これらの訴訟で成功を収めるやクッシュマンは世界中で催される知的財産のセミナーに招待されるようになりました。また、海外の特許弁護士や外国法人の特許部門のスタッフを対象とする特許訓練生プログラムを確立し一躍世界で有名になりました。その後、他の多くの知的財産を専門とする弁護士事務所がクッシュマンに習いよく似た訓練生制度を始めました。

ピルズベリー・ウィンスロップは上記全先行事務所の優れたサービスを伝統として受け継ぎ、今後も継続してグローバルなサービスを提供していきます。

グローバルなサービス

ピルズベリー・ウィンスロップはグローバルなレベルで、知的財産、法人有価証券、電子通商、設備のファイナンスおよびリース、ライセンシング、M&A、合併、プロジェクトおよびインフラストラクチャーのファイナンス、国際税務、独占禁止、労働および雇用、環境、製造物責任、米国移民、会社更生等のビジネス処理の分野でサービスを提供しています。

当事務所は、訴訟、調停および各種代替的紛争解決手続においてもグローバルなレベルでクライアントを代理しています。当事務所の訴訟チームは、今まで数百件もの紛争を陪審評決や判決に至らせ、クライアントのために巧みな説得力で紛争の経済的な早期解決を達成するため、豊富な経験と信頼性を効果的に活用しています。

また、当事務所は革新的な取引の第一線に立つクライアントを代理しています。例えば、エレクトロニクス、エネルギー、パイプライン、有料道路、航空機、船舶、衛星システム、鉱業、原油生産および精製、パルプ・製紙工場、製鉄工場およびその他の工業施設などあらゆる業種における他国間取引を常時取り扱っています。

更に、米国および国際証券市場のリーダーとして、当事務所は証券市場に関与する各当事者を代理した経験から得たグローバルな見地で国際証券取引の企画立案、交渉から、満足のゆく完了に至るまで、法人、政府機関並びに政府教育企業を支援しています。

当事務所のロンドン、東京、香港、シンガポールおよびシドニーのオフィスは、現地の習慣、ビジネス慣行および政策に係わる知識を活用し、環太平洋並びにヨーロッパ地域でビジネスや金融の取引に従事する企業・法人にサービスを提供するため戦略的に位置付けられています。当事務所のグローバル・プラクティスに従事する弁護士は当該地域において豊富な経験を持ち、その地域の言語にも堪能です。また、これら弁護士の多くは現地の法律資格も取得しています。

About Us｜Attorneys｜Practice Areas｜Locations｜In the News｜Publications｜Events｜Opportunities｜Feedback
copyright｜disclaimer｜privacy｜info@pillsburywinthrop.com

FIGURE 9-2. Pillsbury Winthrop's Japanese site

PRINTED GOULSTON   ABOUT GOULSTON   VIRTUAL TOUR   SERVICE AREAS   LAWYER SEARCH   COMMUNITY OUTREACH   JOIN US

en español

DIVISION DE LATINOAMERICA Y EL CARIBE

Goulston & Storrs ha devenido, como resultado de su clientela amplia y diversa, en una firma legal con una cartera activa en Latinoamérica. A traves de la representación de promotores, industrias manufactureras, operadores de cadenas de cine y otros clientes, Gouslton & Storrs participa, y ha participado, en varias adquisiciones, ventas, projectos de desarrollo, joint ventures y financiamientos en toda Latinoamérica. Clientes de la firma con operaciones en Latinoamérica incluyen, entre otros, a General Cinema International, Inc., Hoyts Cinemas Limited, Joan Fabrics Corporation y Manley-Berenson Associates, Inc.

Creemos firmemente que una representación adecuada de clientes operando, o que desean operar, en Latinoamérica exige de habilidades idiomáticas y experiencia internacional. La firma cuenta con siete abogados que hablan español con fluidez y con asistentes legales que hablan tanto español como portugués con fluidez.

Por otro lado, Roberto Laver se ha incorporado recientemente a la firma como miembro de la división de Latinoamérica y el Caribe. Roberto Laver trae a Goulston& Storrs mas de quince años de experiencia legal en Estados Unidos, Argentina y otros países Latinoamericanos. Con anterioridad a su incorporación a la firma, el Sr. Laver era asesor legal senior en la división de Latinoamérica del departamento legal del Banco Mundial. En dicho rol, el Sr. Laver era responsable por el asesoramiento legal y en políticas internas con respecto a las operaciones de préstamo del Banco Mundial en varios países Latinoamericanos incluyendo a Venezuela, Méjico, Colombia, Peru, Bolivia, Ecuador, Panama, Costa Rica y El Salvador. A su vez, el Sr. Laver participó en el diseño y gerenciamiento de projectos de reforma legal y judicial en Venezuela y Peru.

A continuación se presenta una lista representativa de projectos en Latinoamérica y el Caribe en los cuales ha participado recientemente Goulston & Storrs:

"Joint Ventures"

- Argentina. Constitución de un joint venture entre un operador estadounidense importante de cines y un socio argentino para el desarrollo de un cine multiplex en Buenos Aires.
- Argentina. Constitución de un joint venture entre un socio estadounidense y un socio argentino para el desarrollo de complejos de oficinas en áreas suburbanas.
- Argentina, Chile y Brasil. Constitución de varias entidades legales como resultado de un joint venture entre un socio estadounidense y un socio brasileño para adquirir, desarrollar, gerenciar, operar, financiar y poseer bienes industriales y bienes raíces en Argentina, Chile y Brasil.
- Méjico. Constitución de un joint venture entre dos operadores importantes de cine para el desarrollo y operación de cines en Méjico.
- Sudamérica y Centroamérica. Constitución de un joint venture entre dos operadores importantes de cines para adquirir, desarrollar, gerenciar, operar, poseer y arrendar una cadena de cines y actividades relacionadas de entretenimiento y concesiones en Sudamérica y Centroamérica.
- Argentina y Uruguay. Constitución de un joint venture entre un socio estadounidense y un socio sudamericano para desarrollar projectos comerciales de minoristas en Argentina y Uruguay.

FIGURE 9-3. Goulston Storrs's Spanish site

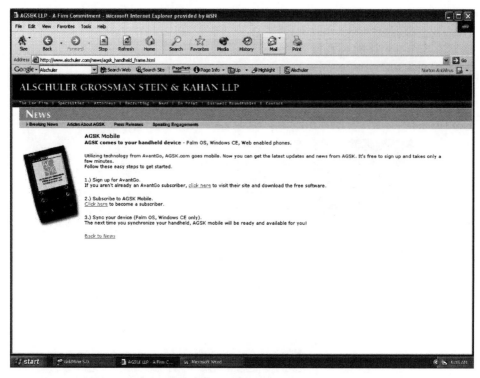

FIGURE 9-4. Alschuler's content for handheld devices

Lawyers.com provides a number of opportunities for lawyers to write articles and respond to reader questions. Sites like **About.com** and **Find-Law.com** provide similar opportunities.

AskMe.com allows people to ask questions of volunteer "experts" on any topic. The questioners then rate the answers they received. The legal topic area alone covers nearly forty areas of the law. As this book went to press, there were over 350 legal experts and a cumulative total of more than 18,000 questions asked and answered, sometimes by multiple experts. (AskMe is the site where a fifteen-year-old boy gave numerous responses on criminal law questions and received the highest ratings by the consumers. This episode is discussed in detail by Michael Lewis in his book *Next: The Future Just Happened* [W.W. Norton, 2001] as an example of how the Internet has changed the traditional delivery methods and controls over professional services, from lawyers to brokers.) Note: Be careful when you call lawyers "experts"—you might be violating ethics rules. (See Chapter Fifteen, "Web Ethics and Ethical Issues of Online Marketing.")

If you want syndication to work for you, you need to do two things: analyze the demographics of the third-party site, and know your target client. If the site targets middle-class consumers and you're a mergers and acquisitions lawyer, you might devote considerable energy, but get little or nothing in return.

Working with other sites to publish your content involves some work:

- Identify the best sites (and the best fit for you) that appear to need content;
- Determine what content will appeal to that site's readers;
- Meet the site's deadlines, size limits, and other publication rules; and
- Make the pitch to get your content published.

Syndication can take a lot of effort, but the rewards can be extraordinary.

CHAPTER**TEN**

Web Site
Design Issues

Standards and Consistency

A well-designed Web site should have a uniform layout and appearance from page to page (see figures 10-1 and 10-2). For example, navigation bars shouldn't jump from the top of one page to the bottom of another— your visitors won't know where to find them. A consistent layout helps visitors navigate easily through your site and find the information they need. If they can't find it intuitively, they'll leave and won't return.

Also, a look that is consistent with your firm's off-line marketing and sales materials will help readers distinguish your site if they are rapidly browsing through law firm Web sites. One of the best ways to maintain a uniform look and make your site easy to update is to make your site dynamic, rather than using the old-fashioned HTML hard-coded page design. For sites that are rich in content, going with a database-driven site is a must. While costs go up significantly with a database-driven site, the maintenance is a breeze and your site's content can stay up-to-the-minute.

To Frame or Not to Frame?

Most first-generation Web sites used frames. Frames were typically used to create a solid-color block on the left side of the Web page to house the navigation buttons. You can tell that a site is framed if you scroll down the copy on the right, and the navigation block on the left doesn't move.

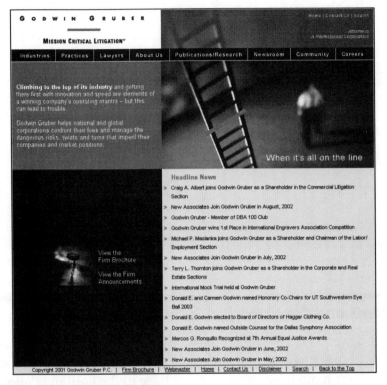

FIGURE 10-1. Godwin Gruber's home page

Frames have become unpopular today for several reasons, but we don't summarily dismiss framed sites. Done well, they can offer clean navigation, consistent presentation, and can aid in having an appealing look and feel.

So, what's the downside? First, search engines do not index frames, so you have to build hidden pages behind the framed pages in order for your site to be indexed by search engines. This is cumbersome and time-consuming, but it can be done. See **http://www.rankwrite.com/framedsite.htm** for a list of tricks you can use to get search engines to do the right thing with your framed content.

Second, visitors may have trouble bookmarking framed sites or forwarding framed content, such as a lawyer resume or practice description.

Third, bringing another Web site into your frame may present copyright issues. For example, if you have a link to an association's Web site and it loads into your frame, you are actually "taking credit" for that site.

Finally, framed pages that don't let you navigate elsewhere in the site (because the navigation options are all in the frameset, not in the page itself) deserve their own circle in Dante's hell.

FIGURE 10-2. Godwin Gruber's Industries page has the same look and feel as its home page

A great reference explaining why frames should be left to the experts is Jakob Nielsen's "Why Frames Suck (Most of the Time)" (see http://www.useit.com/alertbox/9612.html). This article was written in December, 1996, but most of it is still relevant. (Disregard the comments about browser compatibility—does anybody actually remember Netscape 2?) But Nielsen's general observations about usability still hold. If you have an interest in Web design issues, Nielsen's newsletter is a must (http://www.useit.com/alertbox).

Animation and Sound

In the last couple of years, some law firms with big budgets have incorporated animation and background sound into their Web sites. Most use Flash, from Macromedia. The "cool-factor" in many of these sites is definitely high, and the animation adds a little fun to the site. Dewey Ballantine's site has an interesting use of animation (www.deweyballantine.com).

Some Flash presentations look overly cartoon-like and are a waste of time. In any case, use animation strategically (not just to see your logo spin), and consider limiting the use of this feature as it consumes bandwidth and delays your visitor from getting the information he wants.

Some firms force readers to view a site in Flash format. We think this is a big mistake, for several reasons. As mentioned earlier, sound and animation use a lot of bandwidth. If you are a frequent visitor to a site, having to view the animation over and over again can be irritating. Flash cannot be viewed readily on certain kinds of Web browsers, such as those on PDAs and WebTV systems. Having to download a viewer before being able to visit a Web site is a turn-off for many, particularly people in a hurry. Finally, some corporate firewalls are set to screen out Flash transmissions because viruses can be more easily implanted in or attached to them.

Other firms have an initial page offering format choices for viewing the Web site. This is better than no choice at all, but it can still be annoying for frequent visitors to have to pass through the entry page. First impressions count on the Web. We recommend designing a striking home page that can be downloaded quickly on any type of browser, and using Flash for online demonstrations or for interior sections, like recruiting.

There are more subtle forms of animation that can enhance the viewing experience. A popular feature on many new-generation Web sites is mouse-over animation, in which moving a mouse over a button appears to press it, or modify its color or shading. This feature makes a site livelier and adds clarity to your navigation without really slowing a visitor down. The key here is being subtle rather than screaming.

Document Formats

Readers will appreciate it if you post documents in more than one format. Newsletters are usually posted in a Web version, but consider including links that allow them to be downloaded in text, Microsoft Word, and Adobe (PDF). Make it possible to download an entire version of your newsletter rather than just individual articles. This makes it easier for people who want to read your material off-line.

Compatibility and Browsers

Some people speculate that Microsoft would like it if everyone viewed the Web through their Internet Explorer Web browser. Whether this is true or not, there are still many people viewing the Web with other browsers—

various versions of Netscape, WebTV, AOL, Palm, Opera, and others. Before you launch your site, test it using as many browsers as possible to see if it looks and behaves in a uniformly acceptable way. You might not be able to please everyone, but there are ways to create a site that will remain consistent from one browser to the next.

Also keep in mind that people view the Web on screens of many different sizes—from tiny handheld devices to nineteen-inch monitors. Often, what looks good on one size screen looks strange on a different one.

A great resource for verifying that your site works on various platforms and browsers is **www.anybrowser.com**. Here you can check your site on different screen sizes, simulate it in various browsers, and use a number of tools to polish rough edges you might find.

Sophisticated Web programmers can force pages to display dynamically, so that pages change to accommodate the visitor's screen. The look and feel of your site will be affected, however, so this is a decision you must make before your designer starts designing. If you don't care about dynamic display, you are safest designing for an 800-by-600-pixel screen.

There are Web site usability and design articles that address these issues. For information about maximizing viewable browsing area, etc., see **www.webreview.com**.

Tackiness, Excess, and Other Web Site Irritations

Web sites, in general, look better today than they did in the mid-90s. But many home pages, including those of a number of law firms, still go too far—or, rather, haven't gone far enough. Some are do-it-yourself sites. Others are created by Web developers who are more interested in showing off programming skills than in building a differentialting, effective marketing and communications tool.

Remember that the goal of your Web site is to communicate—about the firm, and about what you can do for your prospects. Avoid features that clutter, confuse your communication, or do nothing to differentiate your firm, including:

- ◆ Blinking text and graphics;
- ◆ Overused clip art images (courts, columns, gavels, fountain pens, shaking hands);
- ◆ Background patterns that are distracting or make it difficult to read text on a page;
- ◆ Pop-up browser windows that don't have purpose;

♦ Page bloat (pages that take too long too load);

♦ "Under construction" signs;

♦ Broken links (links that don't take you anywhere);

♦ Unprofessional photos that resemble driver's license or passport images; and

♦ Missing page titles. When a visitor bookmarks your page, the browser will use your page title as the "name" of the bookmark. Titleless pages will be bookmarked using your URL as the name, making the bookmark less memorable and potentially useless.

Testing Your Site

Remember that a good final test for a Web site is to view the entire site on a minimal setup. Find a computer with a small monitor and a dial-up modem. Time each page with a stopwatch as it downloads. If any picture takes longer than eight to ten seconds to load, there is a problem. Reduce the size of the graphics, or break one page into several pages. View every page on the site and click on every link to ensure that everything looks right and works correctly. Seek candid feedback from "beta testers"—people who will constructively test and review the site.

Launching without testing is tempting, because firms may be in month six, month eight, or even month ten of development. Your lawyers are growing impatient. Testing, however, is imperative to site success. There will be problems—wouldn't you rather know about them and fix them before you go live?

CHAPTER**ELEVEN**

Wireless, Extranets, and Other Tools

EARLY ADOPTERS HAVE EMBRACED wireless access to the Internet, but other than wireless email, most law firms haven't explored its uses. There is an elite group of market leaders who have jumped on the wireless band-wagon, and see the growing value of wireless strategies for their firms.

What is the most significant advantage for these law firms? They can give their clients and other Web site visitors time- or location-sensitive access. These law firms will have client relationships that are far ahead of the curve once the rest of the world catches on.

According to Nancy J. Whiteman, a regular contributor to www.clickz.com, in her article "Wireless Advertising's Early Adopters" (see http://www.clickz.com/wireless/ad_comm/article.php/840471), there are three categories of businesses for which having a wireless business model makes sense:

> The first category consists of businesses for which the customer's ability to make time-sensitive decisions, no matter where he or she happens to be, is inherent in the business model. Fidelity's decision to develop a wireless Internet trading platform, for example, is a no-brainer. It extends the real-time, 24/7 mentality of online trading and makes it truly mobile. Perfect. The idea of being able to place a last minute eBay bid from your cell phone is pretty cool, too.

> The second category consists of companies with a market demographic that's a close fit with those of today's wireless devices. As was the case with the Web, this category will broaden as wireless-device penetration increases

and its demographics begin to more closely mirror those of the general population.

The third category includes businesses that are location-sensitive. This category, too, will broaden over time, but there are some obvious fits in the near term. The yellow pages industry, for example, identifies one such fit as "small radius" businesses—businesses that people will not drive very far to frequent, such as fast-food restaurants, supermarkets and dry cleaners.

So, where do law firms fit into this? As wireless becomes more mainstream and your business clients rely on this easy, anywhere access, they will want and perhaps even expect their key service providers to deliver information via this medium. Many of your clients are reading the *Wall Street Journal* and the *New York Times* on their PDAs. Why not let them read your latest labor and employment newsletter as well?

Leverage Your Web Strategy with Wireless

Siskind, Susser, Haas & Devine offers their *Immigration Bulletin* for Palm OS and Windows CE devices. As of 2002, the newsletter had over four hundred subscribers who automatically receive the latest newsletter each time they synchronize their PDAs. Siskind created a specially formatted version of the newsletter that can be read easily on a palm-sized screen. The firm includes instructions for using the wireless service on its Web site (www.visalaw.com), and a link to AvantGo where users can get the necessary software.

Lawyers interested in marketing can also obtain the LawMarketing Portal on a Palm or Windows CE device. Go to www.lfmi.com and click on the AvantGo box on the home page.

How Does Wireless Fit with Your Branding Strategy?

Is wireless just a fad? Lawyers, even if they are keen on the idea of reading the Sunday *Times* on their Palms, may very well be skeptical about the long-term marketing and branding advantages in using wireless delivery of Web content. How could it possibly enhance the firm brand? Doesn't the extreme space limitation inherent in wireless devices make this impossible? In fact, some lawyers may be skeptical about the Internet being a place to brand at all.

The answer to these questions depends heavily on how you define branding. Branding, to us, is much more than an ad in the yellow pages or *American Lawyer*, or a television commercial. It encompasses *everything* a firm does to build awareness and to form the ongoing perception of the firm. Increasingly, corporate America understands that long-term brand development is dependent on the actual experiences that customers have with the brand. Corporations such as Disney, Daimler Chrysler, and Southwest Airlines develop branding campaigns around "experience marketing." There is evidence that a positive experience makes your customers or law firm clients more loyal and more likely to tell others about you.

This leads us to the advantage of wireless for law firms. Used intelligently, wireless advertising and mobile-commerce applications offer firms the ability to interact with their clients and future clients in brand-new ways. By allowing Web visitors to specify what information interests them and developing applications that meet their needs, smart firms have the opportunity to build their brands one person at a time, delivering the services and products that are meaningful to each individual.

Wireless applications of the future will allow your target audiences to define themselves—to tell you what messages they want and how and when they want them. Talk about efficiency! The key to building and reinforcing your brand on wireless is to be able to provide a new level of service and value to your clients and prospects—service and value that they can't find at another law firm.

Wireless Resources for Lawyers

There are numerous resources for lawyers who want to beam down the latest case law or often-used reference books. LexisONE (**www.lexisone.com**) is a Web site for small-firm lawyers and is filled with wireless resources. You can subscribe to these law-related clipping services for downloading to a PDA:

- IPO Express 2 Go 1.0 (2KB);
- DocuTouch (8KB) (see **www.docutouch.com**).

Electronic texts are available, too. Many of the latest and most popular law books and treatises are available from Peanut Press (**www.peanutpress.com**) and MemoWare (**www.memoware.com**). To access these on your Palm or Pocket PC PDA, you must first download the free Palm Reader software from Peanut Press.

Lawyers can create and convert documents to PRC or PDB formats for Palms. With Documents To Go (available for purchase from **www.dataviz.com**), you can instantly view Microsoft Word, Excel, and other files on your Palm organizer. PDocs, available for download at **www.thinkchile.com/alorca/pDocs**, allows you to use Microsoft Word 97, Word 2000, or Word XP as your Palm documents editor. Aportis (**www.aportis.com**) makes AportisDoc Converter, an add-on to their AportisDoc PDA reader, which converts Web pages, Word files, WordPerfect files, PDF files, and text files so that they can be read on a PDA.

Time and Billing for Wireless

You might wonder what time and billing have to do with marketing. We believe that the more time-efficient and organized lawyers are while on the road, the better they can serve their clients—in the office or elsewhere. The following PDA tools are available so that lawyers can use time-and-billing and practice-management software while out of the office:

- Time Matters Palm link (**www.timematters.com**);
- TimeReporter (**www.iambic.com**);
- Abacus Law (**www.abacuslaw.com**), Professional and Advanced editions;
- Timesolv Web-clipping interface (**www.elite.com/ services/timesolv/webclipping.jsp**); and

Email Pagers

The most popular email pager is the BlackBerry™ (or "CrackBerry," as the general counsel of a major corporation called it, referring to his addiction to the device). BlackBerry, a device manufactured and marketed by Research in Motion, is a leading wireless email solution for mobile professionals (see **www.blackberry.net**). It is an integrated package that includes software, airtime, and the user's choice of wireless devices to provide easy access to your email wherever you go. With a wireless service provider like GoAmerica (**www.goamerica.com**), BlackBerry users can browse the Web using a slimmed-down Web browser on the device.

BlackBerry offers a traditional pager-sized device, as well as one that is palm-sized. A lawyer can link the device to an email server at her firm, so that the BlackBerry receives duplicates of email messages sent to her desktop. The messages appear in full, although as of this writing email attachments are not accessible on the device. For lawyers on the go, this device keeps them linked to their offices and clients.

The cost of the BlackBerry depends on how many devices a firm purchases. Monthly service contracts are offered by telephone companies at a rate of about $40 per user per month. (Note: this price is current as of publication, but inevitably will change.) It may be necessary to purchase server software, depending on your configuration. Many law firms require their lawyers to purchase the BlackBerry, with the firms paying the monthly charges, or vice versa.

Relying exclusively on the BlackBerry for email on the road has its downside. You might not find a signal in a remote area, even within the United States. Currently it is not reliable for use during international travel.

Extranets

An extranet is a restricted-access network, not available to the general public. It offers a law firm a way to manage client relationships or other matters of limited duration. An extranet is a flexible, Web-based system that can be designed to meet the particular needs of each client. It can improve collaboration among parties and increase efficiency. Multiple users can share information and exchange valuable and relevant resources—in the same place, and at the same time.

Extranets can be hosted by a law firm, a client, or a third-party company that specializes in these services.

A well-designed extranet enables lawyers to:

- Exchange and manage documents;
- Conduct secure, private conferences;
- Automate calendaring and scheduling;
- Deploy the most appropriate lawyer, regardless of location or practice group;
- Track matters from project management and project accounting;
- Generate email alerts to clients when there are matter updates; and
- Make current clients aware of additional services the firm can provide.

The best extranets integrate with many existing accounting and document-management systems. They can be completely Internet-based and work globally through a Web browser. Traveling lawyers don't have to carry laptops to access the extranet, because they can connect through any regular Internet connection, such as an Internet kiosk or a home connection.

ERoom (www.eroom.com), described as a Web-based digital workplace, is becoming a popular extranet tool for collaboration with clients and co-counsel. External users can enter eRooms, set up for a particular case or client, and share documents, calendar, docket, white board, discussion threads, and so on. Matrix Logic has designed eRoom Service for DOCS, which allows eRoom users to work on documents in DOCS Open, a document-management system, even if they are not registered DOCS users (see www.matrix-logic.com/products/eroom.asp). An audit trail of recent events is kept, so lawyers can see who has accessed, edited, printed, or viewed documents in the eRoom, just as they can in DOCS (see figure 11-1). The greatest advantage to eRooms (and a problem with earlier off-the-shelf extranet products) is the ability to work on a document directly in DOCS. With this feature you always have the latest edits in your document-management system—not one version in the eRoom and another version in DOCS.

More than an Extranet: a "Deal Room"

Four of London's so-called "magic circle" firms that handle major merger/ acquisition and corporate finance matters—Linklaters, Clifford Chance, Allen & Overy, and Freshfields—have all set high extranet standards. They have taken the extranet concept further and are hosting online "deal rooms" where lawyers from both sides of a deal can meet and exchange documents.

Ashby Jones, writing for Law Technology News (www.lawtechnews.com), said that it is noteworthy that the London firms have built these extranets on their own. "Many large U.S. firms, such as San Francisco-based Heller Ehrman White & McAuliffe L.L.P., and New York's Cravath, Swaine & Moore, have outsourced their Extranet platforms . . . on a deal-by-deal basis. By contrast, the London firms have built their own deal rooms. This is more labor-intensive, but the firms believe it gives them speed and flexibility, and offers clients a greater sense of security. . . . These are the firms that compete intensely for the United Kingdom's and Europe's biggest and sexiest clients. Their Extranets are one way the firms try to set themselves apart from the competition. . . . So far, U.S. firms don't seem to have felt the same competitive need to develop Extranet services. Davis Polk

FIGURE 11-1. eRoom Service for DOCs product description

[New York's Davis Polk & Wardwell] is one of the few American firms that has created an elaborate extranet system on par with those of the 'magic circle' firms."

Extranet devotees say that before long, extranets will be viewed as law firm staples, like telephones and copiers.

Beyond Extranets: Pushing It Further Still

In the above-mentioned article, Ashby Jones goes on to say that some British firms have done more than just extranets—they are making splashes with other Web-based platforms: "Linklaters, for instance, launched its Blue Flag 'expert system.' On Blue Flag, clients can get answers to a whole range of basic legal questions. . . .The site functions like a decision tree: Each answer elicits a more specific question, until sufficient information has been taken in. Then the site provides links to pertinent information and even advice."

Law firms struggle to leverage their work product and maximize knowledge management. Linklaters has done both in Blue Flag and it charges subscribers for this service—currently about $200,000 for a one-time initiation fee and an annual flat fee of about $72,000 for each subsequent year. The financial and practical successes of this strategy haven't been reported, but Blue Flag received considerable legal and business media attention when it was introduced (see figure 11-2).

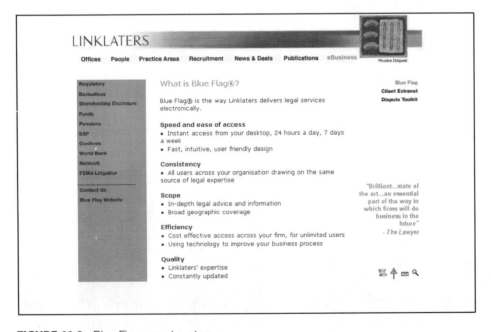

FIGURE 11-2. Blue Flag expert system

Why Bother with an Extranet?

According to David R. Hambourger in a 2001 issue of *The Alert*, the newsletter of the Federal Bar Association's Corporate and Association Counsels Division, there are compelling reasons to make extranets an important part of your practice:

1. **Clients are demanding it**—Many clients who have been exposed to the use of extranets are pressuring their law firms to provide similar services as a means to enhance communications. Corporate counsel are increasingly saying they expect their major law firms to provide extranet connections.
2. **Reduced "friction"**—One of the aspects of Internet technology is its ability to eliminate steps. . . . Now that I can check my credit card balance online, I no longer need to call and wait to speak to a customer service representative. Similarly, an extranet can greatly decrease the number of "Can you send me a copy of . . .?" or "What was her fax number?" type of calls.
3. **Improved client development and retention**—Creating a specialized, customized extranet application can help create a stronger link between clients and law firms and a much deeper sense of partnership. With this kind of integration and sharing of common information, counsel and clients have a better chance to develop a long-term, mutually beneficial relationship.
4. **Decreased costs**—With less information being exchanged through traditional methods, there is the potential for a reduction in costs (telephone calls, postage, messengers, etc.). And the professionals involved will likely spend more time on higher value activities.

(Reprinted with permission from the
Federal Bar Association's Corporate and Association Counsels Division.)

Extranet Models

Transactional or Administrative
This is a site focused on a specific transaction, deal, or administrative filing. It may be short-term and may involve large numbers of third parties (banks, underwriters, etc.) The major functions of a transactional extranet are likely to be document distribution and archives, matter status updates, feedback delivery, and contact lists.

Litigation
This is similar to the transactional model, but it focuses on one or more litigation matters. It may be designed for use by multiple parties (client,

co-counsel, opposing counsel, experts) and would likely include pleadings, hard copy and email correspondence, transcripts, relevant documents, calendar of events, and ongoing case status.

Relationship

This extranet is designed to serve long-term lawyer-client relationships. It can be used to collaborate on current matters, provide an archive of documents and forms from past matters, share pertinent and frequently used information about both the client and the firm, and can include data related to billing, budgeting, and accounting of disbursements.

Lawyers can post recent client-development materials of interest to each type of client, such as labor and employment information, venture capital or REIT industry newsletters, industry white papers, or briefings on late-breaking legal developments. In addition, firms can schedule e-meetings in their extranet space, and post PowerPoint shows or demonstrations used during the meeting.

Marketing Your Extranet

If your firm is willing to make the investment of time and money in an extranet, don't keep it quiet. At LegalTech New York 2001, Rodney A. Satterwhite, a partner in the Richmond, Virginia, office of McGuire Woods, gave solid marketing advice. He stressed that a law firm should not market an extranet as a technology tool, and the law firm's IT staff should *not* be on the front lines selling the extranet. Satterwhite recommended marketing the extranet as an educational tool for hard-to-impress clients.

Lawyers must be comfortable with an extranet and its functions. Satterwhite suggested giving "how-to" in-house presentations to lawyers, and discussing the benefits to the lawyers and the firm's clients. Firm lawyers must be clear on the advantages of an extranet so they can sell the communication-enhancing benefits to firm clients.

After the lawyers are on board, invite the legal departments of firm clients in for personalized demonstrations of the extranet.

CHAPTER*TWELVE*

Using Web Technology to Market Your Firm

WHILE MUCH HAS BEEN made of the use of Web sites for marketing purposes, less has been made of using the broader Web for marketing. What's the difference? Web sites are structured sites that contain content designed by the firm and presented to users. The site is always on (we hope); people stop by, read for a while, and leave.

On the other hand, a number of different Web technologies are increasingly popular for marketing purposes. Whether meeting one-to-one or presenting to a few hundred people, firms are able to use the Web as a virtual meeting place and as a direct communications medium. The marketing benefits can be tremendous—and are too often overlooked as firms put their Internet marketing strategy together.

In this chapter, we'll look at the technology behind Web meetings (often called Webinars, since they are frequently replacing traditional seminars) and Web engagements, discuss examples of how firms can leverage these tools, and give some tips and tricks to help you take full advantage of the medium.

Webinars

Several years ago, a few software companies started trying to make virtual sales presentations over the Internet. The idea was simple: have someone from the software company sit at his desk while the prospect sat at her desk. Connected by the Internet, the salesperson would show the software remotely to the prospect.

Unfortunately, though the idea was simple, the technology was not. The early results were terrible: as often as not, people on the receiving end did not see anything. Or they saw something for a few seconds, interrupted by long pauses and lost signals.

A number of companies entered into this arena, trying to provide a standardized way for companies to make remote presentations. By 1999, the technology had matured. With new tools developed by providers like PlaceWare (figure 12-1) and WebEx, companies could turn one computer into a broadcast center, sharing documents, presentations, and applications. Anyone on the Internet could view—in real time—what was being broadcast from companies' computers.

To prepare your firm to present a Webinar, usually a Webinar provider will install some software on your computer that allows you to connect to the Webinar company's server. Attendees at the meeting connect to that same server. Once everyone's connected, whatever appears on the presenter's computer is then broadcast out to the attendees.

The value of seminars (the in-person kind, not the virtual kind) should be obvious enough to firms. If you educate clients and prospects about your experience that is relevant to them, you increase the odds that those individuals will hire you at some point in the future. The advantages go beyond this. You may be seen as an expert in your practice area, which can also generate leads. Others in the community who learn more about you come to trust your expertise, and this too can lead to business.

There are further benefits to hosting these kinds of events. You often learn a lot from your attendees. By encouraging feedback and inviting questions, you learn valuable information about what matters most to your prospects and clients.

One reason some firms have avoided seminars is cost. It is expensive to do them well. When you add up the cost of the location, printed materials, invitations, time, food, and so on, you could easily be spending $5,000 to $15,000 for a morning meeting lasting only a couple of hours.

By moving your seminar to the Web, you can avoid certain expenses:

1. You don't need to feed your attendees;
2. You don't need to print and collate handouts;
3. You can invite people electronically; and
4. The amount of time you spend "at" the event is much less (more on that in a minute).

Webinars aren't free, but they are often much less expensive than seminars.

In addition to cost savings, you also gain other benefits. The convenience factor should not be overlooked, nor the geographic reach. Think about the people you target for your seminars. In most cases, they are busy people. Taking time out of their days—not just the time to attend your event, but also the time to commute to their jobs or homes—can be a burden. That alone may discourage people who would otherwise be interested in learning from you. With a Web seminar, your attendees can attend from their desks, which means there's no transportation hassle and no downtime. When the seminar starts, they attend. When it's over, they return to their jobs by closing the Web browser. The time savings alone can be compelling.

There may be a number of clients and prospects who are not physically located near your offices who would benefit from your experience—if, for example, your practice mix includes intellectual property, immigration, or securities. In these situations, traditional seminars are hard to manage. In order to attend, people would have to travel, in addition to taking time out for the seminar itself. Making presentations on the Web ensures that anyone who is interested can view your program from any Internet connection.

Finally, your firm benefits by presenting itself as a technologically sophisticated business, and one that is committed to furthering its clients' understanding of issues that concern them.

Provider Choices

It probably goes without saying, but we need to emphasize that in order to use Web conferencing effectively, you need to have a reliable high-speed connection to the Internet. While it is possible to use a dial-up connection to give a seminar online, your attendees (many of whom are likely to have a high-speed connection of their own) will be held back by your slower connection.

There are two major providers of Web conferencing technology: PlaceWare (see figure 12-1) and WebEx. Both companies started in 1996, and have grown so that they now have hosted meetings for thousands of organizations. When selecting a provider (see chart below for options), pay attention to things like customer support, reliability (they need to have a very reliable Internet connection in order to provide your service), and company history. You don't want to do business with someone who

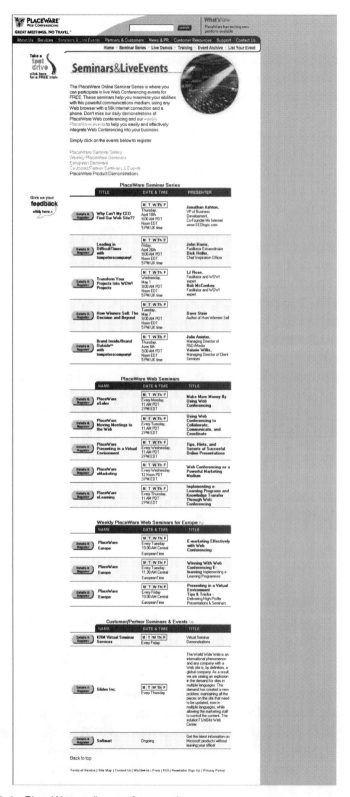

FIGURE 12-1. PlaceWare online conference site

will make you look bad, especially when you're using such new technology. If things go poorly, it reflects on you as the Webinar sponsor.

(Note: prices listed below are current as of publication, but inevitably will change.)

PlaceWare	Supports both large Webinars and small interactive Web meetings. Users can present PowerPoint, share applications, and involve multiple presenters. Can handle up to 2,500 attendees at once. **www.placeware.com.**	From $50 per user per hour. Discounts and flat-rate pricing are available for volume purchases.
WebEx	Interactive Web meetings, mid-sized audience-style presentations. Supports application demos and sharing, polling, and audience chat. **www.webex.com.**	Can pay per use, charged at $.45 per minute per user, or can pay $100 per user per month for flat-rate access.
iMeet	Offers self-service Web conferencing for small business, has larger corporate options as well. Geared to interactive meetings as opposed to large audience-style presentations. Includes PowerPoint support, polling, and other features. **www.imeet.com.**	From $40 per user per month for self-service (minimum 5 users); corporate product priced by user and size of organization.
Raindance (formerly evoke)	Offers both self-service and corporate solutions. Integrates phone control and access with Web conferencing and offers collaboration (interactive meetings) in the "Pro" version. **www.raindance.com.**	From $.27 per minute for phone conferencing, $.21 per minute for Web broadcasting, additional fees apply for archiving, playback, and other services. Corporate pricing based on size of account and number of users.

In addition to companies like PlaceWare and WebEx that focus exclusively on Web conferencing, a number of teleconference companies have either developed technology of their own or acquired smaller companies that can provide that functionality. While generally not as feature-rich as PlaceWare or WebEx, these tend to be more aggressively priced. If you have a relationship with a long-distance phone provider, or have used someone for setting up audio conference calls, you may want to inquire with them to see if they can offer Webinar functionality and a better overall package.

Streaming Audio

In order to have a completely interactive seminar, you will want to provide audio for your attendees. Some Web conferencing companies include streaming audio with their services, which may be good for one-way audio (you to them), but doesn't work from them to you. Streaming audio can be an effective use of technology to save money (you don't pay for the audio connection hours as you do for a conference call), but it requires you to have more-sophisticated audio equipment on your end, as well as a 100% reliable Internet connection.

One other consideration with streaming audio is that your users will need better computers with faster Internet connections. If their machines or connections are slow, they will have inconsistent performance and will likely not hear the entire presentation. Unfortunately, as of this writing, streaming audio over the Internet is still less than perfect. For at least the next few years, you should expect to deal with telephones for the audio and the Web conferencing system for the presentation itself.

Some services will allow you to provide streaming video in addition to the more standard presentations, applications, and interactive tools. Bandwidth considerations aside, ask yourself whether having a jerky video really adds any value to your presentation. Video quality on the Internet is still nowhere near broadcast quality. In most cases, you are better off avoiding streaming video in your presentations—you'll save money, and the resulting experience will seem more polished.

Hughes & Luce's Commerce by Net (**www.commercebynet.com**) offers online video Web seminars in several substantive areas, at low, medium, and high speeds (see figure 12-2).

Tips and Tricks for Webinars

1. **Keep the presentation interactive.** While a Webinar can be far more convenient for attendees, it is easy to be distracted.

FIGURE 12-2. Commerce by Net, Hughes & Luce's Webinar site

Attendees are sitting in front of their computers, which means their phones can still ring, email can arrive, or people can walk into their offices. Avoid thirty PowerPoint slides in a row—engage your audience. Many of the providers offer tools to do this. PlaceWare, for example, gives you the ability to survey your audience. It will automatically tally the results, and can be a great tool for gathering useful information from your attendees.

2. **Practice.** Even if you have a lot of speaking experience, you'll find that giving Web presentations can be very different. First of all, there's no audience you can see. Speaking to a computer monitor is much different than speaking to a room full of people. Make sure that you are comfortable with the interface, that you set a reasonable pace (get someone else from your office to "attend" a dry run), and that things look good on the screen.

3. **Encourage questions and answers.** Whether you get people to ask questions through the conference software, or they simply ask questions over the phone, you'll offer a better overall experience and your attendees will be more involved in the presentation. (This is also a good way to ensure that the audience is getting value from the presentation. Unlike live seminars, you can't see if you are talking to a sea of confused or disinterested faces.)

4. **Get contact information from your attendees.** The value that your attendees get from you is the information you give and recommendations you make in your presentation. The value you get from them is the ability to keep in touch with them—so that they may buy your services at some point in the future. Get as much contact information as you can (without being intrusive), at the very last email addresses and phone numbers.

5. **Use on-screen annotations to draw attention.** Whether you use the digital equivalent of a laser pointer or an on-screen pen to draw on your slides, you should make more of an effort than you might in person to guide attendees along in your presentation.

6. **Record the presentation and archive it.** In many cases, you'll be able to archive the presentation you give, including questions and answers. Save the archive and make it available on your Web site or in a password-protected area available only to clients. If anyone was unable to attend the "live" Webinar, they'll be able to see the recording. Newer clients will be able to browse through older Webinars, introducing them to firm expertise and providing valuable information about issues of concern to them.

7. **Be careful!** If you're presenting content that may be sensitive, know your audience. Every Web conferencing service should allow you to easily identify everyone present. If it looks like there are more attendees than there should be, or you're worried that an unauthorized visitor is in the room, there are ways to check it out.

8. **Encourage your attendees to check their computer configuration ahead of time.** This is ordinarily quite easy, but can save as much as five to ten minutes before the program's start. (A last-minute phone call from a prospect begging for help with an error message on his computer is often hard to handle.)

9. **Make it easy to sign up.** If your seminar is open to the public, advertise the event broadly and provide a simple registration mechanism on your site. Don't make people hunt for the form, and don't require too much information prior to confirming the sign-up. You can always ask for more later, and requesting too much information on the front end may dissuade some interested people from following through.

10. **If using Web engagements, use pre-written replies to make chatting easier.** This will make the discussions happen faster and your visitors won't spend a lot of time waiting for you to type a reply.

Engaging Your Web Visitor

Picture yourself walking into a Home Depot. The store is enormous—
it has everything you could possibly want for your home repair project.
The biggest challenge is finding what you're looking for without getting
distracted.

Compare that with walking into the neighborhood butcher shop. In
most cases, the store is small. The butcher behind the counter recognizes
you from your last visit, asks how you've been and how your kids are, and
remembers the last cut of meat you ordered.

Most Web sites resemble Home Depot—there's ample information,
but finding it can be tricky. Few Web sites (especially among law firms)
allow visitors to customize their experiences, and almost none are capable
of recalling their last visit and presenting them with specific information
based on their prior visits.

Recognizing this problem, a number of companies now provide services that allow you to engage and interact with your site's visitors.

Identifying a Visitor to Engage

For purposes of discussion, we'll assume that the engagement service will
be owned by someone in the marketing department in the firm. This person will have a window on her computer that allows her to see, in real
time, when a visitor is at the firm's Web site. The information the marketing person sees includes whether the visitor has visited the site in the
past, which pages the visitor has viewed on this visit, how long he has
been browsing, from what domain he is browsing, etc. Based on this
information, the marketing staffer can "engage" the visitor. Essentially an
invitation to enter a real-time chat, an engagement establishes a direct
communication link (usually by text messaging) between someone in the
firm and the visitor.

From there, it's up to you what you do with the engagement. Based
on the visitor's traffic at your site, you should have a solid idea of what
interests this person. (Note: this should make it obvious how important
and valuable an intuitive site structure is. You are now able to infer what
your visitors want by their browsing patterns, and do something about it
right away!) Inside the real-time chat window, you can push a visitor to
practice-area descriptions of interest, and capture contact information so
that you can forward printed materials later. If you want to tell him about

lawyers in your firm who can address the issues he has identified, you can display the lawyers' bios with links to more information. For more information, refer back to Chapter Five, "Promotional Content."

The idea is to provide an experience that much more closely resembles that of the neighborhood butcher shop. Rather than expecting a visitor to guide himself through your site, you have someone from your firm "speak" to him directly, and share information and ideas about how the firm can help. It can be a nonintrusive interaction; if the visitor turns down the request to chat, then he can continue browsing the site without further interruption.

From a marketing perspective, this creates a more intimate, informed relationship with the visitor. The visitor benefits by learning more about your firm, and you save him time by identifying more quickly whether your firm is capable of solving his problems.

The chart below lists providers for services that will allow you to engage your visitors. For a nominal monthly fee, the results could easily be a handful of new clients—which will more than pay for your firm's investment. (Note: prices listed below are current as of publication, but inevitably will change.)

NewChannel	Allows customers to define their own criteria for the most serious prospects on the Web site. NewChannel alerts marketing/business development to their presence on the Web site, allows the firm to engage a prospect in real time **www.newchannel.com**	Price varies based on number of internal users and number of engagements. Base price is a few hundred dollars per month.
LivePerson	Several free services, including real-time engagements with Web site visitors. Also includes site monitoring and statistics analysis (see figures 12-3 and 12-4). **www.liveperson.com**	Prices start at $89.50 per month for "pro" service; enhanced services available.

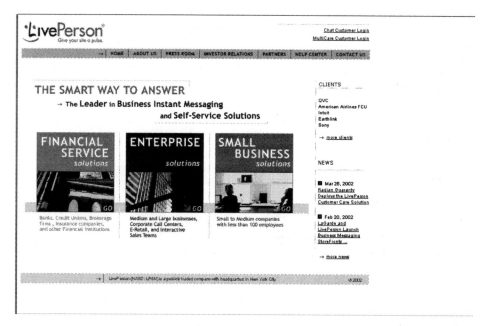

FIGURE 12-3. LivePerson's home page

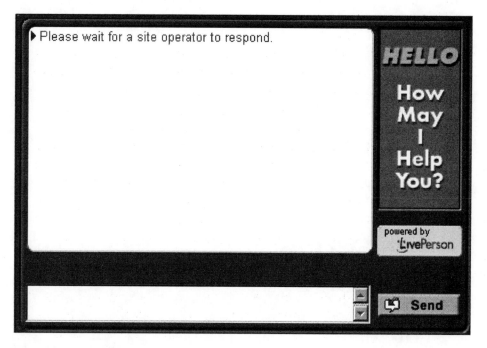

FIGURE 12-4. LivePerson's message window

*CHAPTER*THIRTEEN

Weblogs

What Are Weblogs?

In the early days of the Web, to admit to a personal Web site was to invite any number of groans. Personal Web pages were the antithesis of the Shoeless Joe mantra that we reference in our introduction, "If you build it, they will come." People built them, but the likely visitors (friends and family) knew what was good for them—and stayed away. In droves.

That's all changed, thanks to a relatively new concept called a Weblog. Actually, Weblogs (also known as "blogs") have been around in one form or another since about 1998. But thanks to a veritable explosion of easy-to-use and inexpensive applications, Weblogs are now mainstream. Personal Web sites, rather than groan-inducing vanity presses, are now content rich and legit. Rather remarkably, blogs are proving to be excellent marketing vehicles for lawyers at large and small firms alike.

What distinguishes blogs from traditional Web sites? A few characteristics are common to most blogs:

- Frequently updated content;
- Posts organized chronologically; and
- Posts containing links to news items, other blogs, or Web sites of interest, along with comments about the linked item.

Successful blogs focus on a particular topic or subject and are updated frequently (at least several times a week, if not daily). Most blogs are run by individuals and are often highly opinionated. The advantage is that readers get an honest feel for the blog owner's point of view—and often form a stronger bond with that individual than they would with a more "corporate" site.

A challenge in maintaining any Web site is how to add content without significant effort. Though tools like Microsoft FrontPage made the design of Web sites easier, they did not make the addition of new content simple. The result? Sites look all right, but updating requires a lot of effort. And this, of course, results in stale sites with stale content.

Blogs simplify this. Blogs are designed to publish content effortlessly to the Web, so that your only concern becomes *what* to say. Everything else—formatting, uploading content, linking all of the items—is handled by the blogging application.

Weblogs received considerable attention in 2002, with write-ups in *Newsweek*, the *New York Times*, the *Los Angeles Times*, and MSNBC, and countless articles in the computer press. The articles all focused on the ease of setting up blogs—if it takes more than five minutes, you're doing something wrong.

The proof? Only a few months after all this media attention, dozens of lawyers and others in the legal profession were maintaining their own blogs. Howard Bashman, the head of Buchanan Ingersoll's appellate practice, maintains a blog titled "How Appealing" at http://appellateblog.blogspot.com. His focus on current appeals and trends in appellate practice was an overnight hit: after only two months of existence, the site was receiving thousands of visitors a month. It's too early to predict that this will lead to new appellate business for Bashman and his firm—but early bets say it will.

Denise Howell, a lawyer with California's Crosby Heafey Roach & May, maintains her own Weblog called "Bag and Baggage" (at http://bgbg.blogspot.com). As of this writing, she maintains the most exhaustive list of law blogs (which she calls "blawgs"), with more than thirty-five blogs from judges, lawyers, law students, and law professors. Howell explains that from her vantage point, Weblogs are the "killer app" when it comes to members of the legal profession interacting with each other and the public. "The biggest hurdles attorneys face in letting the world know who they are and what their strengths are," says Howell, "are: (1) the print marketing materials available to them are dry, expensive, and slow to obtain; (2) sending out unsolicited marketing materials of *any* kind is ineffective and annoying [and perhaps unethical]; and (3) people, including other lawyers, are predisposed to distrust and look for the ulterior motive behind most anything a lawyer says."

The advantage of her own Weblog is that it "cuts through all that." A "fast, easy and cheap" mechanism for publishing information of interest to her, Howell found it was also interesting and valuable to fellow lawyers and potential clients. After having a blog for fewer than six months, she was hooked.

Ernest Svenson, a litigator at the forty-lawyer firm of Gordon Arata McCollam Duplantis & Eagan, maintains a personal site titled "Ernie the Attorney" (**http://radio.Weblogs.com/0104634**). As the head of his firm's technology committee, Svenson is always looking for ways to improve the practice of law through the use of technology. Weblogs, Svenson believes, eliminate the bottleneck of getting individuals to contribute content for a centralized site. For Svenson, the marketing benefits aren't bad either: Svenson was highlighted in an MSNBC article about professional blogs in March, 2002.

Other examples of legal blog owners are law professors like Glenn Reynolds at the University of Tennessee, who maintains a high-traffic blog called "Instapundit" (**http://www.instapundit.com**). Reynolds stays on top of the day's news, annotating articles of interest to his readers and adding his own commentary where appropriate. In less than a year, he's become many journalists' go-to guy when it comes to getting information about current events. He used his blog to establish instant credibility—and blog technology means that he doesn't have to spend any additional time maintaining the site. He just contributes to it.

Weblog Technology

There are two components to a blog: the site that the owner sees and the site that visitors see. Blog applications are Web-based tools. You connect to your blog's home page, type in the text for your next post, add links to any items, then click "publish." The blogging software handles the conversion of your text to HTML, the formatting of any links to past posts, and the uploading of the files to your public blog.

The following chart lists the most popular blog applications. (Note: prices are current as of publication, but inevitably will change.)

| Blogger | Credited by many for bringing blogging to the masses, **blogger.com** is a Web site that makes creating, hosting, and maintaining your blog simple. Once at the site, pick a username and password, click on "create a blog," and you're off. If you have an existing Web site, or have space on a Web server, you can simply add your server's settings to your Blogger blog. | Free for basic use; Blogger Pro costs $50 per year. |

	Blogger will take care of uploading your blog to **www.yoursite.com**. Alternatively, you can create a free account on **blogger.com's** partner BlogSpot (http://www.blogspot.com) and your blog will be ready for visitors at **yoursitename.blogspot.com**. You have complete control over the appearance of the site, using templates that apply to all pages in your blog. Creating a new entry is simple—go to **http://www.blogger.com**, type your post into the edit field, click "post & publish," and your new content is now online. **Blogger.com** is free, though "Blogger Pro" is a premium service that provides faster servers, increased functionality, and other benefits. The advantages to **blogger.com** are that its purely Web-based, the interface is exceedingly simple, and it is free. The disadvantage is that there is no software installed on your machine, so if you're a mobile user, you're limited to posting when you're online. See **http://www.blogger.com**.	
Movable Type	Based on a similar model as **Blogger.com**, Movable Type is Web-based software that allows you to publish your Weblog. Where Blogger is maintained on a central server, Movable Type is software that you install on your own server. It consists of "scripts" that install on your Web server, so you'll need to be relatively comfortable installing and configuring Web server software. If you're not, the good folks at Movable Type will do it for you for a small fee. While the software itself is free, a donation is requested and future versions with increased functionality will likely be fee-based.	Free if you can install your own software on your Web server; otherwise you'll pay to have it installed. Future versions will certainly be fee-based.

	Conceptually, Movable Type is similar to **blogger.com**. It offers more for those who are capable of doing some of their own programming and offers more control over the presentation of the content. It's not for novices who are uncomfortable with a little bit of programming. See **http://www.movabletype.com**.	
Userland Radio 8	Userland makes the high-end Weblogging software application, called Radio (see figure 13-1). Packed with sophisticated features, Radio gives a user complete control over page layout, formatting of text, and archiving of posts. Radio is a terrific program that lets users set up a blog in a matter of minutes. Radio turns your desktop into a publishing service—not just for your blog posts, but also for other applications that you want to publish from your desktop (see figure 13-2). Unlike the other applications, Radio is software that installs on your desktop. The advantage is that you can always contribute content to your site. However, if you use multiple computers this can be a hindrance. See **http://radio.userland.com**.	$39.95 per year; includes 40 megabytes of storage.

To use a blog, you don't have to know any HTML. In general, you simply type into the text area, add a title for the post, and click "Post to Weblog."

Marketing Advantages of Weblogs

Much of the marketing advantage behind Weblogs has to do with the popular search engine Google™. When searching, Google gives preference

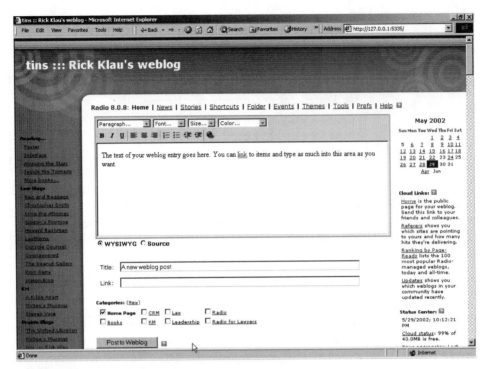

FIGURE 13-1. Radio's page for updating blogs, to be used by blog owners

to current content on sites that are the targets of links from other sites. So Weblogs are ideally suited to capturing high results for searches at Google™.

Each time you post to your blog, your blog's home page gets updated. That means the next time Google™ visits your site, it will see that there is new content. This indicates to Google™ that your site is updated frequently, and it will visit your site more quickly next time. By showing Google™ that your content is fresh, you move up a notch in Google's™ estimation.

Simply updating your site won't make you truly attractive to Google™. In order for Google™ to visit frequently (and if you do it right, Google™ will visit your site every day), it needs to know that your content is relevant. The way Google™ determines relevance is to see if anyone else has linked to you. If there are links to the page, then Google™ assumes that it must be interesting to its visitors.

The ultimate benefit is that your blog will start to appear high in the Google™ rankings for searches on content that is in your blog. Because Google™ weighs both currency and inbound links to the page as barometers of how relevant the content is, your blog may very well show up higher than other, more comprehensive sites that are older.

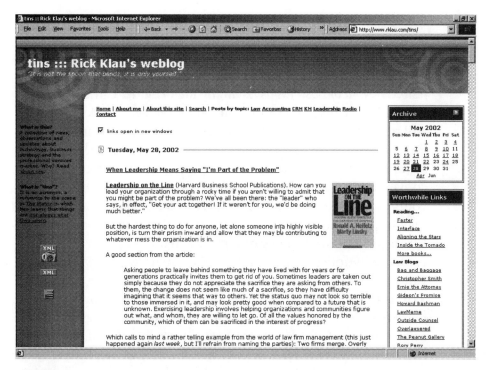

FIGURE 13-2. A blog on Radio's site, which includes posts, a calendar archive of past posts, links to related sites, and (not shown) a search engine to search past posts

For individuals seeking to establish their expertise in a particular area, there is no better way to do so than to use a blog. Within weeks, Google™ will be updating its index of your site daily—type something on to your blog today and anyone searching for that content at Google™ tomorrow will see it. In many cases, it will be one of the top ten search results.

The more focused your area of interest, the more likely it is that Google™ will steer more visitors your way. (Incidentally, these tips are equally applicable if you choose to maintain your Web site manually instead of using a Weblog application. The advantage to using a Weblog application is the ease of use and speed of publication.)

Tips and Tricks for Weblogs

1. **Don't make the site "corporate."** Readers of Weblogs expect to see the personality behind the blog. Blogs, by their very nature, are personal publications. If you make the blog too "official" sounding, you risk diluting the message. Do what Crosby Heafey

does: link to the individual's blog from the firm Web site. (And if you're a lawyer working for a law firm, link back to your firm's site so visitors can find out more about what the firm does.)

2. **Make it interactive.** Readers of the book *The Cluetrain Manifesto: The End of Business as Usual*, by Rick Levine, Christopher Locke, Doc Searls and David Weinberger (Perseus Books, 2001), will remember that marketing is a conversation. (Incidentally, all four co-authors maintain their own Weblogs.) In order to take advantage of Weblogs as marketing tools, you should encourage conversation on the site. Let readers leave comments, then engage your readers in a dialogue. See http://www.rateyourmusic.com/yaccs for a terrific, free "comments" plug-in for Weblogs.

3. **Change the content regularly.** If you don't update the site, readers will notice and Google™ will ultimately ignore you. The value of a blog is directly related to the currency of the posts to it.

4. **Track readership.** It is standard practice among bloggers to reciprocate when someone links to them. Not only does this acknowledge a favor of someone steering traffic to you, but also it can genuinely aid readers of your site. If a blog owner linked to you, presumably it's because you said something that he found interesting. Chances are good that he is focused on similar issues and may have content that is also interesting to your readers. See Chapter Fourteen, "Measuring the Results of Your Internet Efforts," to learn more about measuring traffic and visitors' preferences.

*CHAPTER*FOURTEEN

Measuring the Results of Your Internet Efforts

IF YOUR FIRM IS like most, you will undoubtedly have skeptics when it comes to committing to an Internet marketing strategy. They will want to know the bottom-line value of these efforts. After all, Internet marketing initiatives cost money, and unless you can point to concrete benefits, they'll be unenthusiastic (to say the least) about supporting any future Internet commitments.

So how can you demonstrate success? The good news about many of the strategies discussed in this book is that they are easier and cheaper to measure than their off-line counterparts. In this chapter, we'll look at ways to measure the effectiveness of your Internet efforts.

Web Site Statistics

Each time someone visits your Web site, your Web server captures information about the visit. The server captures the visitor's IP address, the link of the site (if any) that referred the visitor to your site, the page(s) at your site that the visitor viewed, and even details like the browser and operating system that the individual was using. Unfortunately, the raw server logs are often unintelligible (see figure 14-1).

It shouldn't come as a surprise that there's a solution to this, and it doesn't involve having someone in your firm read every line of the log. If your site is hosted by an ISP (as opposed to your own firm's server), your

```
vnnyca-4-g2-12-234.vnnyca.adelphia.net - -
[31/Dec/2001:23:49:47 -0500] "GET /tins/
HTTP/1.1" 200 17073
"http://www.j-marshall.com/talk/" "Mozilla/4.0
(compatible; MSIE 6.0; Windows 98; Q312461)"
vnnyca-4-g2-12-234.vnnyca.adelphia.net - -
[31/Dec/2001:23:50:00 -0500] "GET /tins/bio.html
HTTP/1.1" 200 6964 "http://www.rklau.com/tins/"
"Mozilla/4.0 (compatible; MSIE 6.0; Windows 98;
Q312461)"
vnnyca-4-g2-12-234.vnnyca.adelphia.net - -
[31/Dec/2001:23:50:01 -0500] "GET
/tins/archive/index.html HTTP/1.1" 304 -
"http://www.rklau.com/tins/bio.html" "Mozilla/4.0
(compatible; MSIE 6.0; Windows 98; Q312461)"
vnnyca-4-g2-12-234.vnnyca.adelphia.net - -
[31/Dec/2001:23:50:01 -0500] "GET /tins/rklau.jpg
HTTP/1.1" 200 3455
"http://www.rklau.com/tins/bio.html" "Mozilla/4.0
(compatible; MSIE 6.0; Windows 98; Q312461)"
vnnyca-4-g2-12-234.vnnyca.adelphia.net - -
[31/Dec/2001:23:49:48 -0500] "GET
/tins/archive/index.html HTTP/1.1" 200 2564
"http://www.rklau.com/tins/" "Mozilla/4.0
(compatible; MSIE 6.0; Windows 98; Q312461)"
ACA0D146.ipt.aol.com - - [31/Dec/2001:23:53:26
-0500] "GET /tins/archive/index.html HTTP/1.1"
200 2564 "http://www.rklau.com/tins/"
"Mozilla/4.0 (compatible; MSIE 5.5; Windows 98)"
ACA0D146.ipt.aol.com - - [31/Dec/2001:23:57:51
```

FIGURE 14-1. A typical server log

ISP may provide you with a server statistical analysis. Before investing in statistical analysis tools, check with your ISP to see if they can provide this. They'll often provide the service at a URL like "**www.yourfirm.com/stats**" or something close. (On a related note, if you want to see what traffic is like at other servers, try "**www.yourcompetitorsfirm.com/stats**" and see if you get anything. You'll be surprised at how often you can actually access the stats.)

On a Shoestring

If your ISP doesn't make this analysis available, you do have a couple of options. You can download a free trial of an application like WebTrends Log Analyzer (see **www.webtrends.com**), but after thirty days, you'll need to pay to register the software. Your ISP may provide you with a free copy if they have an agreement with WebTrends. The purpose behind Log Analyzer is to translate every line of the server log and present it in a more understandable, useful view (see figures 14-2, 14-3, and 14-4).

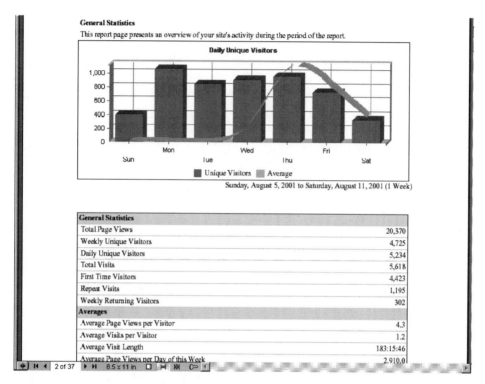

FIGURE 14-2. Log Analyzer site activity chart (Reprinted by permission of NetIQ Corporation. © 2002 NetIQ Corporation. All rights reserved.)

For smaller firms, WebTrends has a "Lite" version that gives less information and limits the number of logs, but is free for use with one Web site.

Another low-cost option is to use a service like SiteMeter (see **www.sitemeter.com**). A free service, SiteMeter displays a real-time overview of your visitors, where the most recent visitors have gone, how visitors are finding your site, and how long they spend at your site.

Unlike WebTrends, SiteMeter is purely Web-based. To make it work, sign up for an account at **sitemeter.com** and you'll receive a few lines of code that your Web master can include in your Web pages. The result is that every time someone visits your site, **sitemeter.com** records a hit and tracks that visitor's traffic inside your site. SiteMeter is less comprehensive than a complete statistics package (see figure 14-5). However, it is easier to implement than other software, and it has the added advantage of providing you with information directly through your Web browser. One

General Statistics			
Total Page Views			20,370
Weekly Unique Visitors			4,725
Daily Unique Visitors			5,234
Total Visits			5,618
First Time Visitors			4,423
Repeat Visits			1,195
Weekly Returning Visitors			302
Averages			
Average Page Views per Visitor			4.3
Average Visits per Visitor			1.2
Average Visit Length			183:15:46
Average Page Views per Day of this Week			2,910.0
Average Unique Visitors per Day of this Week			675.0
Average Visits per Day of this Week			802.6
eCommerce			
Total Revenue			$394,710.73
Total Orders			1,950
Total Unique Buyers			1,621
Most Active Period		**Least Active Period**	
Page Views Monday	4,395	Page Views Saturday	1,076
Unique Visitors Monday	1,058	Unique Visitors Saturday	338

FIGURE 14-3. Log Analyzer summary report (Reprinted by permission of NetIQ Corporation. © 2002 NetIQ Corporation. All rights reserved.)

downside: in return for providing you a free service, SiteMeter requires that you include an image promoting its service on every page.

A note about a number of free statistics packages that are out there: like SiteMeter, many will require that you include banner advertising on your site in exchange for the statistics-monitoring package that you use. This may be all right for a personal Web site, but for a professional site you should avoid including advertising for other sites and providers, especially when you may have no control over the advertising content.

With a Budget

WebTrends and other applications offer premium versions of their statistics packages. Pricing information and details are below. Advantages of paid versions of these packages include:

- ♦ **Increased ability to track multiple sites.** If your firm maintains more than one Web site, you'll want to have more flexibility with your statistics package. The free versions are often limited to one site.
- ♦ **More reporting options.** You can create more sophisticated reports, which provide more in-depth analysis of your site's activ-

Page Views

This section measures the number of times pages from your sites were displayed during the period of the report.

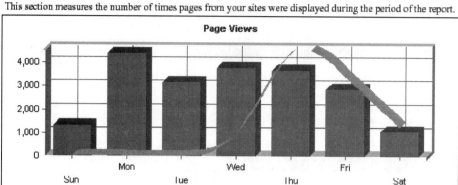

Sunday, August 5, 2001 to Saturday, August 11, 2001 (1 Week)

Day	Average	Page Views
Sunday	0	1,351
Monday	0	4,395
Tuesday	0	3,173
Wednesday	1,018	3,800
Thursday	4,418	3,694
Friday	3,434	2,881
Saturday	1,247	1,076
Total	10,117	20,370

FIGURE 14-4. Log Analyzer weekly report (Reprinted by permission of NetIQ Corporation. © 2002 NetIQ Corporation. All rights reserved.)

ity. Depending on how much information you want to share with others in the firm or how granular you want your analysis to be, this could be valuable.

♦ **More export options.** In general, the default presentation style is in a Web page. More sophisticated packages will give you the option of exporting to a spreadsheet or other format where you can do further analysis and presentation.

♦ **Sophisticated database integration.** Instead of seeing that your visitor was "191.24.21.38," you can see that he was "vipclient.com." By having real-time access to domain-name information, for-pay packages will give you a better idea of whom is visiting your site and from where.

There is much more to these packages. The point is to find one that tells you what you want to know and presents it in a way that is useful and easily understandable. Once you are comfortable with the information in the reports, try influencing the trends you're observing. The basis

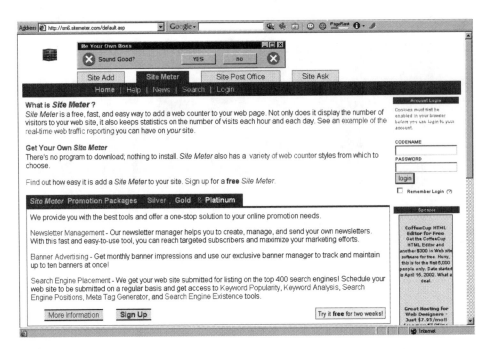

FIGURE 14-5. Site Meter product description

of marketing is measurement, so you should manage your site to improve the statistics that matter to you.

For example, if you are promoting an event that the firm will be hosting, watch how many hits the event page gets. If you want more, highlight the event page on your home page. Include a link to it in all email messages you send. If the numbers start going up, you're doing the right things. If the numbers stay flat, then you need to do something different.

(Note: prices listed below are current as of publication, but inevitably will change.)

WebTrends Lite	Software that installs on your computer. It needs to know where your server log is located, so ask your Web master or ISP where the log is located. Reports include traffic analysis, most popular pages, locations of visitors and referrals to your site. See **www.webtrends.com**.	Free for use with one Web site, limitations on the number of logs you can analyze.

WebTrends	Offers LogAnalyzer (basic site analysis), Analysis Suite (more advanced functionality, can track more pieces of information) and Web-Trends Live (real-time display of statistics). See **www.webtrends.com**.	LogAnalyzer: $499 Analysis Suite: $999–$2499 WebTrends Live: based on size of site and amount of information being tracked.
123LogAnalyzer	Functional alternative to WebTrends; software-based. See **www.123log-analyzer.com/sample** for sample report; **www.123loganalyzer.com** for information about the company and product.	$129
HitBox	Hosted solution (no soft-ware to install), excellent reports. See **www.hitbox-professional.com**.	From $24.95 per month, up to $500 per month for high-traffic sites (more than one million page views per month.)

Inbound Communication

One goal of your Internet marketing strategy should be to increase the inbound communication to your firm. Whether it comes from a visitor completing a form on your Web site, an email sent to someone in the firm, or a phone call after a visitor has been to your site, you should track every one of them.

By tracking email, you'll have a better idea of how much interest your Web site is generating. If you aren't seeing many inbound email messages, look at your site with a fresh eye and make it more engaging for your visitors. If you're seeing a lot of email messages about issues your firm doesn't handle, make the site more descriptive and focused. Pay attention to the volume of email. Is it consistent? If not, ensure that it's easy for site visitors to communicate with lawyers in the firm.

Phone calls can also be generated by the Web site. To track how many phone inquiries your site is generating, consider listing a separate phone number on the site instead of the firm's main number.

With the information collected by tracking these interactions, you can better demonstrate the effectiveness of your Internet efforts. Not only will you be able to show the volume of inbound inquiries, you'll also be able to demonstrate what (if any) business resulted from those efforts. (And if, after tracking this information, you learn that the skeptics are right, then take a hard look at what you've done and whether it can be improved.)

A sample report for circulating inside the firm might look like this:

MONTHLY TOTALS OF VISITORS TO OURFIRM.COM

Month	Total visitors	Number of email messages	Qualified inquiries	Meetings	Client engage- ments
January	750	25	5	3	1
February	895	35	5	4	2
March	1242	57	8	3	2
April	1159	39	4	2	1

Return on Investment

Measuring your return on investment (ROI) is possible, but it takes time and patience. First, there are several ways to define ROI:

- Dollar for dollar return generated by existing or new clients, and referrals from lawyers and other professionals;
- Number of new prospects who have contacted you;
- Number of new law students who wanted to interview with you; or
- More of the kind of business you want (and that you identified in your Web marketing plan).

"All of the above" isn't really practical. Outline reasonable goals and track the results. Below are a couple of realistic scenarios that may help you formulate your objectives.

Scenario 1

Snow & Snow LLP[1] is a business-to-business law firm whose primary goal is "getting more of the client." Its Web strategy focused on cross-marketing

---

1. Although there are law firms named Snow & Snow, this particular one is fictitious.

key practice and industry areas that weren't currently used by the firm's top one hundred clients. They created a matrix that resembled the one below:

FIRM MAJOR PRACTICE AREAS

		Corporate	Litigation	Tax	Labor	IP
Top 100 Clients	Client A	In-house	x	competitor	In-house	competitor
	Client B	competitor	x	competitor	x	competitor
	Client C	x	x	x	competitor	competitor
	Client D	competitor	competitor	competitor	competitor	x
	Client E	x	competitor	x	competitor	x
	Client F	In-house	competitor	competitor	x	competitor

They continued their analysis by determining which competitors were representing the clients in these key areas, or whether the clients handled the work in-house. Snow & Snow leadership figured that as important as these clients were to the firm, they were still vulnerable if the firm didn't do a better job of institutionalizing the relationships.

They created a Web positioning and marketing strategy that focused attention on clients for whom the firm had served as "outside general counsel" and handled everything, or "outside primary counsel," for whom the firm handled most things. In addition, they created a practice-group-centric advertising campaign that drove traffic to specific sections of their Web site (**snowlaw.com/ip** or **snowlaw.com/tax**). Finally, they mailed copies of these advertisements to clients in key areas, inviting them to visit the Web site for more information.

Snow & Snow's strategy demonstrates a good way to track. As mentioned above, they created URLs to drive traffic to specific areas of their site: **www.snowlaw.com/corporate** or **www.snowlaw.com/labor**. If you do this, your tracking mechanism will identify visitors who start at these addresses—you'll know your cross-marketing efforts worked.

If Snow & Snow's top one hundred clients hire the firm in any of these new areas, it is likely that the impetus came from the Web site and related off-line marketing efforts. We know that selling legal services is still a relationship business—but the buyer has to be inspired to want more information. The Web can facilitate this.

Scenario 2
Lopez & Lopez LLP has always regarded itself as "full service." On analysis, however, they discovered that eighty-five percent of their best and

most profitable business was litigation. The firm's first-generation static site listed a dozen practice areas with fairly ineffectual descriptions. Firm lawyers determined that their third-generation site would be database driven and position the firm as a large litigation boutique, with emphasis in product liability, intellectual property, and complex commercial disputes.

Lopez & Lopez's goal was to get more high-end litigation work. They would invest in this area, but would not divest the corporate lawyers and other practices. These would be viewed as support practices for the firm's litigation clients.

The firm created a weekly email "brief" that went to clients, friends, and referral sources and covered the latest in litigation—cases, courts, companies. They published anything that positioned the firm as a go-to source and that kept the firm name in front of key influencers and decision-makers.

Like Snow & Snow, the Lopez firm used traditional "off-line" marketing to push traffic to its site and reinforce the new litigation focus. In order for Lopez & Lopez to meet its primary goal of getting more high-end litigation work, it needed to narrow its strategy and focus its spending.

Don't make the mistake of thinking you can track ROI without being disciplined on the front end of Web site development. The only way you can manage and measure results is to do the research, establish goals, develop a strategy, ensure that your Web design and functionality supports the strategy—and market your site using electronic and traditional means. Then measure. If you aren't getting the results you believe you should, analyze why and make the right adjustments. It takes planning, discipline and commitment.

Web Ethics and Ethical Issues of Online Marketing

TECHNOLOGY IS CHANGING THE practice of law at an unparalleled pace. Firms are using video conferencing to meet with clients and colleagues around the world. Research materials, ranging from statutes to corporate annual reports, are online. Court administrators are making files available electronically, and in some jurisdictions, sets of court forms with instructions. Courts are beginning to accept electronic filings. In 1997, a law firm filed a brief on CD in the United States Supreme Court for the first time.

Many of these changes in technology are fundamentally advances in communication tools. As communication expands, so do the methods of marketing legal services. When lawyer advertising became permissible after the Bates decision in 1977, the various advertising media—radio, television, and print—already existed, and advertising regulations were understood. Once lawyers learned about marketing, they were ready to begin using advertising to promote their firms. Currently, however, the nature of marketing is changing as the new media emerge. As lawyers use the new technologies, they need to assess the role that regulations play in guiding their online marketing.

Communication Through Technology as Commercial Speech

As with any medium, the threshold question is whether a firm's communication over the Internet falls within the parameters of commercial speech. Commercial speech has been defined by the U.S. Supreme Court as that which "proposes a commercial transaction or speech" related solely to the economic interests of the speaker and his audience.[1] If the information being conveyed through technological communication relates to seeking business, it is commercial speech and is governed by the rules of professional responsibility among the states, and by applicable state and federal statutes. If, however, the information is not commercial at all, but would be categorized as political discourse, then an argument could be made that the information is not governed by the rules that apply to the communication of legal services.

Law firms create Web sites, for example, to keep clients advised of developments in their substantive areas, make newsletters and articles available, network among colleagues, and recruit new associates, as well as to market themselves to current clients and prospects. Home pages for law firms adopt a range of styles varying from exclusively informative to exclusively promotional, or nearly so. If a lawyer can demonstrate that the Web site is *not* for the purpose of client development, he may be able to avoid an application of the state rules. In an Iowa ethics opinion, that state's Board of Professional Ethics and Conduct concluded that a Web site or home page is generally designed to promote the firm and sell its services.[2] An exception is noted, however, for the "pure exchange of information." So, it's arguable that informational Weblogs would be an exception.

Discussion Groups and Chat Rooms

Similarly, within a discussion group or chat room, the content of the message should be the dominant factor in determining whether the communication is commercial speech. For example, if a lawyer makes it known that she has some experience in a practice area, but her messages are informative and in the context of a discussion group thread, this communication would probably not be deemed commercial speech by its context and content, even though the lawyer may wish to develop clients as a result of the activity and may in fact do so.

As an analogy to this situation, the United States District Court, in *Texans Against Censorship, Inc. v. State Bar of Texas*,[3] stated that a lawyer

1. *Texans Against Censorship, Inc. v. State Bar of Texas*, 888 F.Supp. 1328 (E.D.Tex 1995).
2. Iowa State Bar Association Ethics Opinion 95-30 (5/16/96).
3. Supra Note 1.

who ran a newspaper advertisement asking people what they thought of judicial selection methods was not involved in commercial speech, even though the lawyer intended the dialogue to be a marketing endeavor.

On the other hand, if someone in a discussion group asks for help finding a corporate and securities lawyer in Denver, and a lawyer who meets these qualifications replies with a list of credentials and a solicitation, that communication would be subject to the applicable rules. If this Denver corporate and securities lawyer directly replies to the inquirer, it would probably be considered an invited solicitation. However, if the lawyer replied through the discussion group and all members of the list see this message, it could be construed as advertising. It would then require application of the rules that apply, such as disclaimers and labeling requirements.

Note that there is scant authority for these positions and the general presumption is that the use of the Internet does include the purpose of marketing the firm's services; therefore, it falls within the definition of commercial speech.

The Emergence of the Internet as a Marketing Vehicle

While the pieces of the technology puzzle have converged to make Internet-based forms of communication viable client-development resources, the rules and regulations that govern the uses of these tools have lagged behind. States are just now re-examining their rules of professional conduct to determine what revisions should be made in light of the use of technology as a client-development tool. As a result of this lag, the rule application depends on the current wording of the rules now in place, along with their interpretation.

The ABA Rules

ABA Model Rule 7.1 prohibiting false and misleading communication is broadly worded, addressing the communication of legal services. The comment to Rule 7.1 states in part, "Whatever means are used to make known a lawyer's services, statements about them should be truthful." Clearly this rule applies to all forms of electronic marketing. This ABA rule and its state bar counterparts are frequently violated when law firms include overly broad representations on their Web sites, such as "a national law firm" or "a full-service firm." Unless these representations are fully accurate, they create unjustified expectations in violation of ABA Model Rule 7.1(b).

Model Rule 7.2 permits advertising through the public media, and written and recorded communications. The Rule provides examples of the media where advertising is permissible, but does not limit the advertising to those examples. Consequently, even though the Internet is not listed, the rule should be interpreted to include it. See, for example, Pennsylvania Bar Association Ethics Opinion 96-17 (5/3/96), stating that a Web site qualifies as "public media" that lawyers may use to advertise under Rule 7.2(a), and in principle there is no difference between a Web site or a legal directory, newspaper, radio, or television.

In addition, lawyers should assume they have an obligation to comply with the specific provisions of the state counterparts to Rule 7.2, such as retention requirements, even though strict compliance may be difficult in some situations, as discussed below. Several states have now issued ethics opinions consistently concluding that lawyers may advertise on the Internet, but also requiring that all current applicable rules must be followed when doing so.[4]

Compliance with Model Rule 7.4 requires lawyers to carefully select the ways in which they indicate practice areas. The rules of individual states frequently require the use of disclaimers in connection with representations of specialty. While lawyers may think to include appropriate disclaimer language on Web sites, they must also be cautious when communicating through the other forms of technology, such as email and in discussion groups. (In general, avoid claims such as "I am a tax expert or an employment specialist," unless your state bar certification permits this.)

The technology of communications can facilitate innovative legal services, such as a "virtual law firm." However, Model Rule 7.5 requires lawyers to avoid the implication that they practice in a partnership when that is not a fact.

---

4. See State Bar of Arizona Ethics Opinion 97-04 (4/7/97); Connecticut Bar Association Ethics Opinion 97-29 (10/22/97); Illinois State Bar Association Ethics Opinion 96-10 (5/6/96); Iowa State Bar Association Ethics Opinion 96-1 (8/29/96); State Bar of Michigan Informal Opinion RI 276 (7/11/96); North Carolina State Bar Association RPC 239 (7/25/96); Pennsylvania Bar Association Ethics Opinion 96-17 (5/3/96); South Carolina Bar Ethics Opinion 94-27 (1/95); Utah State Bar Ethics Opinion 97-10 (10/24/97); Vermont Bar Association Ethics Opinion 97-5; and Virginia State Bar Ethics Opinion A-0110 (4/14/98).

These issues illustrate the difficulty in applying a set of standards that were developed without consideration to the environment that now exists. Some states are now defining the requirements that lawyers should abide by in their electronic communications. California bans lawyers from false or misleading representations through the electronic media, which specifically includes "computer networks." Other states regulate advertising through electronic media, which would probably apply to Internet communications. A question arises, however, as to whether use of the Internet, and in particular email transmissions, are also covered under the application of "written communications." Colorado, for example, has clarified the application to email, for example, by amending Rule 7.3(d), which requires solicitation to be labeled. The rule requires every written, recorded, or electronic communication governed by the other provisions of the rule to be labeled conspicuously with the words "THIS IS AN ADVERTISEMENT" at the beginning and end of the communication.

Florida and Texas have adopted rules that apply to the use of the Internet as a marketing tool. In Florida, Rule 4-7.6 sets out the application of governing rules to Web sites, home pages, and email communications.

In Texas, lawyers must file their advertisements with the state bar's Advertising Review Committee. This includes a hard copy of the "first screen" of a Web site home page, along with a filing fee. Other information on the site must be submitted if it is "primarily concerned with solicitation of prospective clients." Safe harbors list types of information that do not fall under this category and do not need to be screened, including newsletters, articles, editorials, illustrations, questionnaires, surveys, office announcements, requests for proposals, lawyer bios, job openings, legal developments and events, seminar and event announcements, and links. Although lawyers do not have to submit these items for screening, the information must still comply with the Texas rules.

Email

One of the fundamental Internet-based communications tools that has ethical implications when used for client development purposes is email. Email may be information conveyed from one person to another, or it may be part of a discussion group or mailing list, where individuals sign up and subsequently exchange email with all subscribers. Email communication can also be integrated with Web site usage; for example, a Web site may solicit questions or information from the visitor and then follow up with an email response.

Chat rooms or chat groups are a variation of discussion groups—people communicate to all subscribers, but they do so in real time. Discussion groups and chat groups frequently center on issues and lend themselves to an ongoing exchange of information, known as threads.

Since chat rooms operate on a real-time basis, some state ethics opinions have indicated the communications of legal services in chat rooms is equivalent to in-person or live telephone solicitations, as opposed to advertisements or direct mail. The use of chat rooms, therefore, is subject to state bans. See Utah Ethics Opinion 97-10, which concludes, ". . . a chat-group communication is more analogous to an in-person conversation due to its direct, confrontational nature and the difficulty of monitoring and regulating it. We, therefore, find that a lawyer's advertising and solicitation through a chat group are 'in person' communications under Rule 7.3(a) and are accordingly restricted by the provisions of that rule."[5]

The Ethics of Spam

Any uninvited promotional email to individuals, discussion groups, or Usenet groups is considered to be spam (see Chapter Three, Email Marketing, for more on spam). Most Internet users believe that spam is a violation of the etiquette of the Internet. While there are no formal sanctions, those who are offended by spam often encourage recipients to reply in mass, causing breakdowns for the computer servers that carry it. This is known as "flaming" the spammers.

Some lawyers have argued that the Telephone Consumer Protection Act should be construed broadly enough to prohibit uninvited email solicitations, along with commercially faxed ads. Even though this application was debated, the Act did not anticipate email nor was the Act intended to apply to email. On the other hand, there is both state and federal legislation under consideration that is specifically directed toward limiting spam. One alternative would ban uninvited solicitations, and another would give the consumer an option to inform spammers that they do not want these solicitations.

In 1997, Tennessee became the first state to suspend a lawyer for violation of state rules as they apply to email marketing. In 1994, the lawyer spammed more than five thousand Internet groups and thousands of

---

5. Utah State Bar Ethics Opinion 97-10 (10/24/97). See also Virginia Opinion State Bar Ethics Opinion A-0110 (4/14/98).

email lists with an advertisement for his firm's immigration services. As a result of hundreds of complaints from Internet users, the Tennessee disciplinary authorities initiated a prosecution. Tennessee, like other states, did not have a rule prohibiting spam. Therefore, the lawyer was prosecuted for failing to abide by existing rules, including failure to label the Internet message "THIS IS AN ADVERTISEMENT," failure to provide a disclaimer about the status of specialization, and failure to provide regulatory authorities with a copy of the posting.

It should be noted that the lawyer was charged with other ethical violations, and did not defend the charges. These factors not only contributed to the severity of the sanctions, but also made a defense to the application of the rules to the actions merely speculative. This decision, however, emphasized that current rules governing legal services marketing apply to the array of Internet-based client development activities.

To assure that regulations applied to future Internet activities, the Tennessee Supreme Court revised its rules governing solicitation. These regulations set out conditions by which a lawyer may solicit via the Internet, or through "computer online transmission." The transmission must include the phrase "THIS IS AN ADVERTISEMENT" in a prominent place, using a conspicuous font, at the beginning and end of the transmission. Additionally, the lawyer must send a copy of the transmission to the state's Board of Professional Responsibility.

While members of online discussion groups are subject to inappropriate spamming, other forms of promotions are generally part of the protocol established by the group sponsor or manager. Discussions may be restricted by their managers. These restrictions may limit both the participants and the content of the messages. For example, some discussion groups are available only to lawyers. Some group managers screen all messages submitted by members and include only those they deem in compliance with the guidelines of the list. These protocols allow managers to control marketing endeavors. Many groups, however, lack these controls and are more likely to include salesmanship within the messages that are exchanged. (For much more on discussion groups, see Chapter Three.)

Regardless of the extent of formal or informal controls within group discussions or chat groups, the contents of the messages are subject to the rules governing the communications of legal services.

Web Sites

Many Web sites are electronic brochures that are characterized as "pull technology," providing information that the consumer or potential client must seek out. This passive technology is compared to the more aggressive forms of delivering the information, which are brought to and sometimes "pushed" upon the recipient through email.

Through their ethics opinions, states are now addressing use of Web sites and home pages. These opinions commonly focus on informative Web pages that are more analogous to yellow pages listings than to television commercials. As passive forms of Internet use, Web sites are most often considered public media or advertising, invoking the application of the state counterparts to ABA Model Rule 7.2, which governs advertising. On the other hand, Web sites are not considered solicitations, which would be governed by Model Rule 7.3.

For example, Illinois State Bar Association Ethics Opinion 96-10 (5/16/97) states, "[T]he Committee views an Internet home page as the electronic equivalent of a telephone directory 'yellow pages' entry and other material included in the Web site to be the functional equivalent of the firm brochures and similar materials that lawyers commonly prepare for client and prospective clients. An Internet user who has gained access to a lawyer's home page, like a yellow pages user, has chosen to view the lawyer's message from all the messages available in that medium. Under these circumstances, such materials are not a 'communication directed to a specific recipient' that would implicate Rule 7.3 and its provisions governing direct contact with prospective clients. Thus, with respect to a Web site, Rule 7.1, prohibiting false and misleading statements concerning a lawyer's services, and Rule 7.2, regulating advertising in the public media, are sufficient to guide lawyers and protect the public."

Ethics opinions that have examined Web sites, home pages, and email communications tend to conclude the following:

♦ Law firm home pages and Web sites are generally used for promotional purposes and amount to advertising, although they may involve the pure exchange of information;[6]
♦ The use of the Internet is permissible advertising under Rule 7.2, but lawyers who do so must abide by the rules governing their activities, including the limits on false and misleading representations (Rule 7.1), and designations of practice areas (Rule 7.4);[7]

---

6 Iowa Supreme Court Board of Professional Ethics and Conduct Opinion 97-01 (9/18/97)

7. Supra Note 9.

♦ Home pages and Web sites are viewed as passive sites of consumer information and are generally regulated by the provisions of Rule 7.2 and not Rule 7.3, which governs solicitation;[8]

♦ Email, discussion group participation, and other forms of direct communications are analogous to direct mail and are governed by the provisions of Rule 7.3. These provisions may include labeling requirements and the use of disclaimers;[9] and

♦ Real-time communications involving lawyers and lay persons, such as chat rooms, may be analogous to in-person solicitation and are subject to being banned.[10]

Unique Features of the Internet

Because states are applying existing rules to the use of the Internet as an advertising medium, rather than amending them to fit the Internet, compliance is often difficult. The Internet has unique features that have not been considered by policy-makers and regulators.

For example, some provisions of the rules governing legal services marketing may readily apply to traditional forms of advertising, but be particularly burdensome and impractical in their application to Internet marketing. Model Rule 7.2(b), for example, requires lawyers to keep copies or recordings of their advertisements for two years after their last dissemination, as well as a record of when and where the ad was used. This requirement is an administrative convenience for disciplinary counsel who may need to act on a complaint. For print ads, or even traditional electronic commercials such as those on radio or television, compliance is a simple task.

However, this rule can be an extraordinary burden for law firms that maintain dynamic Web sites. A lawyer must decide what must be saved. The first question for a lawyer with a Web site is whether he needs to retain only the home page, the contents of the entire site, or the contents with the links that may be established through the Web. Most likely a

---

8. See, for example, Illinois State Bar Association Ethics Opinion 96-10 (5/16/97), stating, "[t]he Committee views an Internet home page as the electronic equivalent of a telephone directory 'yellow pages' entry and other material included in the Web site to be the functional equivalent of the firm brochures and similar materials that lawyers commonly prepare for clients and prospective clients."

9. Supra Note 9.

10. Supra Note 10.

lawyer should retain all the material where the content is under the lawyer's control. A lawyer must then decide how to retain the material. Sites appear differently when viewed with different browsers. There is no standard or direction for this decision. Since the retention requirement is primarily a convenience for disciplinary counsel, lawyers may want to check to see what the disciplinary agency prefers. Lawyers will then have to decide what to do when making changes in their Web sites. Some firms and we (the authors) recommend that firms modify their sites frequently. There is no clear direction on what justifies a change sufficient to require new retention.

Finally, Model Rule 7.2 requires lawyers to keep a record of when and where the communication was used. The extent of this requirement is also unclear. It could be construed to require retention only of the URL for the site and search engine registration, or it could be interpreted to require tracking to assess who has visited the site. If Web sites are analogous to yellow pages advertisements, the lawyer would have no obligation to track those who come to the site.

In applying the standards of Rule 7.1, prohibiting false or misleading representations, Web sites are analogous to other types of advertising when focusing on the content of the material. However, the Internet raises unique concerns. For example, meta tags can be implanted into Web sites to trigger the placement of the sites when prospects seek out the site or conduct searches. A lawyer must conclude whether it is misleading to plant meta tags of the firm's name so that the firm's home page will surface at the top of a search for that firm. A lawyer must then conclude the reasonable limit on the use of meta tags. If they are appropriate for this purpose, are they appropriate for fields of practice? In other words, may a law firm plant words such as "personal injury" or "workers' compensation"? If that is permissible, may a lawyer use more pedestrian words or phrases, such as "car accident" or "job injuries"? The ethical propriety of using meta tags will probably depend on the content, but no clear direction has emerged on this yet.

Linking to Clients and Client Testimonials

Links on a Web site provide the ability to expand the available information well beyond that which the law firm presents. Yet they raise issues about their propriety under certain circumstances. Firms may want to link to sites of their business clients, for example. Doing so may require client permission. ABA Model Rule 1.6 provides that lawyers may not reveal client confidentialities without the client's consent. The rule may apply to the fact of the representation just as it applies to the content of the subject matter.

Linking also raises the question of whether lawyers are responsible for the content of the links. There are ways in which linking could violate the rules even if the lawyer has no control over the content of the link. For example, if a client issues a press release praising the firm in a way that the firm could not do directly, but the firm links to a site with that information, the lawyer may violate Rule 7.1 (b) by creating unjustified expectations and making unsubstantiated comparisons of services. The link could also violate a ban on client testimonials in those states that have such a rule.

These examples illustrate some of the shortcomings in the application of the current rules to emerging technologies. Perhaps the most difficult compliance issue results from the fact that the regulations are inherently state-based and the Internet has no geographic boundaries.

Multistate Regulation and Disclaimers

As we have mentioned, state rules vary; some vary dramatically and in ways that limit what lawyers can do in their client development endeavors. Therefore, it's important for law firms to understand which state rules apply to their Web sites. Unfortunately, there is no consensus on jurisdiction.

It is possible that future technology will allow filtering that limits the scope of a Web site to specified geographic areas. Intranets and extranets are closed networks that restrict access for various reasons. These may allow lawyers to create sites that comply with the rules that govern the intended jurisdictions. In the interim, however, lawyers must turn to other alternatives.

One possibility is through the use of disclaimers. Most law firm Web sites have disclaimers intended to protect them from malpractice claims. (See the discussion of disclaimers in Chapter Nine, "More Possibilities and Leveraging Your Content.") These statements generally say things like "the material is for informational purposes only; viewers should not rely on the information, but should consult a lawyer about their specific legal issues; the content of the site in no way creates an attorney-client relationship," etc.

However, many firms include information designed to assure their ethical compliance beyond the attorney-client issue. Law firms may be able to limit their need to comply with the rules of restrictive states, if they are not willing to accept clients from those states who come to the firm as a result of their Web site. This type of disclaimer is analogous to those that are used in gaming and sweepstakes promotions that say "void where prohibited by law." In other words, a law firm may state on its site that if its site is not in compliance with the regulations of any particular state, that the firm is not willing to accept clients from that state who come to the firm as a result of the site. If the firm then follows up with enforcement of this limitation, it would be difficult for a state to bring successful proceedings against the members of the firm.

Iowa has rejected the use of disclaimers to avoid compliance, although not specifically on this point. Iowa State Bar Association Ethics Opinion 96-14 (12/12/96) indicated that an out-of-state law firm with a branch office in Iowa emphasized, rather than cured, non-compliance by using a disclaimer stating the Web site was "not intended to promote or sell" legal services from its Iowa offices. The opinion suggested instead that the firm establish two sites, one for its Iowa office and another for out-of-state offices. Given the ways in which Web sites are located and accessed, this may not be an alternative that is technologically sound.

The Internet is causing the issues of jurisdiction to be revisited as a whole, and will be the subject of debate for the foreseeable future.

Banner Advertisements

Banner advertisements are emerging as another Internet advertising method. Banners, which appear as miniature electronic billboards on the Web sites of others, are used in the same ways as more traditional advertising vehicles, encouraging sales and enhancing name recognition. While some firms may find the banners distasteful, they are an established part of the Internet, providing substantial advertising revenues that assist with the cost of the sites that carry them.

One of the current issues with the Web as a research tool is the ability of users to find the material they are seeking. Banner advertisements provide a conspicuous site that allows viewers to link to the home page of the sponsor.

Although there is not yet an authority governing the use of banners that advertise legal services, there is nothing to suggest they are not subject to the rules of the various states governing lawyer advertising as discussed throughout this chapter. Lawyers who use banner ads to advertise their services should be concerned about the requirements of state rules for disclaimers and disclosures. The limited space that is inherent in banner ads precludes statements that are sometimes required by the state rules. Since banner ads also serve as links, one option would be for the ad to link to the required disclaimers or disclosures before connecting to a firm's Web site.

Conclusion

The Internet has created a new medium to advertise and solicit legal services. When the Internet is used as a marketing tool by lawyers, those uses are subject to the state rules governing advertising and solicitation in general. States are just beginning to examine the applications of the rules to Internet-based marketing. A few states have amended their rules to address the issues raised by these uses. Several states have also issued ethics opinions, consistently opining that lawyers may advertise on the Internet, but must follow the applicable state ethics rules when doing so. A few ethics opinions have now concluded that the use of real-time chat rooms for business development is akin to in-person and live telephone solicitation and should be avoided.

The current ethics assessments, either rules or opinions, do not generally take note of the unique features of the Internet, such as domain names, meta tags, frames, and links, and therefore have not addressed these issues in their policy-making or disciplinary-enforcement decisions. The Internet disseminates information without boundaries. Lawyers, therefore, must be sensitive to the rules of those states in which they seek clients, or take measures to protect themselves from possible disciplinary actions in those states where their sites do not conform to the rules.

*EXHIBIT*ONE

Sample Web Hosting Proposal and Agreement

XYZ Law Firm Web Hosting Proposal

Table of Contents
Revision History

Revision History

Version	Date	Author	Description
1.0.0	10/30/2001	Drew Naukam	Web Hosting Proposal

1. About XYZ Law Firm

1.1 Overview
Founded in 1995, XYZ Law Firm is a professional and managed services firm that solves business problems with innovative technology solu-

tions. Our delivery expertise is concentrated on two primary service groups:

- **Network Services**—Providing design, implementation, and managed services to support a company's networked computing infrastructure.
- **Technology Solutions**—Delivering custom technology solutions that automate business processes and improve communication and commerce between companies and their customers.

XYZ Law Firm is not a "new economy" company. We do not try to be all things to all people or the "low cost" solutions provider. What we are, however, is an organization that is truly committed to improving the business performance of our clients through the application of reliable, scalable and cost-effective technology solutions. You expect (and deserve) your technology partner to bring to the table technology expertise necessary to solve today's technology problems.

For the past 6 years XYZ Law Firm has been a full-service provider of value-based technology solutions to enterprises of all shapes and sizes, including such well know names as: **(Insert Names).**

To ensure that we deliver best of breed solutions to our clients, we have aligned ourselves with premier partners including: **(Insert Names).**

1.2 Mission
Simply stated, our mission is:

> To create business value for our clients through innovative technology solutions.

1.3 Core Values
Our success begins and ends with our people. Our core values are the guiding light that directs everything we do at XYZ Law Firm. From the recruiting of new professionals to determining the clients we want to be associated with, our core values are a foundation for our every decision, and are as follows:

- **char·ac·ter** (kăr′ ək-tər)—The combination of qualities or features that distinguishes one person, group, or thing from another. Moral or ethical strength
- **re·spect** (rĭ-spĕkt′)—To feel or show deferential regard for; esteem.
- **in·teg·ri·ty** (ĭn-tĕg′rĭ-tē)—Steadfast adherence to a strict moral or ethical code.
- **pride** (prīd)—Pleasure or satisfaction taken in an achievement, possession, or association.

1.4 Why XYZ Law Firm

We are very proud of our track record of successful projects, happy clients, solid, credentialed professionals and profitability. However, we are particularly proud of the fact that we approach every engagement from a partnership perspective, primarily concerned with the creation of value for our clients, not just the delivery of a single project.

Probably the best testament to this is the fact that approximately 70% of our revenues for 2001 will be comprised of repeat customers. In simple terms this illustrates that our clients recognize the value in our efforts and have elected to engage our services over multiple projects spanning multiple years.

In summary, we believe XYZ Law Firm is the right partner due to the following:

- **Our People**—We employ experienced, certified professionals with a diverse mix of industry and consulting backgrounds, business and technology expertise and drive.
- **Our Culture**—Our culture begins and ends with our people and can be summed up with four words: Character. Respect. Integrity. Pride.
- **Our Approach**—Our proven approach allows us to consistently deploy and manage successful, stable managed services to our clients focused on ROI and risk mitigation in a timely fashion.
- **Our Model**—Our unique business model allows us to be the single point of contact for a company's technology initiatives resulting in increased efficiency and accountability.
- **Our Devotion**—We are devoted to our clients' success—to long-term partnerships rather than one-time projects. As such, many of our clients have engaged us over multiple years.
- **Our Foundation**—We were established in 1995, and profitable since 1997. We are privately held and funded and led by a solid management team.

2. Our Data Center

2.1 Data Center Features

The XYZ Law Firm Data Center was designed and built using the highest standards. We employ a high availability power system, a high-speed network backbone, and advanced monitoring tools. These standard features allow us to deliver the highest levels of reliability and uptime. Specific data center details include:

- Redundant gigabit network backbone
- UPS and backup generator
- Redundant HVAC controlled environment
- 24/7/ server operations monitoring
- Security breach alarms
- Continuous video surveillance

Additionally, our network infrastructure is scalable, allowing us to grow our network capacity to meet your changing and evolving needs. We use reliable, world-class servers from Dell to help ensure network reliability.

Bandwidth into our datacenter comes from multiple Internet backbones, providing you with additional assurance in the event that one provider experiences network downtime.

A state of the art gyroscope generator provides continuous power to the facility in the event of a power outage.

3. *Web Hosting Deliverables and Pricing*

3.1 Detailed Proposal
This proposal outlines the requirements for (Client) for managed hosting of their new web site, **www.(client).com.**

3.2 Server Specifications
The (Client) web site will reside on a shared web server, shared Microsoft SQL database environment.

Based on anticipated site size and traffic patterns, we recommend the following server configuration.

Server Configuration:	Web Server
Server Type:	TBD
Processor(s):	
Memory:	
Operating System:	
App. / Content Storage:	
Log files / Cache:	
Content Fault Tolerance:	
Monthly Transfer:	

3.3 Services

XYZ Law Firm will provide the following services for the (Client) web site:

◆ Placement of the web site on a web server with the configuration as listed in this proposal.
◆ Use of multiple redundant network components to reduce downtime, increase speed and increase connectivity reliability, including:
  ◆ Bandwidth (20 GB of data transfer per month)
  ◆ WebTrends site statistics—real time report showing web site traffic details
  ◆ HP Openview monitoring—HP monitoring package with auto alert features and performance measurement tools
  ◆ Daily backups
  ◆ Checkpoint firewall protection—sophisticated intrusion prevention software

3.4 Pricing

In exchange for the services listed above, (Client) will pay to XYZ Law Firm the following fees:

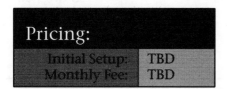

These fees are based on a one year contract. The fee will be billed on a monthly basis, with the initial setup fee billed at the time of the initial monthly fee once the site is live.

Appendix A: Our Maintenance Procedures

The following checklist details the standard maintenance procedures we follow in order to ensure consistent, reliable performance of our web servers and your web site

Weekly Maintenance Tasks					
	Check Server Logs		Check Error Logs		Check Firewall Logs
	Check System Events		Note Hard Drive Failure Warnings		Note Consistent Log on Failures
	Note Dropped Connections		Determine Causes & Possible Resolutions		Note Results/Actions in Guidebook
	Check Dialup connections (i.e.—RAS or VPN if present)		Verify backup completion.		Verify Schedules
	Verify anti-virus signature file dates are up to date. Verify last network scan date of all files. Verify that weekly scans and updates are on schedule.		Test restore function (Mission critical files to different directory)		Verify configuration for proper server shutdown. Check UPS log for recurring power surges/sags.
	Clean equipment screens.		Update backup script as necessary to account for machine name changes, etc.		Verify emergency repair disk for OS is present and updated.
	Verify all fans are working properly; that the server has proper ventilation and is not excessively warm to the touch.		Verify all network hubs, routers and switches are operating correctly. Note any excessive collisions, traffic load, warning lights, etc.		Verify disk space availability. Make recommendations w/ primary consultant approval.
	Verify Software Licensing.		Conduct an UPS test and load check. Verify last date battery replaced. Verify UPS fully charged.		Complete user adds/changes/ deletions & log into Guidebook. Check the guidebook and note any changes or missing information.

Monthly Maintenance Tasks		
Use computer-safe case vacuum to clean internal server components.	Confirm UPS operates properly (unplug from outlet); verify server and scheduled shutdown time process. Schedule a test outage during off-peak hours to test UPS and settings.	Verify NOS patches, device drivers and service packs are all current. Apply only known tested updates.
Complete user adds/ changes/deletions & log into Guide Book. Check the guidebook and note any changes or missing information.		

XYZ Law Firm—Hosting Services Agreement

This Agreement is entered into by and between XYZ Law Firm Solutions, Inc. (**"XYZ Law Firm"**), (address), and (Client), (**"Customer"**), (address).

Whereas, XYZ Law Firm has a background in Internet Web site hosting services and is willing to provide those services to Customer based on this background; and

Whereas, Customer desires to have Internet Web site hosting services provided by XYZ Law Firm.

The parties hereto agree:

1. Description of Services

XYZ Law Firm will provide the following services (collectively, **"Services"**):

(a) ***Equipment:*** Is described under Deliverables and Prices on Exhibit A attached hereto.

(b) ***Hosting:*** Website hosting on the Equipment described in Exhibit A. The equipment and software used by XYZ Law Firm in providing Services are referred to collectively as the **"Products"**.

(c) ***Service Levels:*** XYZ Law Firm will use commercially reasonable efforts to ensure the reliability and availability of all Services under XYZ Law Firm's control; however, XYZ Law Firm does not guarantee or warrant any specific level of service availability.

(d) ***Additional Domain Names:*** Services include hosting for 10 domain names at no extra charge. Additional domain names will be supported at the rate of $25 per month, plus $100 per setup if XYZ Law Firm does the setup or $25 per setup if Customer does the setup for XYZ Law Firm DNS entry.

(e) ***Maintenance:*** Standard server maintenance will be provided by XYZ Law Firm as part of this Agreement in accordance with the procedures attached hereto as Exhibit B. Standard server maintenance includes 24 hour, 7 day support for mission critical problems which will be connected within the time set forth on Exhibit B. Non Mission Critical Support will be provided from Monday to Friday 9 a.m. central time to 8 p.m. central time and Saturday 12 a.m. central time to 5 p.m. central time, exclusive of holidays.

(f) ***Activation:*** The servers to be used to perform Services will be available for Customer to load content (**"Activated"**) within 14

days after the execution of this Agreement if Customer timely supplies all necessary information to XYZ Law Firm.

2. Term, Prices, and Payment

(a) Term: The initial term of this Agreement shall be 12 months from date of activation unless terminated as provided herein. After the expiration of each term, this Agreement will be automatically renewed for successive 12-month terms unless either party gives notice of its intent not to renew at least 90 days prior to the expiration of the then current term. Customer may terminate this Agreement at any time following 90-days written notice.

(b) Setup Payment: Customer will pay a fee to XYZ Law Firm for the initial set-up of the Products in the amount of $500 that is due in full upon execution of this Agreement.

(c) Monthly and Initial Payment: A service fee in the amount of $350 per month will be charged as described in Section 2(d). Charges for Services, if any, supplied prior to the first day of the term shall be determined by XYZ Law Firm, prorated, and invoiced to the Customer. Charges for Services will begin to accrue on the date servers to be used to perform Services are activated.

(d) Past Due Payments: Customer will be invoiced monthly, on or about the 15th day of each month, and payment shall be due on no later than thirty (30) days after receipt of the invoice. Interest charges of 1.5% per month (or the highest rate permissible under applicable law, if less) may accrue daily on all amounts not received when due. Customer will pay or reimburse XYZ Law Firm for any and all taxes and other charges imposed as a result of this Agreement, including sales and use taxes, duties or levies imposed by any authority, government or government agency (but excluding property taxes and taxes levied on XYZ Law Firm's net income). Upon termination of this Agreement, prospective payments under Section 2 shall cease; provided, however, that XYZ Law Firm shall be entitled to payments for periods or partial periods that occurred prior to the date of termination and for which XYZ Law Firm has not yet been paid. If Customer is in Default (as defined below), including termination of this Agreement other than as permitted by its terms, Customer shall immediately pay XYZ Law Firm in one lump sum the product of the monthly service fee stated in Section 2(c) and the portion of the initial or renewal term remaining immediately prior to such Default.

(e) ***Additional Services:*** Charges for additional services as set forth in any subsequent Purchase Order or Service Agreement shall be as set forth in that Purchase Order or Service Agreement and shall be at rates and policies agreed to by the parties.

(f) ***Tariff Applicability:*** If any Services ordered by Customer are subject to a tariff filed with the Federal Communications Commission, or its local equivalent, by XYZ Law Firm or any other network service provider whose services and/or equipment is utilized by XYZ Law Firm to provide Service and/or equipment to Customer, the terms and conditions of such tariff shall govern Customer's use of such Services.

(g) ***Rate Escalation Due to Carrier Increases:*** XYZ Law Firm shall have the right to increase its charges upon 30 days' prior notice to Customer due to increases in the rates of the underlying carrier (**"Rate Escalation"**).

(h) ***Rate Escalation Due to Any Reason Other than Carrier:*** Other than for rate escalation due to carrier increases, the pricing in this Agreement will be valid for the initial term of this Agreement. After the expiration of such term, XYZ Law Firm may change the monthly fees on 30 days' notice by an amount no more than a 5% increase per year.

3. Customer Responsibility

(a) ***Licenses:*** Customer will provide all software licenses necessary to host Customer's Web site other than Microsoft Windows 2000 and XYZ Law Firm System Administration software. For any server designated as a database server, Customer shall be responsible for obtaining all necessary licenses.

(b) ***Passwords:*** Customer will not allow the use of any process, program, or tool on the XYZ Law Firm servers which would be used for the purpose of guessing passwords or that makes unauthorized attempts to access other systems or networks. Customer acknowledges that XYZ Law Firm will assist local, state and federal authorities in the prosecution of any and all illegal activities carried on through the XYZ Law Firm servers.

(c) ***Network Rules; Compliance with Law:*** Customer will comply with the Online Rules of Conduct and other rules and/or regulations adopted and sent in writing to Customer by XYZ Law Firm and its bandwidth providers from time to time. Customer will use Services only as permitted by applicable law, including but not limited to export control laws and regulations. The transmission of any material in violation of applicable law is prohibited. This prohibition includes, but is not limited to, the transmission of bulk e-mail often referred to as "spam" e-mail, the transmission of copyrighted material without permission of the copyright holder, or the transmission of threatening or obscene material and trade secrets.

XYZ Law Firm may terminate this Agreement at any time for violations of its Online Rules of Conduct or other similar rules and/or regulations that it may adopt from time to time or if it determines that Customer is in violation of its obligations set forth under this "Customer Responsibilities" section provided that Customer had been previously notified of such responsibilities and given a period of five (5) business days to comply therewith and fails to comply within such period. Following such a termination, Customer shall immediately pay XYZ Law Firm in one lump sum the product of the monthly fee and the portion of the term remaining immediately prior to termination of this Agreement.

4. Notices

All notices required or permitted under this Agreement shall be in writing and shall be deemed delivered when delivered in person or deposited in the United States mail, postage prepaid, or via FedEx addressed as follows:

If for Customer:
(Customer)
(Address)
(Address)
(City, State, Zip)
Attn: (Name)

If for XYZ Law Firm:
XYZ Law Firm Services, Inc.
(Address)
(City, State, Zip)
Attn: (Name)

Such address may be changed from time to time by either party by providing written notice to the other in the manner set forth above.

5. Title to Products and Services

The title to the Products is the property of XYZ Law Firm and remains the property of XYZ Law Firm during and after the term of this Agreement.

All title to equipment and software licenses provided by Customer (as listed on Exhibit A or which are otherwise or subsequently provided by Customer), if any, and content and log files from the Customer's application are the property of Customer and remain the property of Customer during and after the term of this Agreement.

6. Domain Name Rights

Customer shall be solely responsible for the selection, registration, maintenance and defense of any Domain Name utilized by Customer. Customer will indemnify and hold XYZ Law Firm harmless from any claims relating to or against Customer's Domain Name, including but not limited to any claims with respect to infringement or dilution of trademarks.

7. Treatment of Confidential Information

Customer recognizes that any software and programming provided to Customer pursuant to this Agreement constitute valuable trade secrets of XYZ Law Firm. Customer shall use its best efforts to protect and keep confidential all software and programming used by it and shall make no attempt to examine, copy, alter, "reverse engineer", tamper with or otherwise misuse such software and programming. Notwithstanding any provisions contained in this Agreement, Customer shall not be required to maintain in confidence the following information: (i) information that, at the time of disclosure to Customer, is in the public domain; (ii) information that after disclosure, becomes part of the public domain by publication or otherwise, except by breach of this Agreement; (iii) information that was in Customer's possession at the time of disclosure to Customer, and that was not acquired, directly or indirectly, from XYZ Law Firm; (iv) information that Customer can demonstrate resulted from its own research and development, independent of disclosure from XYZ Law Firm; (v) information that Customer received from third parties, provided that such information was not obtained by such third parties from XYZ Law Firm on a confidential basis; or (vi) information that is produced in compliance with applicable law or a court order, provide that XYZ Law Firm is given reasonable notice of such law or order and an opportunity to attempt, at the expense of XYZ Law Firm, to preclude or limit such production.

8. *Warranties/Disclaimers/Limitations of Liability*

(a) XYZ Law Firm warrants that:

   (A) The Products will be in good working order and will conform to XYZ Law Firm's published specifications on the date installed,

   (B) all work performed by XYZ Law Firm in providing Services shall be performed in a good and workmanlike manner;

   (C) it has good and valid title to the Products; and

   (D) it has sufficient legal rights to provide Services to Customer.

(b) THE WARRANTIES SET FORTH IN THE IMMEDIATELY PRECEDING SENTENCE ARE IN LIEU OF ALL OTHER WARRANTIES, EXPRESS OR IMPLIED, INCLUDING BUT NOT LIMITED TO, ANY IMPLIED WARRANTIES OF MERCHANTABILITY OR FITNESS FOR A PARTICULAR PURPOSE.

(c) Customer acknowledges that information available from or through Services or any interconnecting networks, may not be valid or accurate. XYZ Law Firm makes no warranties of any kind, either express or implied, regarding the quality, accuracy, or validity of the data and/or information residing on or passing through any such networks. The use of any information obtained from or through Services will be at Customer's own risk.

(d) Customer acknowledges that XYZ Law Firm cannot and will not be responsible for any data or the content of such data transmitted over the Internet or stored on any servers or equipment that are used for the purpose of providing Services, including but not limited to Internet connectivity, Web hosting, server allocation or dedicated Web hosting.

(e) CUSTOMER AGREES THAT XYZ LAW FIRM IS NOT RESPONSIBLE OR LIABLE FOR ACTS OF GOD, INTERNET BLACKOUTS AND BROWNOUTS BEYOND THE CONTROL OF XYZ LAW FIRM, SOFTWARE BUGS, IMPROPER APPLICATION ARCHITECTURE, OR IMPROPER APPLICATION

IMPLEMENTATION. IN NO EVENT WILL XYZ LAW FIRM SOLUTIONS BE LIABLE FOR LOST PROFITS OR CONSE-QUENTIAL DAMAGES, EVEN IF XYZ LAW FIRM SOLU-TIONS HAS BEEN ADVISED OF THE POSSIBILITY OF SUCH DAMAGES, OR FOR ANY CLAIM AGAINST THE CUSTOMER BY ANY THIRD PARTY. IN THE EVENT OF ANY DEFAULT BY XYZ LAW FIRM SOLUTIONS HEREUN-DER, CUSTOMER'S SOLE REMEDY SHALL BE THE ADJUSTMENT, REPAIR OR REPLACEMENT OF THE GOODS OR SERVICES AS DEEMED APPROPRIATE BY XYZ LAW FIRM SOLUTIONS. IN NO EVENT WILL XYZ LAW FIRM SOLUTIONS' LIABILITY EXCEED THE FEES PAID FOR THE MONTH IN WHICH THE OUTAGE OR DEFAULT OCCURRED.

(f) (1) If Customer is in Default, XYZ Law Firm may terminate this Agreement and retake possession of any goods provided to Customer and not yet paid for (before, during or after any action to recover sums hereunder), in which case Customer shall provide XYZ Law Firm full and free access to such goods. Further, XYZ Law Firm shall retain all payments made hereunder, and recover charges and costs owed by Customer as well as any other damages XYZ Law Firm may have sustained because of Customer's Default, including but not limited to attorney and collection agency fees. For purposes of this Agreement, Customer shall be deemed in "Default" in the event Customer becomes the subject of a voluntary or involuntary bankruptcy, insolvency, reorganization or liquidation proceeding; makes an assignment for the benefit of creditors; admits in writing its inability to pay debts when due; or fails within 10 days after receiving written notice to remedy any breach of this Agreement.

(2) If XYZ Law Firm is in Default, Customer Solutions may terminate this Agreement and retake possession of any goods provided to XYZ Law Firm and not yet paid for (before, during or after any action to recover sums hereunder), in which case XYZ Law Firm shall provide Customer Solutions full and free access to such goods. Further, Customer Solutions shall retain all payments made hereunder, and recover charges and costs owed by XYZ Law Firm as well as any other damages Customer Solutions may have sustained because of XYZ Law Firm's Default, including but not limited to attorney and collection agency fees. For purposes of this Agreement, XYZ Law

Firm shall be deemed in "Default" in the event XYZ Law Firm becomes the subject of a voluntary or involuntary bankruptcy, insolvency, reorganization or liquidation proceeding; makes an assignment for the benefit of creditors; admits in writing its inability to pay debts when due; or fails within 10 days after receiving written notice to remedy any breach of this Agreement.

9. Indemnification

Customer will indemnify and hold XYZ Law Firm harmless from any claim, demand or cause of action and all damages, judgments, decrees, costs and expenses, including attorneys' fees arising, from Customer's use of Services or any violation by Customer of any of the terms of this Agreement, including but not limited to using Services and publication of any image or information on Customer's Web site in violation of the rights of any other person. Customer acknowledges and agrees that XYZ Law Firm may block access to Customer's Web site if XYZ Law Firm receives notice of any such violation, and Customer agrees to indemnify and hold XYZ Law Firm harmless from any claim, demand or cause of action and all damages, judgments, decrees, costs and expenses, including attorneys' fees, related to blocking such access or such notice.

Similarly, except for claims or actions that arise from Customer's Original Materials, XYZ Law Firm will, at XYZ Law Firm's cost and expense, indemnify, defend and hold Customer harmless, against any claim or action against Customer alleging that the Final Product infringes upon or constitutes a misappropriation of any patent, copyright, trademark, trade secret or other proprietary right of any third party. XYZ Law Firm will have the sole right to conduct the defense of any such claim or action and all negotiations for its settlement or compromise unless otherwise agreed to in writing by the Customer and XYZ Law Firm.

10. General

(a) Customer's rights to use Services and Products are personal to Customer, are non-exclusive, non-transferable and non-sublicensable. Customer shall not attempt to assign or transfer any rights or obligations under this Agreement without the prior written approval of XYZ Law Firm. Any attempt to assign this Agreement in violation of the provisions of this paragraph will be void and of no force or effect. Customer and any attempted transferee shall be jointly and severally liable to XYZ Law Firm for any costs or damages incurred by XYZ Law Firm in connection with attempted assignments not permitted by this paragraph.

(b) Each party's performance hereunder shall be excused where delayed or hindered by war, riots, embargoes, strikes or other concealed acts of workmen, casualties, accidents, acts of nature (including flood or earthquake), or other occurrences beyond such party's control. The affected party shall notify the other in the event of any of the foregoing occurrences. Should such occurrence continue for more than 30 days, either party may terminate this Agreement with no future obligation.

(c) Any legal action arising out of this Agreement must be brought within one year of the occurrence, or is deemed waived.

(d) XYZ Law Firm must obtain Customer's written consent before using Customer's name in its marketing and other materials and to announcing the execution of this Agreement. This consent must be obtained prior to each use.

(e) This Agreement represents the complete agreement and understanding between XYZ Law Firm and Customer with respect to the subject matter herein, and supersedes any other written or oral agreement. The terms and conditions of this Agreement may only be modified in writing and must be signed by XYZ Law Firm and Customer.

(f) This Agreement shall be governed by and construed in accordance with the laws of the State of (State), excluding the conflicts of laws provisions thereof. The parties hereby submit to the exclusive jurisdiction of the courts in and for (County), (State) with respect to any dispute arising out of or relating to this Agreement if brought by Customer and in (County) if brought by XYZ Law Firm.

Accepted by (Client)

_____
SIGNED BY (FULL NAME)

_____
TITLE

_____
SIGNATURE

_____
DATE

Accepted by XYZ Law Firm:

_____

SIGNED BY (FULL NAME)

_____

TITLE

_____

SIGNATURE

_____

DATE

Exhibit A

Services and Fees

Services

In addition to the Services set forth in the Agreement, XYZ Law Firm
Solutions will provide the following Services:

Placement of the Web Site on a server with the following configuration:

- Dual processor 1.13 gHz
- RAID 5
- 3 18GB hard drives
- 1GB of RAM

Use of multiple redundant network components to reduce downtime,
increase speed and increase connectivity reliability.

- WebTrends site statistics.
- HP Openview monitoring.
- Daily backups.
- Checkpoint firewall protection.

Fees

In exchange for the Services, Customer will pay to XYZ Law Firm Solutions
a fee in the amount of $TBD per month for the term of the Agreement,
plus a $TBD set up charge upon initiation of a one-year commitment.

Exhibit B

Maintenance Procedures

Weekly			
	Check Server Logs	Check Error Logs	Check Firewall Logs
	Check System Events	Note Hard Drive Failure Warnings	Note Consistent Log on Failures
	Note Dropped Connections	Determine Causes & Possible Resolutions	Note Results/Actions in Guidebook
	Check Dialup connections (i.e.—RAS or VPN if present)	Verify backup completion.	Verify Schedules
	Verify anti-virus signature file dates are up to date. Verify last network scan date of all files. Verify that weekly scans and updates are on schedule.	Test restore function (Mission critical files to different directory)	Verify configuration for proper server shutdown. Check UPS log for recurring power surges/sags.
	Clean equipment screens.	Update backup script as necessary to account for machine name changes, etc.	Verify emergency repair disk for OS is present and updated.
	Verify all fans are working properly; that the server has proper ventilation and is not excessively warm to the touch.	Verify all network hubs, routers and switches are operating correctly. Note any excessive collisions, traffic load, warning lights, etc.	Verify disk space availability. Make recommendations w/ primary consultant approval.
	Verify Software Licensing.	Conduct an UPS test and load check. Verify last date battery replaced. Verify UPS fully charged.	Complete user adds/changes/deletions & log into Guidebook. Check the guidebook and note any changes or missing information.

Monthly		
Use computer-safe case vacuum to clean internal server components.	Confirm UPS operates properly (unplug from outlet); verify server and scheduled shutdown time process. Schedule a test outage during off-peak hours to test UPS and settings.	Verify NOS patches, device drivers and service packs are all current. Apply only known tested updates.
Complete user adds/ changes/deletions & log into Guide Book. Check the guidebook and note any changes or missing information.		

Sample RFPs

BELOW ARE TWO SAMPLE RFPs for Web design and development.

Sample 1

SNOW & SNOW LLP[1]
Sample Request for Proposal—Web Site Redesign

Goal: Develop a leading-edge Web site that will consistently grow site traffic, provide clients and prospects with relevant information, reinforce the firm's differentiating market positions and brand, and ultimately drive down the cost of doing business.

Request:

Snow & Snow, a multi-practice law firm with more than 120 lawyers in four cities, is delivering this Request for Proposal (RFP) for the redesign of its existing Web site to selected consultants. We have developed a series of specific criteria for our proposed redesigned site, which is described in this RFP. We are open to recommendations on features, options, and alternative designs that we have not considered and that would improve the site.

The ideal candidate will demonstrate the ability to provide innovative, professional, and cost-effective services that translate the firm's conceptual vision into a technically proficient, informative, and leading-edge Web presence. We intend to launch our redesigned site in the spring of 200_.

In addition to new content, we will utilize much of the existing content (lawyer bios, practice group descriptions, etc.) from our current site.

---

1. Although there are law firms named Snow & Snow, this particular one is fictitious.

While the initial redesign should contemplate and take into account the appearance and functionality of the ultimate Web site, the live site should at all times appear complete and fully featured, i.e., no inoperable buttons, "under construction" messages, etc.

It is our intention that once the site has been redesigned, we will maintain and host the site internally.

Submission:

Please submit a proposal for professional services that is concise and to the point. You may include company brochures and promotional materials as support for your proposal. This proposal is voluntary and does not commit Snow & Snow to compensation for any costs you have incurred in preparing the proposal. Snow & Snow reserves the right to accept or reject the consultant's proposal in part or in its entirety. All responses to the RFP shall become the property of Snow & Snow and disseminated as Snow & Snow determines in its sole discretion.

Submit two (2) copies of your proposal, one via hard copy and one via e-mail, by December 31, 200_ to:

Marketing Director, Snow & Snow LLP, address. Questions regarding this RFP should be submitted to your name via e-mail to **marketingdirector@snowlaw.com.**

Criteria for Redesigned Site

A.) Services

The consultant should perform all or some of the following duties:

- ♦ Provide design consultation for developing a leading-edge Web site that best promotes the firm.
- ♦ Advise on features that can improve the site in functionality as well as in its technical capabilities.
- ♦ Provide training to designated Snow & Snow staff to permit revisions to the site in-house.

B.) Goals for Redesigned Site

- ♦ Establish Snow & Snow as leaders in customer service and accessibility through technology in our major markets (or the cities in which we have offices.)
- ♦ Increase first-time and repeat traffic to site.

♦ Send a message to all visitors of site that the firm is technically proficient.

♦ Fit within firm's current branding and image strategies.

♦ Reduce cost of doing business by taking advantage of lower-cost electronic delivery methods.

C.) User Profile

The Snow & Snow Web site should be redesigned with the following user groups in mind:

♦ **Clients and potential clients.** Existing and potential corporate clients are the principal targets. The ultimate design should include features and content that will attract the targeted group to visit the site.

♦ **Legal recruits.** Law students, paralegals, and lawyers considering a career with Snow & Snow. The site should convey the firm's culture and identity to this audience.

♦ **Non-legal recruits.** We also anticipate that other potential employees will visit the site to learn about career opportunities.

♦ **Employees.** All Snow & Snow employees (lawyers, paralegals, and staff) will have access to internal (intranet) information.

D.) Specific Features in Redesign

In addition to the information already on the site, the firm would like to include the following items in its redesign:

1. Extranet
   ♦ Pleadings
   ♦ Documents
   ♦ Docket information
   ♦ Case information
   ♦ Exchange drafts of briefs, memos, etc.
   ♦ Billing information
   ♦ End of matter surveys, etc.
   ♦ Other miscellaneous documents
2. Case law alerts
   ♦ Frequent updates made by internal marketing staff. To keep the firm's clients and friends updated on important legal decisions that may affect them, we will include recent case law and developments in an "online library" through written text and links.

- ♦ <u>Legal and other links.</u> Carefully selected links that appear in pop-up windows that enhance the firm's image as well as make the site a convenient resource for its clients and prospects.
- ♦ <u>Online sign-ups.</u> To allow users to request the electronic transfer of newsletters and white papers.

3. Recruiting section
- ♦ Current recruiting page
- ♦ Benefits page
- ♦ Job openings for lawyers and staff
- ♦ Locations with maps
- ♦ Person(s) to contact when applying for a job
- ♦ Summer program
- ♦ Associate program
- ♦ Online applications

4. Intranet
- ♦ Office phone and e-mail directory, including pictures of all employees
- ♦ List of lawyers by practice group
- ♦ Detailed practice group descriptions
- ♦ Top fifty clients
- ♦ Lawyer biographies
- ♦ RFP collection
- ♦ Successful transactions and litigation results
- ♦ Practice development newsletter
- ♦ Templates for letters of engagement, end of matter, etc.
- ♦ Marketing materials available (newsletters, monographs, etc.)

5. Registration of site with major search engines and search engine optimization

E.) Required contents of your proposal

- ♦ Provide a list of other sites you have done for other law and professional services firms.
- ♦ Provide a brief description of your proposed design for the site.
- ♦ Submit a timeline for the redesign of the site.
- ♦ Propose your fees and costs for the redesign. We understand that, given the uncertainty of the scope and timeframe for this project, you may not be able to fix fees and costs with precision. However, the successful proposal will provide the firm with a favorable and complete pricing package for all of the requested services that you are able to provide.

Sample 2

SNOW & SNOW LLP
Sample Request for Proposal—Web Site Redesign

PRODUCT:

Firm Web site

OBJECTIVES:

+ To display a site that positions Snow & Snow as a highly qualified, Texas-based regional law firm.
+ To take advantage of technology that enables us to make changes in key areas quickly and cost-effectively.

BACKGROUND:

Snow & Snow has had a Web site for a few years but has not kept pace with its competitors. The site currently requires a lot of maintenance by the Web host, which is time-consuming and costly. The site now appears to be outdated and does not reflect the respect and stature that Snow & Snow possesses in the industry. The firm name has recently changed, providing an opportunity to change the look and feel of the site.

ROLE OF ADVERTISING:

A. Target

First and foremost we are targeting corporate counsel of medium to large corporations and second, other skilled lawyers who wish to join a dynamic firm.

B. Web site Communication Objectives

Snow & Snow is a major regional law firm that effectively handles large corporate legal matters. We want visitors to find the site dynamic and observe that it is updated frequently—ensuring that they will return. We want users to inquire about our services and learn more about Snow & Snow.

C. Creative Considerations

   1. Home Page: The home page will be dynamic. It will contain a "News from the Firm" scrolling bar that will display one line of story headlines that users can click on to link to another page that contains the full story. In addition, the site will have links to an:

a. Articles Page

b. Employment Opportunities Page

c. Offices Page

The home page will clearly display links to three main focus areas:

d. Lawyer Profiles

e. Firm Profile

f. Practice Areas

Please ensure that you are complying with the state bar rules and that appropriate disclaimers are included.

2. Firm Profile Page: The page will clearly display information that enables the visitor to quickly access information about the legal services that Snow & Snow offers, the long history of the firm, the commitment of the firm to its clients, and the fact that the firm has the capability to handle the legal matters of large corporate clients. From this page, users can click to link to other pages that contain detailed information to all areas listed above.

3. Practice/Industry Area Page: The practice/industry area page will clearly display all practice and industry areas. The user will click on the practice area headings to link to other pages that contain detailed information on all practice areas.

4. Lawyer Page: The lawyer page will enable the user to quickly search for a lawyer or group of lawyers by full name, office location, practice area, and/or by clicking on a letter of the alphabet. After searching for a lawyer or group of lawyers, the user can click on the name of a lawyer to link to the lawyer's resume.

5. Articles Page: The articles page will display the titles of all articles on the site as well as the author of the articles. (We also want to link the author to a lawyer biography.) The visitor can search by a word or a group of words to locate the key words of interest in the articles. The titles will all be linked to the articles.

6. Offices Page: The offices page will display our office locations, addresses, phone number(s), and fax number(s). Visitors will be able to click on an office location to link to more detailed information, such as pictures of the office and a list of lawyers who are located at the office. This section will include maps and directions to each office.

7. Careers Page: This page will include information regarding legal recruiting and staff opportunities, and should be divided accordingly. From the staff "intro" page, which will contain important information about employment at Snow & Snow, visitors will have several options to consider, including "Current Openings," "Benefits Information," "FAQs" and "Submit Your Resume."

8. Contact Page: The page will enable the visitor to submit a request to a specific office and/or department. The page must require the visitor to enter a name, e-mail address and phone number. The visitor will have the option of entering a company name as well as any comments and/or suggestions.

TECHNOLOGY:

In addition to the technology features identified in the individual page descriptions above, the site must have the following attributes:

1. The site must contain databases that enable Snow & Snow to make immediate changes to lawyer resumes, practice-area descriptions, employment listings, and articles from anywhere on the Internet.
2. The site must allow the visitor to utilize a "response form" to contact the firm. The response form will be programmed to deliver visitor information to the appropriate individuals within the firm.
3. Appropriate meta tags should be added to the site.
4. The site should enable the visitor to search globally for any word or group of words.

OTHER CONSIDERATIONS:

1. **Photographs:** We will include photographs of all lawyers.
2. **Timing:** Our launch date is January 1, 200_.
3. **Industry:** We expect that you will familiarize yourselves with the best law firm sites, as well as sites that are considered "best practice" in corporate America.

EXHIBIT**THREE**

The 2002 IMA Awards

A Review of the Top 250 Law Firm Web Sites (and Nifty Fifty 2002)

From Internetmarketingattorney.com™

The 2002 IMA (Internet Marketing Attorney) Web site reviews and awards feature thumbnail reviews and scores for the *National Law Journal* (NLJ) 250 law firms in the United States. The IMAs—with 2002 top finishers Faegre Benson, McGuireWoods and Morrison & Foerster—were launched online in January 2002.

The top scoring firm sites have been given IMA Platinum, Gold and Silver awards. Each firm score is based on a maximum of fifty points. All sites were individually visited during the months of December 2001 and January 2002. On average, twenty minutes was spent surfing each site. Each review was based on five categories—design, content, usability, interactivity and intangibles.

Any U.S. and foreign law firm Web site is eligible for the 2003 awards (and beyond). The NLJ 250 firms will automatically be reviewed, but other firms must be nominated (you can nominate yourself). Visit **www.internetmarketingattorney.com**, the IMA site, and e-mail your nomination. All sites will be reviewed during November and December of each year. If you have questions, contact Micah Buchdahl at **micah@HTM-Lawyers.com**.

Note: These reviews and the opinions of the Internet Marketing Attorney are independent of the authors of this book and the American Bar Association.

TOP 250 LAW FIRMS WEB SITE SCORES AND AWARDS

PLATINUM AWARD

Firm Name	Design	Content	Usability	Interactivity	Intangibles	Total
Faegre & Benson	8	10	9	9	9	45
McGuire Woods	8	9	9	9	9	44
Morrison & Foerster	9	9	9	8	9	44
Hale and Dorr	9	9	8	9	8	43
Winstead Sechrest	9	9	9	8	8	43
Jackson Lewis	9	8	9	8	8	42
Mayer Brown	7	10	8	7	10	42
Smith Gambrell	7	9	9	9	8	42
Wilson Sonsini	9	8	9	7	9	42
Milberg Weiss	8	9	9	8	7	41
Palmer & Dodge	9	8	9	7	8	41
Williams Mullen	9	8	8	8	8	41

GOLD AWARD

Firm Name	Design	Content	Usability	Interactivity	Intangibles	Total
Holland & Hart	8	8	8	7	9	40
Holland & Knight	8	9	7	7	9	40
Stoel Rives	8	9	8	7	8	40
Testa Hurwitz	8	8	9	7	8	40
Thacher Proffitt	7	9	8	7	9	40
Arent Fox	6	9	7	9	8	39
Bryan Cave	9	7	8	6	9	39
Latham & Watkins	8	9	8	6	8	39
Seyfarth Shaw	8	8	8	7	8	39
Hodgson Russ	8	7	8	8	7	38
Jones Walker	8	7	7	8	8	38

SILVER AWARD

Firm Name	Design	Content	Usability	Interactivity	Intangibles	Total
Akin Gump	7	9	7	6	8	37
Davis Wright	8	7	7	8	7	37
Dickstein Shapiro	8	7	6	8	8	37
Fish & Richardson	9	7	6	7	8	37
Greenberg Traurig	7	8	8	6	8	37
Harris Beach	7	8	7	7	8	37
Kirkland & Ellis	8	7	7	7	8	37
Pennie & Edmonds	8	9	8	7	5	37
Perkins Coie	7	8	8	8	6	37
Baker Botts	7	8	8	7	6	36

Firm Name	Design	Content	Usability	Interactivity	Intangibles	Total
Heller Ehrman	7	8	6	8	7	36
Littler Mendelson	6	7	8	8	7	36
Piper Marbury	8	8	7	7	6	36
Preston Gates	8	7	6	7	8	36
Robinson & Cole	7	8	8	7	6	36

TOP 250 LAW FIRMS WEB SITE REVIEWS

Firm Name	Design	Content	Usability	Interactivity	Intangibles	Total
Faegre & Benson	8	10	9	9	9	45

A member of my law firm Web site "hall of fame". Clever, unique, detailed. One of the first (if not the first) law firm to offer the ability to customize your home page, based on your individual interests. Sign up for legal news by e-mail. Pay for seminars with your credit card. The site's news-style home page makes it an added-value component to clients, and a free on-line resource to any interested party.

McGuire Woods	8	9	9	9	9	44

Few firms "got" the Internet, seemingly from day one. MW did. From generation to generation, each re-do of their Web presence has been a constant improvement, following the ever-changing rules of the Web. Just a sampling of the strengths include a unique legal ethics opinion database (for Virginia), a homemade extranet demo and program for clients, separate sites for consulting and capital group businesses, the right way to show representative clients (linking out) and e-mail subscriptions.

Morrison & Foerster	9	9	9	8	9	44

Glad to see a redesigned look to go with some unique Mofo features, such as talk radio and an excellent press room. The revamped site lifts it to the elite status among law firm Web sites. One of the best "related content" organizers out there. It offers the best of everything among law firm and Web site content types. Clean, quick, easy to use, pleasing to the eye. Kudos!

Hale and Dorr	9	9	8	9	8	43

An outstanding mix of information, interactivity, and design, making the Hale Dorr site one of the strongest in the Northeast. The home page is fresh with current news. The site uses clever images, rather than worn-out clip art. Every type of end-user should be able to find what they are looking for. Good use of on-line forms for e-mail alert registration, events and surveys.

Winstead Sechrest	9	9	9	8	8	43

When I first saw the home page, my first thought was all design. Boy, was that wrong. I could write a few pages on this site's virtues. However, I'll just say that the media kit, e-alerts and searching mechanism were particularly good. Worth a visit for any firm, prior to developing something new.

Jackson Lewis	9	8	9	8	8	42

So often in law marketing, I ask firms to think about what the client wants, not what you wish to offer him or her. The layout, design, interactivity and components are perfect for the individual or company seeking workplace law guidance. The firm points the user, first, to the appropriate location. Then, you have area events and informative publications. The e-mail subscription form provides strong intake info to the firm, and good complimentary services to the visitor. No points are lost for the bios linking out to the

Firm Name	*Design*	*Content*	*Usability*	*Interactivity*	*Intangibles*	*Total*
appropriate page on Martindale, because this is a rare instance where those credentials do not play the same selling role that accompanies most practices. And a great nifty touch, offering up a button to "bookmark this page" or "add office to address book". Why not?						
Mayer Brown	7	10	8	7	10	42
The firm continues to have a strong Web presence, with numerous specialty sites to choose from. You can see the struggle on the home page of what to highlight, because there are so many options. I still prefer navigation to be more consistent, especially with so much to choose from. I would love to be able to do searches throughout all the MB sites, but also see where that might take away from some of the ability to not fall into a boiler-plate rut. Not all practice areas on-line are created equal, and that is fine as well. For those departments that wish to develop further on the Web, nobody seems to be stopping them. Better yet, it is clearly encouraged. Antitrust, e-commerce, pro bono, securitization, venture & technology and appellate are among the many uniquely domained sites. They bit off a lot to chew, and are doing it well.						
Smith Gambrell	7	9	9	9	8	42
What a treat! Smith Gambrell manages to use the best part of "the Web" and incorporate its traditional marketing materials in putting forth a unique Internet presentation. Even the flash "recruiting" site is the right combo of bells, whistles and usefulness. Live news from Yellowbrix. Lots of interactivity. A tool that would be found helpful by all end-user audiences. Believe it or not, the weakest link was the home page itself. It simply does not do the rest of the site justice. You have no idea there is that much good stuff inside. Let people know what awaits. It would be nice, too, if the practice areas provided access to related materials elsewhere in the site as well. But, one thing we've all learned is you usually can't have everything.						
Wilson Sonsini	9	8	9	7	9	42
The correlation between the firm's Web site and its Silicon Valley location and clients such as Google and Blue Mountain are no accident. It is clear that this firm knows how to market on-line, and attract clients that do the same. The look is different, yet very user-friendly. The scrolling navigation bar, on the left-side, with options for printing, e-mailing the page and turning off the frames, increases its friendliness. Everything is well organized, from the publications section to recruiting, and solid case studies and testimonials. A home run.						
Milberg Weiss	8	9	9	8	7	41
Few areas of practice have been more positively affected by the Internet than those handling class actions. The Web is a better way to post updates, find people to join in, and organize matters and materials. Cuts down on mailings, phone calls, and increases your audience base. For a consumer audience, attorney bios, recruiting and firm overviews take a back seat. But, make no mistake; Milberg goes to great lengths to show expertise in a multitude of areas, from Enron to Big Tobacco. Detailed forms allow you to sign up for class actions report fraud, or request info. No e-mail addresses or phone numbers for attorneys. Or e-mail for specific offices. They know what they want, from whom, and how. Impressive use of the Web.						
Palmer & Dodge	9	8	9	7	8	41
What a well-balanced site. Clean design, friendly navigation, and strong content. I'm not a big fan of using the term "Specialties" for practice areas, but that is reaching for something to complain about. PDF offerings—in addition to the Web pages—where appropriate. The biggest standout is the very friendly database search structure and						

Firm Name	Design	Content	Usability	Interactivity	Intangibles	Total

organization for the attorney, publication and events sections. Nothing over the top here, just a well-executed transfer of firm credentials to the World Wide Web.

Firm Name	Design	Content	Usability	Interactivity	Intangibles	Total
Williams Mullen	9	8	8	8	8	41

So, if I were to tell you that Richmond, Virginia is one of the "law firm Web site" capitals of the country, would it surprise you? Williams Mullen is another of the outstanding Internet presence from the South. Excellent design, content, navigation and interactivity. A textbook professional service site.

Firm Name	Design	Content	Usability	Interactivity	Intangibles	Total
Holland & Hart	8	8	8	7	9	40

Before entering the site, I took a Web-break, knowing that there would be lots to see and do here. The Web site is called "Holland & Hart Interactive", with the tagline "Partnering Law and Technology." It is one of the most user-friendly of the law firm sites, with a constantly updated "front-page news" home page. On top of that, there are three sister sites listed—one for the IP Group; another for CaseShare, their extranet and litigation support company; a third for Persuasion Strategies, a litigation and arbitration consulting company. H&H does not just say they use technology to do business, they show it. Big difference.

Firm Name	Design	Content	Usability	Interactivity	Intangibles	Total
Holland & Knight	8	9	7	7	9	40

You've got a great site. Get rid of the worthless splash screen!! A perusal of the home page offers a nice overview of options and features. The firm does a lot of great pro bono work, and as they should, do an excellent job presenting it. Because HK has a consulting arm, it is probably more important to show an affinity for the way the Web works. The site also offers Webcasts for viewing. While there is not much in the area of careers or recruiting, any interested potential hire should be more impressed with the overall display of firm credentials and information than a flash show set to music. The information for each office location is also quite impressive, and easy to use. And I still like the use of "banner ads" to promote HK consulting and some of the firm's unique pro bono sites. They almost make me want to go back to practicing law—almost.

Firm Name	Design	Content	Usability	Interactivity	Intangibles	Total
Stoel Rives	8	9	8	7	8	40

Knowing the firm's marketing partner, the inimitable Sanjiv Kripalani, there was little doubt before getting to Stoel that the site would be a standout. Clever, creative and unique in putting itself forward. Just the Internet Law Group's separate site, at www.estoel.com, is better than many of the 250 sites reviewed here. The join.stoel.com site is also a strong recruiting effort. Stoel manages to take much of the same content that every law firm puts out, and tweak it just enough to give it a different feel. The great Northwest provides some of the best firm Web sites out there.

Firm Name	Design	Content	Usability	Interactivity	Intangibles	Total
Testa Hurwitz	8	8	9	7	8	40

"What's your role?" the site asks on the home page. This way, you know if you and the firm are interested parties, or not. The Web traffic reports also will give THT a better idea of end-users to further enhance the site value. Excellent resources, navigation and search capabilities. Even a video section. A very good Web site.

Firm Name	Design	Content	Usability	Interactivity	Intangibles	Total
Thacher Proffitt	7	9	8	7	9	40

The consummate news and information-oriented destination. I had not heard of developer www.intercounsel.com prior to TPW, but it is a well structured site. The firm, of course, has chosen to input data of all types, making it a tool for clients, as well as other interesting parties. More firms, especially in New York, should take a lesson. No firm had a greater excuse not to maintain a top-level (and updated) presence, but somehow they are back in action—fast. They understand the concept of keeping up with the professional services industries, in regard here to on-line presentation.

Firm Name	Design	Content	Usability	Interactivity	Intangibles	Total
Arent Fox	6	9	7	9	8	39

Another of the "classics". One of the first firms to jump in and take advantage of the Web. Still strong, with Discussion Forums, E-Mail Alerts, "Special Focus" sites and home page headlines. Many firms have followed the Arent Fox lead.

Bryan Cave	9	7	8	6	9	39

The new Bryan Cave home page manages to pull off the best of all worlds—techno-design elements, latest news, and entry into the rest of the site—without any feel of over-load or crowding. Few sites are better organized. The eCave legal solutions continue to show off the use of technology for building firm business. The Cave Trivia is a creative touch. A definite upgrade in the firm's online presence.

Latham & Watkins	8	9	8	6	8	39

This is still one of my favorite law firm sites. Clearly, the Web presence is a priority. From having obtained the tough-to-get two-initial "LW" domain name, to the tons of content and choices on the site. A digital press kit for visiting media. Every type of information content imaginable, from handbooks, to newsletters, clippings, seminar materials. This is a site that can truly be used as a resource by all different types of end-users. On top of all this, the separate recruiting site offers a different look and content types. The recruit-ing home page begins with a drop-down box for finding out when LW will be at your school. Instead of trying to design a site to meet all needs, they wisely set up a separate site for the recruiting pitch (as many firms have successfully done). One area of improve-ment—interactivity.

Seyfarth Shaw	8	8	8	7	8	39

Easy to use, good information, something for each user group. The site unites all relevant content from the appropriate databases, and offers plenty for anyone seeking out Sey-farth. Areas such as "Seyfarth Shaw at Work" and the links to extranets and "Trademark View" show they are using the Web effectively, and beyond simply providing a Web site.

Hodgson Russ	8	7	8	8	7	38

A smart set-up, with focus on getting visitors to the appropriate practice area. Combined with a nice intro design, and some changing highlights, it is an effective intro to the firm and the site. Each practice area, in essence, becomes a mini-site. And the categories allow flexibility in what a department wants to do. Having said that, tell a few of them to get off the schneid, and make some members get some content out there. Use a carrot and stick, if need be. The rest of the sections provide good materials as well. And lots of good forms!

Jones Walker	8	7	7	8	8	38

The star of this site is the E*Zine Center, offering a variety of on-line firm publications to both subscribe to and/or peruse on the site. This site is not far from being one of the very best. Consider showing more of the subcategories on the home page (either mouse-overs or listings). I needed the site map to find everything. Also, more of the events and publi-cations should link to more information or the article itself. The continual updating and freshness is outstanding.

Akin Gump	7	9	7	6	8	37

Lots of plug-ins needed to see and use everything on the site, which can be a good thing and a bad thing. The good part is that Akin Gump is using all types of Web technologies; the bad part is that not everybody will see everything. The site might be better served in combining the "enter our site" which includes news items, with the home page itself. The same "senior partner focus" has been up for at least a year and a half. Let's give somebody

Firm Name	*Design*	*Content*	*Usability*	*Interactivity*	*Intangibles*	*Total*

else a chance! But, the addition this year of **www.akingumpcases.com**, showing off their litigation prowess, is unique, informative and educational. The organization of the site could use some improvement, but it is still nice in that it is different and uses the Web well.

| Davis Wright | 8 | 7 | 7 | 8 | 7 | 37 |

More firms need to take this approach to providing professional services on the Web. You feel like this is a law business, not a law practice (that is a compliment, in case you are unsure). Nobody ever said you have to give everything away on-line. Just offer enough to show what you know, and use the site to sell yourself, services, books, seminars, etc. Davis Wright does that. The home page makes you want to come back, and has that e-commerce feel. Improve the lawyer directory, with better search terms.

| Dickstein Shapiro | 8 | 7 | 6 | 8 | 8 | 37 |

When I saw the site, I remembered the "puzzling" ads, and the **www.legalinnovators.com** domain in them. A clever print campaign in which you need to visit the site to see the answers to the puzzles. Besides the solutions, the site offers an array of helpful resources. I found the site refreshing; amidst a sea of sameness. I would have just liked a little better coordination among the materials. Without a site search (although there is a site map), you need to poke around to find all documents related to a particular topic.

| Fish & Richardson | 9 | 7 | 6 | 7 | 8 | 37 |

Two of their main areas of practice demand a strong commitment to the Web—IP and Technology. Otherwise, you are not walking your own walk. The telling home page map lets you know they have the country well-covered as well, Northeast, West Coast and Midwest. The **fr.com** domain shows they were on the ball years ago. All these messages come just from the front page. One of the best selling features is the link to a page on the USPTO site, showing FR filings. Good data without any work on your own site. The Recruiting section was a little soft.

| Greenberg Traurig | 7 | 8 | 8 | 6 | 8 | 37 |

It might seem like a small thing, but it is such a useful component that can not understand why more sites do not include it. When going through the many GT publications (which also are nicely archived back to 1995), they include icons showing me whether it is a hyperlink, a pdf, video, etc...before I click. Designed to put forth information that someone would seek in a professional services capacity, GT also has a number of powerful "special focus" sites, including a separate Spanish version, one for business immigration, technology and others. Especially useful and powerful on the World Wide Web is **www.gtamericas.com**, which helps you connect with legal counsel all over the globe. One change I would make, however, is to either eliminate the splash screen or make sure that "home" means the front page of the site, not a continual return to the splash page.

| Harris Beach | 7 | 8 | 7 | 7 | 8 | 37 |

Not sure about that "Lawyers you'll swear by" slogan. Don't most people swear "at" lawyers? However, HB does a great job showing why they should be your lawyers. I swear. Extensive detail for each practice. Changing news items. Good employment section. And a touching "In Memoriam" by a firm directly effected by loss of life on September 11th. As terrible it is to say, the Web site becomes a major place for gathering of information and news during times such as these.

| Kirkland & Ellis | 8 | 7 | 7 | 7 | 8 | 37 |

Of the many large firm Web sites that Hubbard One has developed, few manage the same level of success that Kirkland has reached. From the interactivity of the recruiting

Firm Name	Design	Content	Usability	Interactivity	Intangibles	Total
section to the scrolling representative client list and on-line Web page rating system, this site presents the firm credentials well. While not as content rich as some sites, it is clear that the firm has selected priorities for the site and focused. Some sites try to do too much, and end up with a mess. Keep building on.						
Pennie & Edmonds	8	9	8	7	5	37
An outstanding display of the firm's "intellectual property". Amazing organization, from the home page inward. Pinpoint navigation and searching. The home page "quickfinder" allows you to quickly send an e-mail, if you know who you are looking for. Otherwise, the attorney bio db breaks things down. Additional browsers open where appropriate, and choices (pdf or html, for example) abound. You could strengthen the contact capabilities, and try to grab some intake info or work to get "subscribers" to return.						
Perkins Coie	7	8	8	8	6	37
Another site that shows improvement from one year ago. Easy to use, and with a strong focus on what makes sense—Internet law and e-commerce. The Internet Case Digest accomplishes one of the great goals—something unique and useful to set your site content apart. Like Morgan Lewis' HSRSCAN for Antitrust, Perkins' Internet law database provides a true resource for interested parties. They also take advantage of on-line registration with payment capabilities, including check or credit card, for upcoming seminars. One peeve. I knew there was a nice Washington, DC site for political law, but had trouble getting to it. It is not highlighted on the site map. If you do not know it is there, you will most likely miss it.						
Baker Botts	7	8	8	7	6	36
As I surfed for what seemed like forever through hundreds of law firm Web sites, the "Breakzone" in the Student Center proved quite a diversion. I played Yahtzee for 20 minutes. There was legal stuff too, of course. The practice profiles were strong, offering a breakdown by suits, news, publications, attorneys and related areas. The only problem was that it took me awhile to notice that some of those components were to my left, and some, part of the graphic design above. A little confusing. But, the site "feels" like the firm, carving out four highlighted areas of concentration off the home page.						
Heller Ehrman	7	8	6	8	7	36
Well structured, with friendly navigational elements. The only drawback is that without a speedy connection to the Web, the download time can be painful. If you have a quick connection, though, you probably enjoy surfing through the content.						
Littler Mendelson	6	7	8	8	7	36
When everything is focused on one major area of practice, it should be easier to operate on-line. "The National Employment and Labor Law Firm" as they call themselves do a good job of taking advantage of the Internet—selling a best-selling book by a firm attorney on Amazon (link over; the firm can get an extra piece of the pie for directing the referral buy), secure on-line credit card purchases of firm product, promotion of seminars and product. Knowing that the audience is often non-lawyers, a glossary and legal dictionary (linked up through **Law.com**) makes the site a tool for people seeking employment law direction.						
Piper Marbury	8	8	7	7	6	36
Focus on the presentation of information makes this site work particularly well, rather than trying to be too fancy. Nice layout. Easy to navigate, search and read. The events calendar is actually a calendar, with the further option of breaking events down by practice area. The office sections not only provide necessary location information, but good						

Firm Name	*Design*	*Content*	*Usability*	*Interactivity*	*Intangibles*	*Total*
links and services for those visiting from out of town. An excellent Web presence that appears to be kept fresh.						
Preston Gates	8	7	6	7	8	36
Something about computer stuff and Washington State that just goes together. Preston Gates accomplishes the unheralded task of putting the same type of stuff together, but making it look different and better. Why is it so hard for so many of us? Strong structure and design. "Client Services" links into the firm extranets, if the client chooses to use it. The firm's link to, and affiliation with **www.allianceofangels.com** is just what investors, banks and start-ups want to see. The home page also has the logos and links out to ratings on **Law.com** and Vault. I would have had it open a second browser, but not enough firms link out to positive "ink" on other sites.						
Robinson & Cole	7	8	8	7	6	36
I remember being fond of the R&C Web site five years ago. Today, I am pleased to see another firm show continued growth in exploring ways to use the Web creatively. Three specialty sites (plus client extranets), at **www.deregulation.com**, **www.votingrightslaw.com** and an oldie but goodie, **www.businessvisalink.com**. Another cool tool is the use of electronic vCards (contact) with each attorney bio.						
Hughes & Luce	6	6	6	7	10	35
First of all, thank you for putting the flash introduction at my option under the firm overview, rather than ask me to sit through it before hitting the site. There is nothing that special about the firm site itself. The usual. The "Client Comments" section is good. Think about having the links to other sites open up a second browser (the Akamai site would not let me return to yours). However, the outstanding specialty site, at **www.commercebynet.com**, was a treat. Lots of on-line seminars to view. Good articles. But, my favorite had to be the ability to buy logo merchandise on the site—now that is e-commerce. The firm also allows attorneys to create their own sites, including **www.lawyerware.com**, **www.coplaw.com**, and **www.lawspider.com**. Some firms worry about "renegade" sites taking away from the general firm site. In this case, it enhances the on-line presence of the firm. I would promote these sites on the HL home page.						
Long Aldridge	7	5	7	7	9	35
Easy to use, well structured and well organized. The home page had lots of new scrolling headlines. I was a bit surprised by the lack of depth in publications (newsletters for environmental and HR only) and articles, although there is great detail in regard to events, press releases and general firm news. Clever and unique was the alumni map, in flash. It was also strange not to see greater promotion of the firm's acquisition of **www.redhotlaw.com** as its technology and IP practice. It is a well-known tech law brand, and this is the Internet. Get a link to that site on the home page.						
Milbank Tweed	7	8	6	6	8	35
You just read your firm's review, smoke is coming out of your ears, and you can not believe I'm now saying that I like the Milbank site—a lot. In a business in which we all play it tight to the vest, and follow the leader, Milbank goes all out in playing on the Web. They offer both an HTML version and a souped-up Flash Shockwave 5 one. Without high-speed access, the Flash version will make you cry. Otherwise, prepare for a barrage of bells and whistles. And lots of information. It is not always set out in an easy to use manner, and I really hate the frames and the color scheme. But for those seeking learning, they offer up a separate "Knowledge Center", chock full of links and writings. Maybe not one of the top law firm sites in the country, but definitely one of the most creative.						

Firm Name	*Design*	*Content*	*Usability*	*Interactivity*	*Intangibles*	*Total*
Thompson Hine	8	8	7	6	6	35

Above-average showing of firm knowledge. The home page allowed for full-blown design, but also incorporated space for a changing "hot topic" and other highlights (including room for changing images). Numerous quality links and written materials. The best page on the site is the "Resources", which offer drop-down boxes for a variety of site categories. This would be better incorporated with either the Search and/or Site Map features, because it is a good starting point for finding what you need. Lots of Rep Client links (open a second browser instead of leaving your site), always a good way to sell yourself.

Dechert	8	7	7	6	6	34

Hooray! I always hated the old Dechert site, and was thrilled to see that they have caught up with their brethren. Gone is the hokey "brochureware", and in is the standard large-firm, data-driven, and database-driven site. Good design and structure. Nothing unique, but everything that needs to be there is in place.

Epstein Becker	8	8	7	6	5	34

From the standpoint of pure dissemination of firm knowledge, the Epstein Becker "Newsstand" is one of the best in the business. Powered by a backend that appears superior to some of the legal industry providers. I bet the "Search" capabilities could be a lot better, increasing usefulness. Interesting that "Recruiting" consists of a single contacts page. No pro-active "marketing" here, but the design, navigation and content make it extremely friendly to those who visit.

Goodwin Procter	8	6	8	5	7	34

GPH manages to succeed here with a brochure-like approach that actually works. It is appealing to the eye, not too cluttered and easy to move through. The greatest strength is in the "Careers" section, which combines information and design, without resorting too much to either. The link to a relationship at "Job Find" allows the firm to post, and the user to search, for non-legal positions without the firm Web site having to recreate the wheel twice. Most firms have found that on-line postings generally only work for non-legal hires anyway.

Haynes and Boone	7	7	6	6	8	34

A site with soothing colors, well constructed, with enough interior design to make it just different enough that I would probably recognize it when I see it again. I liked the concept of the "KnowledgeConnect" section, housing publications, articles, seminars and other informative items. One suggestion, tell the user what the section is, its purpose and how to best use it. You do not want a visitor either missing this section, or the different components under the same or related practice area. Simply follow the same introductory approach as the description to "ClientConnect", the firm's extranet entry point. Nice move getting the **www.clientconnect.com** domain for yourselves. I bet there are extranet companies who would love to have grabbed that one.

Hogan & Hartson	8	7	8	6	5	34

The H&H site is well organized and pleasing to the eye. It has just the right amount of branding on the front, with colors that make it easy to read. The information is easy to find and presented in a way that is not too overwhelming. Sometimes, we do too little. Sometimes, we try and present too much. This is the type of site that should provide just enough information for any type of Web visitor.

Katten Muchin	7	7	9	5	6	34

Colorful, user-friendly and detailed. Love the scrolling left-hand navigation bar, making it that much easier to keep me surfing through the site. Just enough design elements to keep it interesting. Even-keeled for audiences of all types.

Firm Name	*Design*	*Content*	*Usability*	*Interactivity*	*Intangibles*	*Total*
King & Spalding	7	7	7	6	7	34

K&S does a good job blending information and technology to deliver its message. The Recruiting section offers video clips (in varying degrees of resolution for the download-challenged), and virtual tours for each office location. The International map offers a view of the firm's practice as it pertains to each continent. The practice areas each offer a list of relevant attorneys and a detailed list of representative matters. K&S University shows the firm's detailed approach to CLE. Good mix of graphics and photos throughout.

Womble Carlyle	5	9	7	8	5	34

Winston the Bulldog is still around. Yes, the site has some bite. Thanks to content feed and supplement from YellowBrix, and interactivity from companies such as Triton Technologies for conducting surveys, the Womble site is one of the most likely among law firms to assume "bookmark" status among visitors. Many firms say they want their site to be a destination. Womble clearly dedicates that staffing and resources to continually refresh the site.

Bradley Arant	6	8	7	7	5	33

It is always good to see another firm increase its Web presence, with a new, improved site. An excellent example of building a second-generation site. Changed the domain name, moved from HTML to database-driven, and increased the content levels. One of the best parts should receive more acclaim. The "Multimedia" section offers free seminars (they could also offer them at a charge, if they wish) provided through a relationship with **www.legalspan.com**. Once again, you do not need to invest major funds to do some creative things. Outsourcing to an expert is often a better move.

Covington & Burling	7	7	8	5	6	33

Yet another site that has shown "Web growth" over time. Like the firm, the site takes a no-nonsense approach to answering your inquiries. Extremely user-friendly, with simple design, crisp font size, printer-ready pages, detailed search capabilities, related-content and helpful instructions for the computer-troubled. Simple things like explaining the difference between an HTML and PDF document, and doc size and proportionate download time are useful to some audiences.

Edwards & Angell	8	7	7	5	6	33

A well-orchestrated and successful blend of presentation and text. The "NewsFlash" area of the home page is just the way you want to present "What's New". The drop-down box for foreign languages is easy to find, for interested non-English reading visitors. The Toolkit Series looks interesting, but I would like to know a little more, such as a sampling demo of some type. Dump the annoying mouse-overs on the nav bar. It is unnecessary, especially since a click breaks down the subs. Also, I expect more from the "Contact Us" and "Help" buttons than opening up my e-mail.

Finnegan Henderson	5	8	6	5	9	33

Pretty large firm for an IP boutique. J Straight-forward presentation of firm credentials. The most impressive component is the "Federal Circuit Decisions", updated a few times each week. Many firms say they update this kind of info all the time. Finnegan does. Combined with other fed circuit site materials, this should be much better promoted on the site. Why not have an e-mail subscription to boot?

Gray Cary	6	7	7	6	7	33

Lots of things to like about the way this site is set up. The "Links" and "Representative Clients" sections both provide a title, description and hyperlink, as opposed to a static list of links or clients. The "site search" allows you to choose by sections and query, with

Firm Name	Design	Content	Usability	Interactivity	Intangibles	Total

helpful results. They pick out areas to focus on-line, such as M&A and Internet Law. The "Journal of Internet Law", which offers a taste of an issue, but requires a paid subscription (nothing wrong with that), really should offer on-line subscription capabilities. After all, the target audience generally likes to do business on-line. The biggest downfall is the inconsistent navigation. The subcategories in some sections sit in the middle of the page, and requires you to go back to find the list, losing some stickiness.

Firm Name	Design	Content	Usability	Interactivity	Intangibles	Total
Kilpatrick Stockton	6	7	7	6	7	33

The domain name suggests a butcher, perhaps? Or maybe someone is shorting an investment? In fairness, the firm name also brought me to the Web site. Google brought up the Kilstock domain. And Greenfield/Belser's design is Web-like, and not some theme that requires psychoanalysis to understand. The site, though? Well done. Detailed information on all areas. The separate recruiting site, at www.ksrecruits.com, is clever, and includes a private recruit log-in section. The only peeves are that the general site navigation was a touch disjointed. And, one thing in need of correction, the recruiting site does not link to, or back to the firm site. There needs to be some sort of connectivity between them.

Firm Name	Design	Content	Usability	Interactivity	Intangibles	Total
Lowenstein Sandler	8	6	6	6	7	33

A mixed review. Great design. The insurance outpost site was very cool. Good job promoting firm publications on the home page, as well as gathering "subscription" e-mail addresses, and entrance to the firm extranets. There is just no coordination between the practice area info, the related content and the attorney bios (which again is limited to alphabetic searching). It is a matter of taste and what you are seeking, because some will find this site quite impressive, I'm sure.

Firm Name	Design	Content	Usability	Interactivity	Intangibles	Total
McKenna & Cuneoe	6	7	7	7	6	33

Do not be fooled by the home page look and feel, which has remained basically the same since 1996. Unlike some sites that have grown stagnant, McKenna has continued to build and grow the site, including the addition of numerous databases, a separate site for events (at www.mckennaevents.com), moderated discussion forums, and extranets. Some hate it, but I actually have always been fond of the clip art used, which is different. And, in the early days, it did not slow down your experience. A good reminder for many firms that you do not necessarily need to throw out your old Web site, but can replace the engine and interior, and keep it running.

Firm Name	Design	Content	Usability	Interactivity	Intangibles	Total
Orrick Herrington	7	7	7	6	6	33

Guess what? This firm's careers section consisted of a one-page overview and a few office recruiting contacts. Guess what else? It does not hurt the firm's score here. The site is clean and easy to use, with good navigation that includes an ever-present keyword search box. The home page has a newsletter layout, with the latest news, events and publications. On this day, there is a lot devoted to the Enron bankruptcy, easily making the site useful to thousands of interested parties. Tell people what you do, and what you are working on. That message reaches all appropriate audiences.

Firm Name	Design	Content	Usability	Interactivity	Intangibles	Total
Pepper Hamilton	5	7	7	8	6	33

Another firm with dedication toward updating. The home page "hot stuff" features news, events and publications that have been posted in the last few days. While the design is so-so, and I do miss that red hot chili pepper, it is easy to use and find what you are looking for. The Construction Law practice still has a specialty site at www.constructlaw.com, with a Lexis association now. One of the components I found especially smart was having a generic e-mail address for each practice group at the top

Firm Name	*Design*	*Content*	*Usability*	*Interactivity*	*Intangibles*	*Total*
of each practice page (i.e. tax@pepperlaw.com), followed by the attorney list, other related materials and the description. Make it as easy as possible for an interested party to now interact with the firm.						
Wiley Rein	8	8	9	5	3	33
Very tasteful design. Beautiful organization of materials and ability to navigate through them. A site in which it is easy to find what you are looking for. "Guest Books" are way out. Replace with some meaningful on-line forms.						
Arter & Hadden	7	7	8	5	5	32
I've always been fond of the Arter Hadden site. "A Moment in Time" on the home page was different, and kept the site feeling fresh. Little things like the form for employment interest have always made it seem like a useful source. It could use a little jolt of something new, a little more interactivity (sign us up for those newsletters). And that "True Professionals" page...a little hokey.						
Brobeck Phleger	7	6	6	5	8	32
One of the most visible and aggressive firms in the new economy, Brobeck coordinates its other forms of media buy—TV, print—with the Web. The www.joinbrobeck.com site was one of the first to separate recruiting efforts from the other elements of professional services Web sites. The design and layout have more of a high-tech brochure feel, making the site more valuable to one seeking out a law firm for representation than one who already uses Brobeck. It is sleek and well presented. You can see their commercials on the site. Also, excellent use of video testimonials from representative clients. They do certain things very well, and give you solid examples of their successes.						
Dow Lohnes	7	6	8	7	4	32
Until I reached the home page, I forgot that firm attorneys write the @Law column for WSJ.com. Links opening up a second browser take you to the most recent and past columns on the Wall Street Journal site. That is great content (and PR) to highlight. I wonder how many people visit the Dow site from WSJ? The site offers good detailed overviews of each practice, with a link to the appropriate attorneys at the top of the page and a smart "Request Info" link (to an on-line form) at the bottom. The "Career Opportunities" was impressive. And they treat their non-lawyer personnel quite well—free Starbucks, ice cream, popcorn every day, and of course, a free on-site health club. For recruiting, prospective clients and overview info, the site is just right.						
O'Melveny & Myers	6	6	7	7	6	32
The OMM site is about average. Clean layout. Easy to navigate. One of the best components was the search results. For each keyword search, the results are divided by category, with attorney listings first (including phone and e-mail), followed by each of the other site sections. So often, the search results on sites are a jumbled mess. Not the case here. Also, the easy to use subscription form for publications helps obtain and retain interested clients. The site would be even better with icons showing whether a hyperlink is to another Web page, in PDF, etc.						
Paul Weiss	8	7	7	5	5	32
If you like sites that use flash throughout its design, you should like Paul Weiss. The flash is understated and tasteful. Unlike sites that use the flash to cover up for a lack of quality information, PW has its sections and content well coordinated. Like many New York firms, the associates are kept hidden in the attorney listings (NYC firms are always crying to me about cherry-picking of associates). One of the better efforts in NYC. Accomplishes that "conservative" but "slightly different" goal that seems to prevail.						

Firm Name	Design	Content	Usability	Interactivity	Intangibles	Total
Pillsbury Winthrop	4	8	7	7	6	32

Once one of the elite, the Pillsbury site is still solid, but a bit stagnant. The home page is bland and crowded with text. Overall, it is still well stocked with publications, events and strong content throughout. A portion of the site is in Japanese and Chinese. The attorney bio database has good search selection choices, key with 900 attorneys in 17 locations. The client registration form allows users to select areas they wish to receive e-mail information on.Blank Rome

Mayer Brown	6	8	5	7	5	31

Lots of stuff. Different images, fonts, colors, sections. The negative is total inconsistency in layout and surfing your way through. The positive is that all the info you might seek is probably there, if you can find it. For example, "Contact Us" lists each office, but only provides address and phone numbers. No e-mail or directions. They are all in the "Offices" section, which actually has all that "contact" information. Blank Rome offers "Headline News" from Capitolwire.com, with newsworthy media feeds.

Brown Rudnick	4	7	6	6	8	31

Repeat after me. "We are building a Web site, not a sleek print brochure." Repeat. Some attempts at cute categories ("Beneath the Surface" means "Awards and Honors") fall flat. Once again, the attorney listings could be better presented. There are some very sharp and unique efforts here. Few firms offer a "For In-House Counsel" section, featuring a ListServ and other tools. And you should better highlight the pro bono site, at www.brownrudnickcenter.com, an impressive showing of charitable efforts.

Cooley Godward	5	6	6	7	7	31

A little different in look and layout, this can be a good thing. The home page is actually one of the weaker portions of the site. Hopefully, people take the time to peak in and see the rest. The recruiting site opens up into a separate browser. The "search" mechanism is stronger than most, in functionality and detail. I am always a big fan of highlighting key clients in a "client profile."

Crowell & Moring	5	6	6	7	7	31

The splash and dull, dark home page does not do justice to the rest of the site. A (rare) winning combination of brochure-like design and Web-like content aggregation. A new home page that highlights the highlights would be an inexpensive and easy improvement. Highlights include the history "timeline", and the interactive events calendar with on-line registration capabilities.

Duane Morris	6	6	6	5	8	31

The attorney search does not offer "practice area" as an option? What gives? This site has been relatively the same for more than a year. Helpful "e-mail to a colleague" and "printer-friendly" buttons. Decent blend of information and detail. The home page highlights four "news" highlights, which is always smart for the returning end-user. Probably the highlight of Duane Morris on-line is the prolific writings of attorney Eric Sinrod. His high profile in media circles, detailing the world of Internet law, gets the DM name and expertise on the Web in ways that money and marketing can't buy. A powerful "intangible."

Foley & Lardner	6	7	6	5	7	31

Typical—in a good way—of the large firm use of the Web. A conservative, information-oriented home page and site. A flashy, hip separate site for recruiting at www.foleyrecruiting.com. All of the information you expect to receive, displayed in a clean fashion. Some pages offer the ability to e-mail to a friend, or are printer-friendly. Offers related content,

Firm Name	Design	Content	Usability	Interactivity	Intangibles	Total
which makes surfing easier and stronger. Those moving square on the left-hand side, though, were more distracting than pleasing to the eye.						
Fox Rothschild	5	8	7	5	6	31
"This Just In" on the home page was more than three months' old. What is with having so many pages open into a second browser? The strength of the site is in the articles, news and newsletters. The "center" for each practice group has excellent detail. "Employment Opportunities", including recruiting, was limited to one long page.						
Gardner Carton	7	6	7	8	3	31
The law firm Web site version of the white album. Lots of open space. Well organized, easy to use. On-line registration through **www.signmeuponline.com** service. Good related content among categories in the practice area section.						
Hunton & Williams	7	6	6	5	7	31
The Hunton site takes more of the on-line brochure approach than a bookmarked resource. I like the fact that each practice area includes a list of the appropriate firm contacts in each relevant office. I do not like the fact that the related content (i.e. newsletters, articles, etc.) is not linked, and most of the publication materials are in PDF form. However, if I am just trying to get a feel for the firm and its expertise, the site accomplishes that. One nice touch was the "timeline" of firm history, a little more interesting than reading a long narrative. There is a nice mix of graphics and photos through the site. Another good feature—promoting the "client workroom" extranet with a demo, off the home page—showing the use of the Web for client collaboration.						
Kirkpatrick & Lockhart	7	7	6	5	6	31
I'm always proud of firms that were quick enough "in the beginning" to secure a two-initial domain. The biggest problem on the site is too much "stuff" on one page, which leads to too much scrolling. It would take very little tweaking to make this site more functional—better division of content and a keyword search function would go a long way! Overall, the KL site is a good reminder that simple design and navigation can go a long way.						
Lathrop & Gage	8	5	6	6	6	31
People familiar with my critiques and seminars know that I have cheered this site for a few years, offering that the design and structure goes against everything I teach. Yet, it is the uniqueness of presentation that sets it apart. There is no reason that the insides can not grow a little more. The shelf life suggests that it is time for redevelopment. No reason not to keep the theme and message of the look & feel, but it is time to mix it up a little, and add a feature or two. Keep it light. Keep it bright.						
Nelson Mullins	6	6	6	5	8	31
This is happening way too often, where the latest "News" is more than six months' old. When I look at the navigation bar, I see that there is a recent posting, less than a month old (and on the home page). Be careful here. Not everyone checks these things out. They take one look and move on. The size of some of the pages created some download-time issues. One of the more creative "Locations" sections out there, with lots of help for visitors to any of the Nelson Mullins' seven offices. Give the "Germany" angle a little more play.						
Powell Goldstein	5	8	6	5	7	31
It is hard to put my finger on exactly what I liked so much about this site. The content was slightly different than most sites. The information was detailed for those interested						

Firm Name	Design	Content	Usability	Interactivity	Intangibles	Total
in their practice areas. Antitrust and bankruptcy information that I would bookmark, if relevant to my business. A tie-in to industry and world news from NewsEdge. Too many firms get caught up with making sure they post the standard "law firm Web site" information. It feels like Powell was more concerned with providing news of interest in their marquee areas of practice. Good idea.						
Sutherland Asbill	8	7	8	5	3	31
Another strong mix of design and content. The home page offers a different "practice highlight" each time I return to the home page. This not only gives me a little something different each time, but for those visiting once, gives each practice group a shot at front page news. Easy to read, surf and follow. Particularly effective.						
Troutman Sanders	8	7	5	5	6	31
A major improvement over their previous site. When you operate in the same regions as McGuire Woods, you better have a decent on-line presence. The merger with Mays & Valentine probably increased the difficulty in getting this site off the ground. Lose the splash page. The look and feel of the site is quite nice. The "Media Center" was a good touch. The office locations offer a live weather report from **Weather.com**. Biggest problems are no searching or site map, the publications are separate from the practice area descriptions (although the attorney lists come up). I'm assuming it is still a work in progress.						
Venable	4	7	6	8	6	31
If I were to require co-counsel on a technology or e-commerce issue, my first call would most likely be to Venable. I registered for e-book updates of "So You Want to be on the Internet", which is a section of the firm site, as the firm's e-lawyers have made sure their expertise is on display on the WWW. The cutesy interactive "law quiz" is still there. Unfortunately, many of the non-tech practice areas are not as well represented. It is probably time for a redesign, which will be more about organization and navigation than filling it up with meaningful content.						
Fenwick & West	7	7	6	5	5	30
This might sound strange, but I expected to be blown away. Having so often seen their creative ads, and in that Northern CA locale, it was going to be one of the sites that ate up an hour of my time to surf through. It was good, and if it was in another part of the country, I might say it was very good. Above-average for the nation, but not as good as some other similar firm offerings.						
Gibson Dunn	7	6	7	5	5	30
Simple, yet elegant. The design incorporates a touch of artwork, which I assume belongs to the firm. So much nicer than the standard legalese clip art. The font and colors make it easy to read, and the keyword search box is ever-present, for finding something particular. One weakness was the "Who's Who" attorney search, which required some sort of name, rather than searching specific credentials or location.						
Honigman Miller	7	7	8	6	2	30
Sharper new look, and better display of "knowledge" than the old Honigman site. Nothing extraordinary here, but everything you need to have, and find, is well organized and structured.						
Howrey Simon	5	7	4	6	8	30
The site's strength is the level of detail that accompanies each area of practice. If I'm seeking expertise, and want to see a thorough overview of Howrey's work in the area, I get it. The separate site for the Howrey Bootcamp (**www.howreybootcamp.com**) allows the summer associate program its own look, feel and approach. The shortcomings are in basics such as lack of detail in office locations, and no site map or keyword search.						

Firm Name	Design	Content	Usability	Interactivity	Intangibles	Total
Leonard Street	8	8	7	6	2	30

Smart home page. The "client log-in" is always on the top-right, encouraging that audience to use the site for entry. Just below it, grab that sign-up info for newsletters. Then, the PDF brochure for newcomers. In the middle, beneficial firm news headlines. In Minnesota, you've got to keep up with the Faegres.

Miller Canfield	7	7	6	6	4	30

The visual appeal, organization and information make this a success. Easy to use, with an above-average "Newsroom". The best part about it being a Hubbard One site was that I did not know it until getting to the site info section, avoiding the cookie-cutter pitfalls that so many fall into in this market (not just design, but also database implementation).

Patterson Belknap	6	7	8	6	3	30

My guess is PBWT associates do not race out the back door at the first hint of dissatisfaction, because the firm is not afraid to display their credentials on-line. And in NYC no less. The best way to describe the site is "helpful." One of the better "Contact Us" sections. A decent array of legal resources. And descriptive recruiting info. In a city weak on the Web, a better-than-average showing.

Quarles & Brady	5	6	6	7	6	30

Found the design a little stuffy, but the information provided well-organized. The home page offers strong content and timely scrolling headlines. A separate careers site, broken down into lawyer and non-lawyer interests. The site coordinates each practice area with relevant attorneys, publications and offices. The "Firm Events" comes with a request form where you can check off those that you would like further information on. Also, the site is clearly kept up to date. I'm amazed how so many large law firms seemingly have only "made the news" once a month for the last year. Quarles is keeping it fresh. Others should consider a little more updating.

Reed Smith	7	6	6	6	5	30

"It's not just business. It's personal." Personally, I hate the hokey taglines. The site is another solid, functional one by Hubbard. Nicely displayed, database-driven, user-friendly. Each practice area offers a separate link to sub-groups in the practice category, as well as link to the appropriate attorney list, publications list and the form to sign up for newsletters.

Smith Helms	6	7	7	5	5	30

Some firms fail in trying to be too cute with names and categories. Smith succeeds by doing the opposite. The Facts. Who, what, why, where, bottom line and news. In the attorney section, the ability to search by state admission is a smart category to have. Each section relates well to one another, and all the info you expect and need to have is in place. I also liked the specialty site promoted on the home page, a glitzy presentation at www.emerginglaw.com.

Sonnenschein Nath	8	7	6	4	5	30

Like the name and brand, the site has a sunny disposition. They take advantage of radio interviews, articles on legal sites, and their own annual report and brochures, to present themselves. E-business gets its own advanced treatment. Recruiting includes a "day in the life" component. While not original (Akin Gump did it a few years ago), it is still a useful tool. The firm colors and style translates well onto the site, which includes good graphics and layout.

Thelen Reid	5	7	6	5	7	30

Too much scrolling in some areas. Once again, a common theme, where you have to surf around the site to find all the relevant information. Overall, the site is average for a Top

Firm Name	Design	Content	Usability	Interactivity	Intangibles	Total
250. They are wise to promote the www.constructionWeblinks.com affiliate site. If you happen upon this firm or site, and are interested in construction law, they show off that expertise in top form.						
Altheimer & Gray	7	6	6	6	4	29
Yet another white on black background site. It is easy to find what your way around. There were some disconnects between the publications and practice area listings. In other words, not all the pubs in the database were linked up with the practice group. That is probably human error on updating the pages. Not as detailed as many similarly situated sites, but keeping it simple has its benefits too.						
Ballard Spahr	7	7	6	6	3	29
It was not that long ago, when I picked on Ballard in my seminars for having one of the worst large-firm sites in the U.S. The firm's on-line highlight was www.virtualchase.com, a legal research resource (which is still a highlight). Today, the new site is quite snazzy. The navigation is a little distracting, and the Hubbard developers seem to be getting away from effectively using the whole page, and playing with too many shapes and colors. With this site, though, the firm is in the Internet big leagues.						
Barnes & Thornburg	6	7	6	5	5	29
Classy. A well set out description of the firm and its' services. One oddity is that the practice area descriptions do not offer links to related content, yet the attorney resumes do. Fix that. The attorney bios, obviously, are a strength with this important feature. One other minor shortcoming is that the main categories in the left-hand navigation bar does not lead to a page showing the subs. You need to scroll back over the nav bar for that. The first page of each section should highlight the subsections, getting me deeper into the area that I've already expressed interest in. The foreign language pages, offering an intro to the firm, are always a good touch on the World Wide Web.						
Briggs and Morgan	6	8	6	6	3	29
Briggs new design is a marked improvement, and allows the site to focus on the strength in content. From the front and center news of the home page, to fully developed sections of content that relate to one another, the site is a success. Also, good use of forms. The navigation bar was a little annoying, and the "search" provides a bunch of categories that do not exist on the site (i.e. white papers, paraprofessionals), but they make the most of limited database capabilities.						
Crosby Heafey	6	6	7	5	5	29
I expected something a little different from a developer called Atomic Tangerine. Unfortunately, it appears the tangerine got nuked in dot-com land, which could affect the Crosby site's ability to grow. The site is a little different in look and layout. One of the pages says they "don't always think like lawyers" which is a good thing in working with corporate clients. Nothing really out of the ordinary on the site, but the slightly different look and comments help set them apart from the large-firm stereotypes.						
Fried Frank	6	7	6	7	3	29
Outside of some navigation inconsistencies, the Fried Frank site represents itself well. They parcel out their "specialty pages and services by e-mail", which lets the user know the difference between a practice area description or publication, and a concentrated effort to provide extensive information on a particular area of the law. The design look and style of the home page does not match the internal site pages, and is missing any type of disclaimer information. Those are easily corrected.						

Firm Name	*Design*	*Content*	*Usability*	*Interactivity*	*Intangibles*	*Total*
Gibbons Del Deo	4	6	7	7	5	29

Once you get past the old collage-look home page, you find a finely constructed large-firm site. The cold fusion-driven application includes quality sections for all the important areas (i.e. bios, practice areas, etc.). The news alerts allow for e-mail subscriptions in text or HTML. They are also posted on the site. A few other wise things on this site that are often forgotten by many. First, placing the dates after each data entry. It is nice to know if a presentation, article or newsletter was posted yesterday or three years ago. The little things. I also noticed that some bios had photos and others did not. Instead, there was a logo holding that place. Photos on a Web site should be at the discretion of the individual. There is no reason that everyone has to have one, or not. On an earlier site, I also noticed some bio e-mails were simply info@lawfirm. Another good idea for attorneys that do not check or use e-mail. Again, no need for total consistency.

Firm Name	Design	Content	Usability	Interactivity	Intangibles	Total
Hinshaw & Culbertson	5	6	6	6	6	29

Give me a little more meat. Do not give me a list of published articles, either link out to them, or get reprint permission. The bulk are generally available on-line. The weakest part is the practice area descriptions, many of which offer no description at all. Force an attorney to write one page on his or her area of expertise. It would be more helpful if the related sites/events/client alert section of each page related to the section I'm on, rather than stay the same (it makes you think they relate to the page you are on, and it does not). Nice job with the related sites. "Mold—The Next Asbestos" sounds like an elementary school filmstrip, but I was interested enough to read on.

Firm Name	Design	Content	Usability	Interactivity	Intangibles	Total
Holme Roberts	7	7	6	5	4	29

Great site, but the updaters are asleep at the wheel. The front page "Headlines" (scrolling and static) were two months' old, at best. A prerequisite for HRO opening an office in a locale must be the natural beauty. Colorado, Utah and London photos make the design so easy to do. You already feel like it is not a law firm environment. Better-than-basics displays of credentials. The "Video" section offers a variety of topics, available for both Realplayer and Quicktime end-users. The attorney listings allow you to reorganize by alphabet, practice, location or law school. Get rid of the splash page. It adds nothing. While there is plenty of information available on the site, there is also a clients-only section for additional materials. The advent of extranet use has eliminated many of these, but it still makes sense to provide content exclusively for your paying audience.

Firm Name	Design	Content	Usability	Interactivity	Intangibles	Total
Kenyon & Kenyon	7	7	7	5	3	29

It is a wonder anyone ever has to search for IP data on Lexis when the specialty firms provide comprehensive articles and guidance on-line, in presenting themselves. A very pleasant design. The navigation has some inconsistencies, and I hate "under construction" (for Links and Events). "Under Construction" was much more tolerable three or four years ago. The "Library" is loaded with helpful articles, searched by topic and/or author. It is always interesting to see what a firm considers important in presenting attorneys. In this case, alphabetical, office...or foreign language (from a drop down selection).

Firm Name	Design	Content	Usability	Interactivity	Intangibles	Total
Lane Powell	7	8	7	4	3	29

Must be back in the old Northwest, where law firm Web sites have to be good. The best way to describe this site is "pure." The home page—from the colors, to the photo, firm name, news and navigation—are textbook. Everything is easy to find, and related appropriately. The "latest news" on the home page is actually current and updated often. The

Firm Name	Design	Content	Usability	Interactivity	Intangibles	Total
only weakness is in the lack of interactivity relating to contacting the firm, or getting on the mailing list, outside of the general e-mail addresses.						
Locke Liddell	7	8	5	4	5	29
A warning. I have a bias against right-hand navigation. Not because I'm a lefty. But, because the left is where you expect to navigate from on-line. I've learned to live with top-nav, if I have to. The site was much more user-friendly when I surfed using a mirror. Good depth of information and smart use of interspersed images. Finally, if you are going to refer to your clerking program as **LLSClerkship.com**, make sure you have the domain point to that section of your Web site. It is just a dot-com thing.						
Morgan Lewis	4	8	5	6	6	29
While the site lacks organization, the quality of the content is good. The font size makes it easier to read than many sites, and it is easy to navigate through. However, some sections contain too much scrolling. The wait on some pages were painful. Attorney biographies were simply alphabetical, which is not too useful if you do not already know who you are looking for. You are at least warned that much of the content is in a PDF format. A little bland for a firm of this size, but better simple and easy to read than full of flash with nothing behind it. Outside of giving major league baseball the **mlb.com** domain, and switching to **morganlewis.com**, not much has changed on this site over the years. Hate the frames! Like the fact that the home page offers connections to on-line meetings, workspaces and Web mail, showing good use of technology and interactivity on the Web. HSRScan remains a unique database component. The recruiting site is totally different from the firm site, yet can be a little confusing with the top-navigation bar taking you to sections in the regular Web site. The content, as always, is very strong. The presentation and design needs better focus and consistency.						
Robins Kaplan	6	6	6	5	6	29
It is always a little harder when you are reaching out to both consumer and corporate audiences. Robins Kaplan has a smart home page, offering a smattering of what exists on the site for each type of end-user. A little too much scrolling in some sections. Break it up a bit. I'm not sure you need the e-mail click-through disclaimer, but the firm offers many ways to get in contact throughout.						
Simpson Thacher	5	8	6	5	5	29
A disclaimer—I know STB and their Web site well, having participated in its' creation. That does not mean they listened to me. Also, they were limited by the database development of West Group, where all of its FirmSites have a certain cookie-cutter, mass production approach. The splash page frustrates me, but the content is king here. STB does not fall in line with recruiting shows or bells and whistles, but sticks to showing people what they are doing. The front page is loaded with firm news and articles. They do not need to tout themselves, but can simply say what they are up to, and get the message across. A private site for alumni and another for summer associates are nice additional pieces.						
Baker Donelson	5	5	5	5	8	28
Nothing particularly interesting stood out on the main Web site for the firm. For the most part, thumbnail type info. However, the firm did offer two strong and more interesting specialty sites, for e-business, and for Tennessee public policy law at **www.tnpublicpolicy.com**.						

Firm Name	Design	Content	Usability	Interactivity	Intangibles	Total
Blackwell Sanders	5	7	7	6	3	28

A functional site with decent content. The design and set-up (frames again) is a little bland. Good search capabilities. Some of the sections, such as "Seminars" need to be added to the navigation bar, rather than set on the other side of the page. The best part was the E-QUIZ demo. I got each of the questions right, and would have loved to finish the exam.

Lord Bissell	5	7	5	5	6	28

Once beyond the home page, the right side of the site was dark, blurry with an unintelligible navigation bar of some sort. I found it easier to just go back home each time to navigate further. Better-than-usual legal links sections, divided by practice area. The "Events" calendar added a little juice to the site. Sufficient related content and descriptions. Another over-the-top recruiting section, loaded with bells and whistles. I'm now officially bored by the "Day in the Life", which is going to tie the "flash movie" with most repeated Web site feature. Look, they pay first-years $125k. You visit the Jelly Belly Factory and Wrigley Field during the summer program. I'm sold.

Morrison & Hecker	6	6	5	7	4	28

Sometimes stock photos work and other times they do not. I've seen these a million times, but it works here because they are an understated part of the overall design. The site is attractive, easy to read and peruse. No searching, though. Some good publications (and the ability to subscribe). A few nice features thrown in, such as a real audio from an attorney interview, and a power point from a recent seminar. The home page would be much-improved if it featured the publications, or highlighted recent additions. Otherwise, it looks inactive to repeat users. Also, why do you offer "additional information" at Martindale, on the attorney page? Why would you have more in terms of credentials there than on your own Web site? Make no mistake, M-H is KEY to getting your credentials out there, and bringing people to you. But, you should not send people off the site when they've already found you.

Ogletree Deakins	5	6	5	6	6	28

Looks like this site fell into the same disease that most of us experience from time to time—updateitis. This management/labor firm built a good site, seemed to be adding content with some consistency, including tie-ins with seminars and other firm works, only to either stop producing new information, or not getting it up on the Web. By general law firm Web standards, it is competitive. However, a number of similarly-situated (practice area and location) firms have them beat in terms of on-line presentation. The firm does have an impressive immigration site, at **www.visatrax.com**, including a demo of the way the site and the client interaction works.

Schulte Roth	6	7	6	6	3	28

Another site showing improvement in the last year. The "Contact Us" is smart in offering links to each relevant contact component on the site (i.e. Alumni forms, registration, guest book, directions). Also, the Alumni section lets you know who and where. On many sites, the most a user can see is that there is either a private section or a form for submission. The home page "News" item regarding an office relocation is more than a year old—not news anymore. However, the virtual tour of the new digs is a nice touch. Love those Associate bios. Education and practice area only. Not exactly promoting their credentials.

Firm Name	*Design*	*Content*	*Usability*	*Interactivity*	*Intangibles*	*Total*
Shaw Pittman	5	6	6	6	5	28

They make their point (I think). Shaw Pittman is a business-oriented firm focused in D.C. If that is not the message, subtract five points. Good overview of what they do, the way they work with clients and what areas of law is the firm focus. Nothing really was annoying, and nothing stood out as utterly unique. The ability to send an interesting article on to a colleague is always helpful. And the client services section offers some helpful info on how you will work with the firm. Alumni sections are more an more prevalent in this generation of law firm Web sites. The attorney bios could be more searchable.

Strasburger & Price	6	8	6	5	3	28

Outside of the top frame, the site worked well (although a little slow). The layout of the "Publications and Presentations", with the drop-down boxes on top and the on-line subscription form below works. Display of firm ads work too. The Careers section was just the right combo of fun and facts. Just need to up the updating a tad. The scrolling headlines leading to news releases were stale.

Thompson & Knight	7	5	8	4	4	28

The color, design and firm name (branding) are all according to the rules of usability that I was taught. Plenty of useful buttons for bookmarking, sending, printing or searching. Room to grow, in regard to quality and quantity of additional information.

Verner Liipfert	7	7	6	5	3	28

The home page has changing photos (very professionally done) of some firm members and what they do. Guys like Senators Bob Dole and George Mitchell. Some dude who worked with LBJ. You get the idea. They follow that up with some newsletters, news and events. A rather straight-forward presentation. A press kit with high-resolution photos of some firm folks. A wise approach to the Web for a venerable D.C. presence. How about an alumni section?

Vorys Sater	7	7	6	5	3	28

Another much-improved site. Healthy design, nicely set out. The navigation bar subcategories were a little annoying, opening onto the main page, and the search results are not as useful as many, giving alphabetical returns instead of relevance. The Welcome front page does not do the rest of the site justice. Change it up a bit.

Calfee Halter	8	7	6	3	3	27

Look ma, no recruiting section! A law student will have to settle for learning about what the firm does and who works there. A polished design and appearance. The "practice areas", besides providing links to related publications, attorneys and latest news, also has a drop-down box just listing related practice areas. Updated with decent frequency. Very professional feel.

Chadbourne & Parke	8	6	6	5	2	27

Definitely one of the sleeker marketing-style sites. While not my personal style, I am sure that this carefully packaged site is impressive to many. And one of the better among the NYC-based efforts. It screams high-end, sophisticated, "we've been around a long time and are 'players' in this business." Am I right? And again with the lame attorney section. Is it really that hard for firms to hold on to their star associates? It should not be.

Dykema Gossett	4	7	7	6	3	27

Very simple and straight-forward. A little misleading in that it takes awhile to realize there is really a lot to the site. Once you've surfed around, you will find everything from the general to copies of firm logos and brochures, as well as access to all publications and seminars. Another "it is what's inside that count" site.

Firm Name	Design	Content	Usability	Interactivity	Intangibles	Total
McCutchen Doyle	5	7	6	4	5	27

Look, you can not have left, top and right navigation on the home page. Pick one. The rest of the site is detailed, and generally intuitive. I'm not sure why one section is titled, "Portal", and every other section had a mouseover description. Strong press room (especially the "contacts" offerings) and recruiting materials.

Proskauer Rose	3	7	5	6	6	27

I never understood why you would want to make your Internet presence look like an old-tyme print publication. Personally, coming from a sports background, I have always been fond of the Proskauer firm, but the Web site could use a little work. The layout of the pages makes it difficult to read, and cumbersome to print (they could really use a "printer-friendly" feature). The "Table of Contents" is an inappropriate means of Web navigation. But, the information is strong. Lots of newsletters, articles and other materials. The separate recruiting site begins with the "standard" flash show, but actually plays out into a more unique interactive experience for the potential hire. Another site that would be much stronger with a little reorganization and redesign.

Shearman & Sterling	7	6	6	3	5	27

Part of me hates the flash home page, with no news or information, part of me likes the cleanliness and the colors. The "lawyers" section, with numerous search options was a little different than most, and quite helpful. If you prefer brochure-style sites, this one is excellent. Pleasing to the eye, with some nice touches graphic touches. A good alumni section. Well organized. While not the type of site I would bookmark for repeat visits, if you are looking for a good overview of what you get with Shearman, it accomplishes that.

Sidley Austin	5	7	6	4	5	27

Fully-functional, with the typical breakdown of databases and content types. While not a big fan of the black background, I do like the ability to print the page with a reformatted white background in a second browser window. They keep the flash reserved for the careers site—a good move—and the information is generally well organized, consistent and easy to find. For the large firm, in which approvals, style and upkeep can be painstaking, Sidley does a good job in presenting itself on-line.

Snell & Wilmer	4	7	6	5	5	27

A more user-friendly home page, and a little less crowding on some of the page sections, would move the site up in functionality. Otherwise, things appear to be in order.

Baker & Hostetler	7	5	4	4	6	26

The navigation drove me insane. While the look and feel is different, and focuses on solutions in the corporate world theme, the chances of making it a destination are slim. Best serves the recruiting audience.

Baker & McKenzie	5	6	5	6	4	26

Professional, conservative and functional. Clean home page, focused on providing Baker "info" as the domain name suggests. I would prefer a stronger keyword search, to better narrow sections of the site, especially in regard to attorney biographies and the size of the firm. Nothing flashy or unique. However, when dealing with a firm of this size, you can only get so creative in your approaches. The careers section could use an upgrade. "Client Sites" shows a willingness to use the Internet for interactivity and work product. Good on-line registration for newsletters and events.

Butzel Long	7	5	5	3	6	26

There should be more meat on the bone, such as the Immigration practice's resource page, linked off the practice description, and the "College Savings Plan" info. They both deserve front-page links on this site, as marquee content. "Contact Us" needs to be more

Firm Name	*Design*	*Content*	*Usability*	*Interactivity*	*Intangibles*	*Total*
than opening my e-mail. Have the "Lex Mundi" link open up a second browser, rather than have me leave the Butzel site. "Search Tools" should involve the whole site, not just attorney bios. That page is repetitive. The design and navigation are good. A few fixes will take it up a notch.						
Foley Hoag	6	6	7	5	2	26
If I'm an FHE client, I'm not likely to see a lot of added-value here. However, for those checking them out, the site is more than adequate. It is wise to explain the meaning of the gyroscope theme as well. The site is well constructed, with good organization and search results that are actually useful! Also, the drop-down box in "Contact Us" for choosing the recipient is a good touch.						
Jenkins & Gilchrist	4	6	6	3	7	26
The site is still static HTML (except for the attorney database), which makes accessing pages a little more cumbersome. The home page look is "last-gen", but the overall content is decent. The firm flexes some Web muscle with a separate site for the technology law group at **www.jgsolutions.com**. Also, the ability to participate in free on-line seminars is an advanced touch. Some practice area sections were significantly stronger than others. I would also encourage subscribing to some of the excellent newsletters, with an on-line subscription form.						
Jenner & Block	3	7	6	5	5	26
The firm just launched its third-generation site. I actually liked the second-gen better. But, the industry-standard database structure and flashy recruiting site seems to be especially prevalent in Chicago. The colors and page layout are just weird. The home page just seems too brochure-like, sending the wrong message to the visitor. Good info, suspect delivery.						
Michael Best	3	7	7	6	3	26
The home page "Daily Features" are truly daily, and that is impressive. I also liked the "Archive" buttons in many places, rather than get hit with a scrolling list of every article or newsletter for the past five years. The look is dated and a bit worn. What is on the inside is much more important than the way you look or dress—to say anything less would be shallow. My father-in-law, a plastic surgeon, might suggest a redesign, though.						
Vedder Price	3	6	6	7	4	26
Here is what I immediately take away from Vedder Price. We are skilled practitioners that know what we are doing. This is why. Nothing fancy in design or presentation, just the facts. We speak, write, publish and present. A password-protected alumni section. A separate site, at **www.constructionlaw-lawfirm.com**, for that practice. Conservative, but effective.						
Buchanan Ingersoll	4	6	6	5	4	25
Yet another site with organizational problems (the site, not the firm—as far as I know). Nothing out of the ordinary. Solid information.						
Davis Polk	6	4	5	4	6	25
I still like the site's color scheme and simplicity. The latest news item is front and center on the home page. Intuitive left-hand navigation. The site just needs to go deeper. On this day, "Publications" consisted of three. The practice area sections are skimpy. Most offer a brief overview, and a link to the practice area brochure in a PDF. The alphabetical attorney bios are worthless if you do not know who you are looking for. It is possible that the "Clientlink" provides current clients with details and content not visible to others.						

Firm Name	Design	Content	Usability	Interactivity	Intangibles	Total
Frost Brown	6	6	6	5	2	25
Nothing stands out—good or bad—except that the bios are all only in PDF form. Create Web pages for your attorney credentials.						
Kaye Scholer	5	7	6	3	4	25
Decent database-driven presence. All the expected categories are there. Always a nice touch having a search box in the navigation bar, which in this case is on top, as part of a frame. Nice move by the Technology group putting its' U.S. Privacy Law Deskbook on-line, as a complimentary resource. It would be of even greater use out of the PDF format and into the Web context, for easier searching and printing of partial sections.						
Kutak Rock	8	6	4	2	5	25
This is not meant as an insult, but two years ago, I would have loved this site. The art-work is original and a breath of fresh air. The site is limited, still an old HTML. On this day, the search engine was not working, and I encountered a bunch of dead links. The content types can remain, keep the artwork, and convert to .asp.						
Montgomery McCracken	5	6	6	5	3	25
Another site that just needs a little tightening up to move up in class. The home page allows you to customize your sidebar by attorneys and practices. The "Sample Cases" were a good touch. They would be even better if the attorneys and practices listed were hyperlinked. The practice pages are potent, but could use a little better organization. They feature related content and attorneys, but why do you have the descriptions broken out in a PDF? Strange that IP offered no related content at all. The front page "What's New" news was nearly three months' old on this date. Cut down on the overuse of PDFs and input more into the databases. Streamline the navigation.						
Saul Ewing	5	6	4	5	5	25
Somebody shrunk my page? Not the best use of space. Or organization. The site map is a necessity, not a luxury. Some of the site wants to be introductory (old-fashioned print style language), and other parts want to be Web-trendy. When you get done perusing, you realize that there is a lot more here than you thought. A sound site map—prior to rebuilding—and a more unified (marketing) theme would go a long way in taking the site to the next level.						
Schnader Harrison	4	7	5	4	5	25
The scrolling headlines and "In the News" were all months old. The site has taken a few steps back in recent years. Adding "Law" to "Schnader" seems to be the latest project. It was wise when they went from SHSL to Schnader a few years back. Stop tinkering with the name and update the site! The site also needs better navigation and organization. There were some high-quality presentations and materials, if you surfed long enough. Once a Web site front-runner, now in the middle of the pack. I tinkered with giving the firm a few intangible points for playing a role in setting me up with my wife, but that would not be fair to everyone else, would it?						
Stites & Harbison	5	6	6	5	3	25
Outside of a few pages that should be broken down (i.e. the home page should click over to the "Quick Find Index" and the "Contact Us" should separate office locations and the on-line form), the format and content are fine. Relevant articles and events should be linked from the appropriate service area. The color and style of the home page does not						

Firm Name	*Design*	*Content*	*Usability*	*Interactivity*	*Intangibles*	*Total*
really match the insides of the site. The "Gallery" was a nice display of firm ads. Think about adding a few more forms, instead of generic e-mails, to some of the site sections.						
Warner Norcross	5	4	5	5	6	25
The impressive stuff is in the four "featured" sites—environmental, trusts and estates, human resources, and recruiting. These need to get more play on the home page, and internally. The offices, attorneys and practice areas provide little in terms of detail. The news section provides much greater levels of "expertise."						
Winston & Strawn	4	5	5	6	5	25
Too much "loading..." waiting for the graphics. Also, the frame is too large, limiting the space for actual quality content. The materials are not placed in an intuitive fashion. Once I got used to the site, I found there was a lot more there than originally met the eye. The www.whywinston.com recruiting site offered the "standard" flash movie. Okay, but nothing particularly unique or different.						
Arnold & Porter	4	6	5	5	4	24
The site is simple, focusing on providing an overview, and not worrying about bells and whistles. All the necessary "basics" are there. In many places, there could have been useful hyperlinks to related information. The "continue" button on many pages was a little misleading. The "Publications" told you if it was a PDF file—thank you!						
Baker & Daniels	6	6	2	3	7	24
I liked the first messages the home page offered. An Indiana firm. Since 1863. Headlines/Newsstand. Chinese Site. If I need a firm that is Indiana based and/or I want people that have been around awhile, this might be it. Come here for news, not just a firm brochure. And, we obviously have some focus that requires a Chinese-language version of the site. The negative is that the navigation through the site is an atrocity, and it was a struggle to get around. Outside of the Newsstand, it lacked fluidity.						
Bell Boyd	6	6	4	3	5	24
This site has been up there for awhile. Among early sites, it was well above average, and one of the early firms to use video on the site, for recruiting efforts. BB has definitely gotten its money out of the model, and now it probably time to advance. The navigation buttons at the bottom of the page is a hassle. Things like the "Guest Book" are outdated. You need a search engine. The on-line BB was once ahead of the Internet curve. Time to get back.						
Cadwalader Wickersham	6	5	5	3	5	24
All the basics are there. A little less focus on presentation, and more on providing materials would be an improvement. The "hide the Associate credentials" theme that prevails in NYC continues, although all bios provide a link to authored publications for the attorney, if they exist on the site.						
Coudert Brothers	3	6	6	6	3	24
The newest version of this site retains the home page map, but the insides of the site have improved dramatically. I like the fact that the navigation bar is at both the top and bottom of each page, for those that scroll down a page. That corrects what can be a major weakness of top-page navigation. Unfortunately, the meatiest part of the site, "News", blends in with the rest of the site. It should be highlighted, and given much greater play. The other sections are relatively bland. The attorney listing only offers partners/counsel, in alphabetical order. Good on-line registration forms for alumni and retired partners.						

Firm Name	Design	Content	Usability	Interactivity	Intangibles	Total
Fulbright & Jaworski	5	5	5	5	4	24

The site has definitely improved, but it remains average. The attorney bio database, which opens up into a pop-up window, is better than a year ago. The home page could provide a little more value, and as always, the splash page is just a waste of time. Like so many sites, it is helpful to someone seeking additional information about the firm, but not likely to be used as an ongoing resource or added-value to current clients.

Godfrey & Kahn	5	6	4	7	2	24

A little slow on the download, dragged down by some images on every page that made me feel like I was on a five-second delay. This is a design flaw that needs fixing, seriously effecting usability. You would probably see a major jump in page views per visit. The "search" is somewhat hidden in the site map. Some good us of interactivity with sub-scriptions to pubs and registration for seminars. With the practice area descriptions, besides linking to the attorney list, also think about linking to the matching publications and seminars, for maximum effectiveness.

LeBoeuf Lamb	5	6	4	4	5	24

The layout is a little convoluted, and that is not helped by the lack of a search component or a site map. The www.insurelegal.com Web site spin-off would be better off staying within the firm's site. It had not been updated in some time. The Russian site, at www.russianlaws.com, was a stronger secondary site, but again would be better off with the firm's on-line brand. Recruiting features what must now be the obligatory flash show, and regular tidbits and info. I almost missed one of the best sections, featuring speeches and presentations, as it was not part of the navigation bar, only found on the home page's "Just Arrived" news.

Patton Boggs	6	4	5	5	4	24

A little inconsistency in the site navigation. For example "Events" appears on the home page and on some of the other sections, but not all. I only found it after heading back home again. Also confusing to people not familiar with the firm or law firms in general, are the practice "categories" on the left-side vs. the "practice areas". Many firms I've worked with have debated over how THEY divide up groups, sections, areas, categories, etc. On the outside, we do not care about that—only finding the relevant area of law we seek guidance on. Easy to read, but more like print put on-line than an interactive resource.

Porter Wright	5	6	6	5	2	24

The most current "News" is two months' old, sending an immediate message to the end-user that the site is not exactly priority one. The expectation at a firm of your size is weekly updating. The site does offer a nice mix of graphics, photos and video throughout. The "History" is interesting. The "back" buttons to maneuver on pages were a pain in the butt. Strong searching and site map.

Reinhart Boerner	2	7	4	4	7	24

Up until now, I've kept domain name criticism to myself. But, this is one of the worst. Do you think everyone will intuitively remember all those initials? I was so happy when my friends at MDWCG took my advice and became marshalldennehey.com. Think about it. The design is a bit crude, and the site is just not real pretty. A few frames. Some wallpaper. Two words—paint job! But, it actually has some quality content in "Resources" and "Legal Developments". The "Why are these people smiling?" campaign was effective on the Web as well. Even the "Links" offer added-value, updated fresh each month. And, I stumbled across the Trial Science Institute (www.trailscience.com), which should get a home page link as well.

Firm Name	Design	Content	Usability	Interactivity	Intangibles	Total
Ropes & Gray	6	4	4	3	7	24

You get the message immediately upon arrival, in which "Associate Hiring" is the first tab, a section which includes some of the greatest detail and depth among recruiting efforts. The "practice area" sections run from thumbnail (environmental, real estate) to extensive (health care, labor). That better match up with the areas the firm focuses on. Again, an improvement on the drab look of the old site. However, the end-user audiences here are limited. Not that there is anything wrong with that—if that is the intent.

Firm Name	Design	Content	Usability	Interactivity	Intangibles	Total
Sullivan & Cromwell	5	5	4	4	6	24

Not the easiest of sites to maneuver through. The navigation and layout are confusing. Too much of a print-publication approach. The recruiting section offers both a Web brochure and a virtual tour, which are both well presented. If I had never heard of S&C, and was checking them out, the site would be passable. My guess is that very few recruits and/or prospects are not already familiar with them, though.

Firm Name	Design	Content	Usability	Interactivity	Intangibles	Total
Taft Stettinius	4	6	6	5	3	24

Too much quality material is stuffed under "News". The page layout is poor for on-line reading and printing. There is a site map, but you need to surf to find all related content. Okay for a one-time visitor, but not likely to bring you back. One quality touch is the Alumni Directory, available to all. The attorney db is top-notch. There is also information for Japanese visitors.

Firm Name	Design	Content	Usability	Interactivity	Intangibles	Total
Wilmer Cutler	4	6	5	5	4	24

The word "vanilla" comes to mind. The most colorful page is the site map. Now, I know the Wilmer firm, and they are one of the most impressive in D.C. The site also includes many informative and expertise-presenting printed materials, available in PDF form. The site is okay, but they can do better.

Firm Name	Design	Content	Usability	Interactivity	Intangibles	Total
Bracewell & Patterson	3	6	4	4	6	23

The old "Web site that looks like a file cabinet trick". That is the second time I fell for that one this week. The look (and clip art) are a little dated. Browsers kept opening up at the most inopportune times. Maybe I caught the site on a bad day, but getting through the obstacles was annoying. It actually made me homesick for a nice cookie-cutter, db-driven site.

Firm Name	Design	Content	Usability	Interactivity	Intangibles	Total
Ice Miller	4	7	5	4	3	23

There were some server issues plaguing my trip through the site, and the search mechanism was not working effectively. Simply offering attorneys by alphabet is not helpful enough. The Sports & Entertainment Group site was cool. Why is it not highlighted on the home page? I stumbled across it. The secondary navigation on the top was also difficult to see. The home page was a little crowded, but the array of content types and frequency of updating is strong.

Firm Name	Design	Content	Usability	Interactivity	Intangibles	Total
Moore & Van Allen	6	6	5	4	2	23

Decent display of firm's data and skill set. The one thing that appeared unique, a diversity calendar, was not working. Otherwise, nicely packaged.

Firm Name	Design	Content	Usability	Interactivity	Intangibles	Total
Nixon Peabody	4	6	5	4	4	23

Solid. Typical. Nothing stood out as especially strong or weak. The "usual suspects" databases of information. The home page provides current issues, and links to the expected areas of description. Not an in-depth resource, but Nixon Peabody provides all the necessary data to someone investigating the firm.

Firm Name	*Design*	*Content*	*Usability*	*Interactivity*	*Intangibles*	*Total*
Nutter McClennen	6	5	5	4	3	23

One of the cooler firm logos I've seen. The home page could use a little more (recent additions, news) to give it a less static appearance. The news and newsletters need some type of organization, either by date, or preferably by practice group (and date). Too much on one page in certain areas. Not enough value to bring me back again. Although, for an initial visit, the firm paints the big picture. Nothing stands out—good or bad—except that the bios are all only in PDF form. Create Web pages for your attorney credentials.

Sheppard Mullin	3	5	6	5	4	23

You've got over 300 attorneys and you are adding about one article a month? The home page "newsroom" latest edition was nearly two months' old on this date. I saw that legal "clip art" five billion times during my days at West Group. Turn it up a notch. Brighten the look, but most importantly, increase the attorney buy-in. The structure of the site is fine.

Shook Hardy	3	4	5	6	5	23

No matter what any "marketer" tells you, the core selling feature of any firm are the credentials and experiences of your attorneys. SHB always keeps the "Attorney Look-Up" in view. The ability to apply for jobs on-line strengthens the employment section. The site is a little light on content, and the design colors and structure somewhat disjointed. Many of the snippets of info are of no interest to visitors. A few pages offered a "printer version" button, but when I dug deeper into the site, it was nowhere to be found. With the color scheme and design, that button should be consistently presented as an option for end-users.

Steptoe & Johnson	4	5	4	5	5	23

Give more play to the site strengths, such as the E-Commerce Law Week (which offers a free on-line subscription) and the Tax Center. The attorney bio db could be much more helpful, like offering "practice areas" as a choice. Since the practice areas do not list attorneys or other related materials, it makes finding things tough. You don't have a NYC office. Why are you hiding the lawyers?

Vinson & Elkins	4	6	4	4	5	23

Clip art, right-side navigation and a dark background got me off to an unfriendly start on the home page. Some sections contained too much scrolling. There was detailed information for each section, and all the necessary components in a large firm site. However, the inconsistent navigation and layout sometimes had me trying to figure out where to go. A little reorganization would go a long way in making the site more user-friendly.

Carlton Fields	5	5	5	4	3	22

Even after all these years, I still like that Florida palm tree theme that greets you. It looks like a day at the beach. Probably a reason that the recruiting section does not put on a show. I just want to know, is every day biz-casual? The site itself is still in intro-mode, html static and limited in usefulness.

Cummings & Lockwood	3	6	5	4	4	22

If I took some of the all design/no content sites from NYC and mixed it with a site like this one, which is no design and some decent content, I'd have a pretty good presence. There is some solid info and materials, but the presentation is just plain dull. Even the jazzed-up new recruiting section was low-key. Wake me up when it is over.

Firm Name	Design	Content	Usability	Interactivity	Intangibles	Total
Debevoise & Plimpton	3	7	6	4	2	22

Blue, bland and boring. It was so conservative in look and approach; I nearly fell asleep on the keyboard. Developer Hubbard, one of the best in the biz, either had an off day, or simply followed marching orders. Don't get me wrong, simple navigation, database-driven, typical sections and content type. Just too vanilla. The info is there, just wake the site up a bit.

Drinker Biddle	2	6	6	6	2	22

First, I had to get over the graphic design, circa 1995. I then got confused, suddenly finding myself at **www.drinkerbiddle.com**, which was a flash recruiting site. Finally, I had to remind myself that I've always cried, "it is all about the content" to firms such as these. And the data is there. The best part is the option of many documents in HTML AND/OR PDF, rather than just one way or the other. Or worse yet, making me guess. Take the **drinkerbiddle.com** domain for the firm, and put a new coat of paint on the home page.

Gardere & Wynne	4	6	5	5	2	22

After a few lame-o "attorney directories" on some of the site reviews, it was nice to see a good database on the firm's attorney knowledge bank. The design does not really use the screen effectively or efficiently, but the site provides a fair representation of firm offerings and credentials.

Jackson Walker	4	5	5	5	3	22

Yet another simple site. Presents all the basics. Good search engine, which was necessary, since the "Articles" are not separated by topic. Just a list. There was an e-mail subscription box for newsletters. There was mention of a second site, at **www.jwtechlaw.com**, which must have been down on this day. Get rid of the splash page. It was annoying.

Kennedy Covington	5	6	3	3	5	22

This is one of those rare occasions where the firm probably tried too hard to develop something different. It is a mix of fancy brochure and Web site that does not really work. While it helps to have "navigate the site" always visible (back to a site map), it is not user-friendly, and the various frames have me searching for what I'm trying to find. There is content, and it is different, but it just does not work on the Web.

Manatt Phelps	7	4	4	5	2	22

One of the early sites to adapt flash as a design and information component—not just for a quick show. The attorney bios available in both flash and html format. If you have a slow dial-up, the site can cause some stress. The depth of content needs to be improved. Too much flash, not enough flesh.

McDermott Will	3	6	3	5	5	22

The look is a little like 1998. But, the content is decent. The display of information is a little hodge-podge, and that is made more difficult without the ability to do searches on the site—practically a must on today's sites. A move to a database-driven site with a little redesign would solve most of the problems. The content is there. Also, some use of interactivity, with some on-line registration for events and Webcasts.

Miles & Stockbridge	8	5	4	3	2	22

Hey, how about putting some navigation where I can see it? The look and layout are clean and easy to read. The artwork is unique and blends in well. You probably would not even have to jump up from HTML to accomplish a lot more. It just takes the updater longer. Add links from practice descriptions and bios to relevant articles and pubs. I found some data buried in the long-scrolling "firm developments" section.

Firm Name	*Design*	*Content*	*Usability*	*Interactivity*	*Intangibles*	*Total*
Phelps Dunbar	5	6	5	4	2	22
More detail than a print brochure, but nothing unique to the Web. The graphics are a little different. The firm offers up a number of strong newsletters. Lots of scrolling. No searching.						
Phillips Lytle	4	6	5	5	2	22
Solid display of appropriate categories. It was good to see the constant reminders to "subscribe" or "contact us" throughout, taking you to an on-line form. Some sites are not proactive enough in asking for intake and visitor data, although the form could be a little more comprehensive. Beef up the office descriptions, with directions and additional regional info. Add some searchability.						
Plunkett & Cooney	4	5	5	4	4	22
Working my way down the navigation bar (which was one of the best parts), I was ready to just say ho-hum, when I hit a Yellowbrix news feed, showing a spark of firm interest in getting people to return to this Web site. This site, with some reorganization could be so much better. With so many seminars, it could be used to cross-sell with much greater effectiveness. Some paint, a few forms, a new platform.						
Squire Sanders	5	4	4	4	5	22
More on-line brochure than interactive resource. The site has all the basics, but nothing "above and beyond." A year ago, I commended the good attorney biography section, which is still there. Outside of that, not much more than on-line name, rank and serial number.						
Bingham Dana	4	6	3	2	6	21
The home page itself offers nothing of value or introduction. There seems to be some lack of a game plan in putting the site together. Some sections contain too much scrolling. You can not easily match up the publications and related information with the appropriate practice group or attorney. Coupled with no search mechanism, the usability is weak. The left-hand navigation is nice, though. And better to have information that takes some surfing than not having it available at all.						
Marshall Dennehey	4	5	5	3	4	21
I stumbled across "Firm News" and "Speakers Bureau", which were not on the front page navigation or most inside navigation bar listings. The appearance is static, and more firm overview. If you dig a little, there is some good updated content, such as the "Defense Digest." Approach and style are a little dated.						
Robinson Silverman	2	8	4	4	3	21
Ultra-conservative design. The conference room photo that makes up the "splash screen" is also the one photo used in the inside design. This firm is all-business, and has no time for bells, whistles or neon colors. They are too busy dealing with major matters, which are on full display. There is lots of detail, but it can be tough to find what you are looking for. There is a site map (which wisely is displayed when you look to return "home", rather than the "home" photo of the board room). However, the materials are not organized anywhere by practice group, and there is no "search." The attorney IP is easy to find, and can be searched. They are also listed with the appropriate practice area. A detailed recruiting section rounds things out. A little more usability and interactivity launches you to the next level.						
Swidler Berlin	6	5	4	3	3	21
Very cut-and-dried. Nothing stands out particularly positive or negative. Simple design, good navigation and page layout. More of an overview-type presence.						

Firm Name	*Design*	*Content*	*Usability*	*Interactivity*	*Intangibles*	*Total*
Weil Gotshal	3	5	5	4	4	21

After getting past a weak splash page and home page, everything gets better and stronger. There is lots of content there, and the Web is used to provide exclusive access to certain things for recruiting as well as clients. Again with the frames! Get rid of them! So many sites have very similar content and resources, but being able to display and organize is the difference between user-friendly and somewhat frustrating.

White & Case	5	5	4	3	4	21

While the site lacks organization, the quality of the content is good. The font size makes it easier to read than many sites, and it is easy to navigate through. However, some sections contain too much scrolling. The wait on some pages were excruciating. Attorney biographies were simply alphabetical, which is not too useful if you do not already know who you are looking for. You are at least warned that much of the content is in a PDF format. A little bland for a firm of this size, but better simple and easy to read than full of flash with nothing behind it.

Curtis Mallet-Prevost	6	4	4	5	1	20

What happened to your (quarterly) newsletters? August 1998? Come on. At least there were articles from 2001. The home page looked so promising, with recent firm news, and some highlights. Inside, too introductory. How about a little foreign-language action? Offices in a number of countries? Just a page in the appropriate language with some description of practices and an e-mail link.

Dorsey & Whitney	3	5	5	4	3	20

The home page color schematic is a bit off-kilter, and difficult to read. Most of the site publications are in the "Firm News" section, which is not part of the navigation. If you missed it on the home page, you will probably not get around to it. The attorney bios are either alphabetical or location, which is a little limiting. Less is more on the home page. And, do a better job promoting the published materials. "Firm News" and "Firm Publications" are not synonymous.

Loeb & Loeb	5	6	5	3	1	20

Straight-forward. The usual suspects—overview, attorneys, practice areas, news & articles, recruiting. Site search engine. The feel is static, although there is a decent library of articles and alerts.

Sedgwick Detert	5	5	5	4	1	20

On the first two days that I visited, the site was down. Not good. The third time was the charm. There was no firm "Latest News" between July 9th and January 1st? It looks like the site was set up with the best of intentions, and goes through stretches in which decent content is added. A basic large firm presence.

Stevens & Lee	5	5	4	4	2	20

The home page offers up a little different look at "headlines", offering some graphic design and a teaser to bring you in. Unfortunately, it is conservative snooze-city after that. Very plain. This goes for a lot of firms—please archive the old stuff! And stay on those practice groups to stay current with content. A few of the most recent newsletters were quite ancient.

Stroock	5	3	6	4	2	20

Clearly not a firm priority. Good structure, but not much there. The only item in the "News" category was an 11-month old press release.

Firm Name	Design	Content	Usability	Interactivity	Intangibles	Total
Thompson Coburn	2	5	4	4	5	20

An okay showing. Clear energy placed on recruiting. Design is dull, and again with the frames. Not a "destination site", but I could do some respectable research on the firm and its' expertise here. Next design, I might focus on the Midwest locale.

Allen Matkins	4	5	4	4	2	19

The standard presence. This is a good time to remind readers that there is nothing wrong with that. Decent design, coupled with the practice areas, bios, some pubs, recruiting and news, are expected. The bulk of the NLJ 250 accomplishes that. Very few do not. And the ones at the top have chosen to make the Internet a more exceptional part of the firm's business development efforts.

Eckert Seamans	4	3	3	4	5	19

This site has some major problems. First, the only way to find the publications is from "What's New", which is not included on the navigation. Unless you were to find it on the home page, or look on the site map, you assume it is not there. "Upcoming Seminars" was empty. The biggest area pushed on you is the "practice areas", which range from a paragraph overview to a few with decent detail and links to additional information on the site. There are a few standout pieces to the site. A "legal terms" dictionary for non-lawyers. A litigation management slide show. Their **www.productdefenders.com** specialty site is better than the main firm one (and earned some intangible points for the firm Web site score).

Greenebaum Doll	4	5	4	4	2	19

Another site with navigation that makes it difficult to take full advantage. The home page is static. Is it really big news that all attorneys at the firm have Blackberries? That earns a red highlight on the front page. Part of the site seems to be on the verge of taking it to the next level; other sections, with poor layout and old-fashioned buttons, seem like an elementary effort. It screams MS Front Page.

Irell & Manella	8	2	4	3	2	19

Excellent layout, in terms of firm brand, coloring and navigation set-up. Strong attorney bio db, with some unique search components. Lacking in-depth materials. Extremely limited publications and press news. The last addition was more than six months ago. Just focus on adding materials. The foundation is fine as is.

Lewis D'Amato	4	6	4	3	2	19

Yet another firm still in first-generation Web mode. A very basic and simplistic presence. No search mechanism. The bios are links to Martindale. The best part is the firm publications. And it is nice they are in HTML, as opposed to just putting them in PDFs. If you could search the site, including bios and pubs, that would be a step in the right direction. Another firm where I assume that redevelopment is in the cards already.

McCarter & English	4	4	5	4	2	19

One of the other firms I used to pick on for being "way-bad" has launched a much-improved site. Still room for improvement. Much too little focus on the practice area offerings, and way, way too much scrolling. Flush out that "Areas of Service" more. Good move in having client and employee access to services via the Web site.

Mintz Levin	6	4	3	3	3	19

The home page has the right idea, but has too much going on. The Mintz site falls into the same problem area as many firms that are still doing HTML sites, getting the compo

Firm Name	Design	Content	Usability	Interactivity	Intangibles	Total

nents posted in an easy-to-use fashion. The bottom navigation made it clunky, and the biggest annoyance was that the attorney biography pages did not contain a navigation bar or return to the site. You had to hit your "back" button. It was not user-friendly, and I hit on a number of dead links. My guess is that keeping it updated is a chore.

Firm Name	Design	Content	Usability	Interactivity	Intangibles	Total
Alston & Bird	2	5	3	3	5	18

I was sure...sure...that when I hit upon the A&B site this year that I would see something new and different. I was wrong! The home page is still a very weak first-generation design. The site is difficult to navigate through. The sections and content are inconsistent. If you dig, you will find that many sections (i.e. E-Business, Products Liability) have created their own sites. This is a case where the sum of the parts is greater than the whole. There is content. However, the site is not user-friendly and seems in desperate need of an iron fist person or committee to rein it in.

Choate Hall	5	4	3	4	2	18

Poor navigation hampers the effectiveness of this site. The subcategories are in the middle of the page, and disappear when you enter one, losing track of what other options existed. The Firm Directory, with phone and e-mail, is useful if you know the name of the person you are looking for. "Alumni", generally for alumni of the firm on most sites, is a list of where attorneys went to law school. Many of the Boston-based firms raised the Web site bar for themselves this year. Choate needs to do the same.

Dickinson Wright	7	3	4	3	1	18

Very basic presentation, with slightly more info than you would get in a print piece. Practice area descriptions with attorney listings (which offer listings by alphabet, practice or office as well). The "News", which is press release-style, is updated often.

Fredrikson & Byron	1	6	5	4	2	18

It is not pretty (visually), and I had to get over the drab and elementary appearance. The truth is that content-wise, it was excellent. For those that prefer a more vibrant experience, they will not be impressed. If news and information is all you seek, the site will satisfy. Maybe they pass the graphic design savings on to clients.

Hughes Hubbard	4	4	5	3	2	18

Nothing fancy. A rather straight-forward HTML site.

Kelley Drye	5	2	3	3	5	18

The good news is that the new Kelley site is an improvement on the old one. Another firm that spent too much time (and probably money) on the glamour and not enough on the insides. The "Recruiting Show" was typical. The practice descriptions were extremely bare-bones. The "Intellectual Property" description was coming soon, for goodness sakes! Best part was the "Navigating the IPO Waters" video presentation, which thankfully was referred to in the Securities law description. On my high-speed connection, I found myself watching the video. It was impressive. Let's do more of those. And I KNOW KD has lots of published stuff to put in.

Luce Forward	5	4	4	3	2	18

The home page is improved, with some foreign language pages. The navigation is a bit inconsistent. The "Legal News" was without news, and the "mailing list" was under construction. What is there to construct? Put something there for interested parties to fill out. Lacks some of the strengths that a good db-structure offers. Finally, why would you send someone off the site for a Martindale bio, as an option? The resumes are right there.

Firm Name	*Design*	*Content*	*Usability*	*Interactivity*	*Intangibles*	*Total*
Oppenheimer Wolff	3	5	5	4	1	18

The first thing I did was go to "This Month's Feature", which told me that it was September and it dealt with Environmental. It is January, and the topic is Antitrust. Hey, just an error by the updater. Actually, there is some decent content on the site. It could be much better structured. My favorite part is one of the most simplistic. In the navigation bar, the bottom two items are "e-mail us" and an 800-number to call. Always make it easy for a surfer to simply get in contact with you. Call or write.

Ruden McClosky	4	5	4	3	2	18

It is always nice to see something a little bit different. In this case, the navigation bar look, and use of some different icons was a change of pace. Unfortunately, that same navigation is a little tough to decipher and use effectively. Frames and those dreaded "back" buttons spoil the party. The information provided is adequate. A decent amount of press release, articles and a few newsletters. You view the bios in HTML, but have the option of downloading a PDF for printing.

Andrews & Kurth	2	5	4	3	3	17

A&K on the Web just was not my style. Kind of like going into a friend's home and it is just not decorated the way you like to live. Wallpaper, frames, bad art. There was a splash page followed by an introductory page before I got to the first page of any interest. The articles and attorney databases look good, once you get past all the junk around them. Strip out the design and flush out the credentials.

Cozen O'Connor	5	3	4	3	2	17

The home page is a dark, black "brochure" cover. As much as I rail about splash pages, they would be better off making this a splash with a timer taking you to a main page. The site is light on substantive materials. A form allows you to subscribe to newsletters and the like, but this approach limits the visitor from doing some legwork without providing personal data. The site is more introductory to the firm than anything (except for a solid recruiting section). Show me expertise! One touch I did like was showing the number of attorneys practicing in each particular field. This way, you know if it is a major area for Cozen or something one or two attorneys do. The back-end seems in place; the site itself needs better organization for an on-line audience.

Dewey Ballantine	3	3	2	3	6	17

It is very courteous of DB to offer some options before entering the site. Flash or HTML? Need plug-ins for Flash or Acrobat? I am sure there are some who love the different look, style and flash of this site. Not me. I'll grant it a few points in "intangibles", but I found myself trying to reach into the computer to clobber the annoying little people running across to music as I tried finding information. "Publications" was under construction? Please. What were the developers thinking here? Last time I looked, this was a law firm!!

Fish & Neave	6	3	3	3	2	17

You better have a fast connection and flash plug-in if interested in learning a little about Fish & Neave. I stress "a little." For those that like a glitzy flash dance (without Jennifer Beals), this site is for you. Then, if you really want more of a show, you can see the "Discover the Power" show. If you do not visit "What's New", you miss all the firm info on victories, events and publications. Of course, there are visitors that will see this firm as Internet-hip, and non-conformist, which also can be a positive to some.

Firm Name	Design	Content	Usability	Interactivity	Intangibles	Total
Husch & Eppenberger	3	4	4	3	3	17
Basic overview of firm and credentials. Good "job opportunities" for legal and non-legal positions.						
Jones Day	4	4	2	4	3	17
The first screen asks if you want "General Access" or "Restricted Access". The second screen, the home page, offers up a description of a random Jones Day office location. Nothing particularly exciting or informative pops out at you. It reminded me of the typical large law firm "first-generation" site of the late 90s. That is not all bad. Quick download, easy to read white background, left-hand navigation. On this day, the site "search" function was inoperable. The most useful part of the site was a strong attorney bio database, with multiple search categories. It may be quite intentional that the site does not offer "bookmark" quality info, as this may be provided in the private client-access sites. But, the "What's New" included items 18 months old. That is not new! There was also much too much scrolling on many pages and sections. Too close to brochure ware. I do know that a new site from JD is on the way, though.						
Riker Danzig	3	5	5	3	1	17
Remember the McKenna site that looked the same for years, but was substantively different under the hood? Well, Riker looked the same, and was the same. The traditional first-generation Web site, at a time when most firms are working on site number three, has not changed in look or features. The site is continually updated, but is limited by technology and set-up.						
Schiff Hardin	4	4	4	3	2	17
I'm not an idiot (although many of the firms reading these reviews will differ, I'm sure). The front page tells me what "Home", "Firm", "Practice Areas" mean? We know. Also, you tell me to acquaint myself with the firm, immediately turning off anyone that already is familiar with you. This is what you use in the key home page space? The recruiting "section" is one long, long scrolled page. Just like I stated in regard to Fenwick & West, you do need to have a presence that is competitive not only in practice, but locale and client-type. The Windy City is a tough town with lots of good firms with great sites. Upgrade. This is not a 2002 presence.						
Steel Hector	5	3	4	2	3	17
For a 200+ firm, there needs to be more here. On some pages, there was no navigation back, or forward. The attorney listing, by practice group, was only e-mail addresses. Why not just hyperlink back to the bio? It doesn't make sense. This Florida-based firm did provide some good information translated into Spanish. "What's New" did say to watch for the new site, coming in February 2002. My guess is that this one was abandoned while efforts are put into something new.						
Wolf Block	3	3	3	3	5	17
Zzzzzzzz. Outside of "The Wolf Institute", describing the firm's employment-related training, this was a snoozer. Very basic. No office descriptions. One generic e-mail address. Not a very good effort.						
Cleary Gottlieb	4	4	3	2	3	16
The firm overview begins by telling you this site is for law student and lawyer recruiting. It is highly unusual to limit your Web audience to simply recruiting, and not assist the other major end-user audiences—clients, prospects, referring attorneys, media. The site basically appears to be an on-line version of a print brochure.						

Firm Name	*Design*	*Content*	*Usability*	*Interactivity*	*Intangibles*	*Total*
Cravath Swaine	2	2	2	2	8	16

I often use the term (disparagingly) "brochureware". In this case, that would be too nice. It is a freakin' brochure put on the Web. Okay, so some firms do not need the Web for the same purposes as most professional services businesses. I can just see them sitting around saying, "If they do not know who we are, we do not want to do business with them anyway." Am I right? Are you? HOWEVER, the firm has put together extranets (DealSpaces) for clients, where added-value information is probably posted. And, if you are an alum, there is a special place for you as well. We all use the Web in different ways.

Dinsmore & Shohl	2	5	5	2	2	16

The site looks old-tyme HTML, but it is db-driven. Outside of the tired clip art, the site is set up in a user-friendly fashion with perfect left-hand navigation structure. However, not much beyond basic "expected" overview materials. No searching.

Fowler White	2	5	5	3	1	16

Another site that would be much better-rated and effective, say in 1996. A first-generation site with all the expected accoutrements that many will probably recognize from their firm's original site. Still, the firm has kept it up to date in terms of adding news, publications and seminars with appropriate frequency. There are plenty of fancy, "throw money at it" sites with less meat on the bone.

Pitney Hardin	3	4	4	3	2	16

When displaying a splash page, always have a timer to automatically take you to the home page! I was going to let it go when a link to more information on an upcoming seminar was dead, except I then was interested in a video presentation, which also no longer existed. A few good power point shows were still there. Do you think law students checking out the firm for recruiting realize that associates are nowhere to be found on the site? Just wondering.

Rosenman & Colin	3	4	3	4	2	16

Wake me up when it is 2002. Once an above-average presence that has not kept up with the times. The "Recruiting" and "Pro Bono" sections comprise of a PDF-link. There are some good publications and link resources, as well as an on-line subscription form.

Skadden Arps	3	4	3	3	3	16

This site was a design nightmare, starting with a flash intro page that offered no real substance. The navigation was inconsistent—top, bottom, right...where do I turn? There was the use of frames, pop-up windows and I never knew whether I was going to open up Acrobat when seeking information. The font size and colors made it tough to see where I was going. The "events" section showed nothing current, which I find difficult to believe. Crowded, cluttered and tough to use. The "Opportunities" section was stronger, offering much better use for prospective hires and summer associates. The home page itself offered highlights and headlines, which is good and to be expected. Next time, simpler with stronger content.

Chapman & Cutler	3	3	3	4	2	15

For starters, a very simple site improvement. There are publications from three practices. Be sure to highlight these pubs and provide a link from the appropriate practice area description. The directory is virtually useless, unless I am looking up a phone or e-mail for somebody I already know. The best move is having the practice areas listed on each page of that section. The recruiting area seems to have gotten the most attention. But, why is the Chicago weather on that page? It would take very little to improve the usability on this site dramatically.

Firm Name	Design	Content	Usability	Interactivity	Intangibles	Total
White and Williams	3	3	4	3	2	15

Yet another site that has not caught up with the times. Typical, cookie-cutter categories and display. It has been a bunch of reviews since I said "on-line brochureware". Good bios (although not searchable, and only alphabetical), but beyond that a few publications, a little practice description and some recruiting info. The audience here is going to be limited to people seeking an overview of W&W.

Ross & Hardiess	3	5	3	2	1	14

There is simply no excuse for poor navigation in this day and age. Having the click around to find your way around makes for a clunky experience. The search results did not make things easier. While there was some quality information in areas such as publications and seminars, the overall display was technologically inept. Even the registration forms for seminars needed to be printed and faxed.

Willkie Farr	6	2	3	2	1	14

Not a firm priority or focus. Bare-bones. Short attorney bios, practice area descriptions, a little more detail in recruiting. If you are looking for a thumbnail sketch of the firm, this is it. And, yucky frames! Not a bookmark destination, or of value to clients.

Wyatt Tarrant	3	4	4	2	1	14

The standard law firm Web site, complete with that blasted "column" look. Outside of a few good newsletters in a couple of practices, this is as vanilla as it gets.

Wachtell Lipton	5	1	2	2	2	12

Another brief, fancy overview. Outside of the attorney listings (each a few lines), the whole site is about ten pages. "Our Practice" is a total of seven paragraphs long. I love New York.

Wildman Harrold	1	5	3	2	1	12

Not exactly a next-gen presence. Minimal practice area content. Where there is some material, such as in Recruiting, it is all shoved on one page. The design is 1995. You're in Chicago. Call Hubbard, for goodness sake.

Adams & Reese	2	3	2	3	1	11

Not a stalwart effort. Terrible looking home page. The "News and Events" on the side do not fit with the page. The descriptions for practice areas, recruiting and community service are minimal. Why do I need a "back" and "next" button for the practice area descriptions? My browser and your navigation should provide adequate movement. The bios are alphabetical and never listed by office or practice group. And there is no "search" to help me find whom or what I seek. Try again.

Armstrong Teasdale	1	3	2	2	3	11

Not user-friendly at all, with yucky first-generation frames and design, tough-to-maneuver navigation. Not the type of site you would want to return to. While design and structure does not replace solid credentials, there are limits!

Kramer Levin	3	3	2	2	1	11

Bland and basic. The recruiting section looked like a scanned-in print brochure. No searching. Weak navigation. The site appearance and structure say 1998.

Wilson Elser	2	3	4	1	1	11

Too first-generation! Weak design (wallpaper, scrolling welcome java at bottom, frames...phew!). Only display attorney bios of partners (by name). Publications are not on the site, but must be requested. I sense paranoia.

Firm Name	Design	Content	Usability	Interactivity	Intangibles	Total
Cahill Gordon	4	1	2	1	2	10
"This Website is intended for use by law students considering a career at our firm." A flash opening and a few pages of firm overview, limiting the audience to potential summer associates. Even for this one purpose, you could provide a little more background. Although noting a trip to see "The Producers" on Broadway did grab my attention.						
Paul Hastings	2	2	1	2	2	9
You have to see it to believe it. One of the most painful surfing experiences of the year! At least, you have a choice upon entering of the HTML or Flash versions. Either way, the user experience is awful. What was once a solid informational site is now a bell & whistle, flash-filled, pop-up window, on-line brochure horror show. Yikes.						
Akerman Senterfitt	1	2	2	1	1	7
Horrendous first-generation cookie-cutter. This would be questionable for a solo practice effort. You get points for having a presence, but you've got to give a little more effort. I will assume that you have a new site under construction. Please tell me you do.						
Mendes & Mount	1	2	1	3	0	7
Hey, you are in the Top 250 now. Time for a site upgrade! The splash page is bad. The home page is worse. There were a couple of good newsletters, and an on-line form.						
Lewis Rice	1	2	1	1	1	6
U-G-L-Y. Who picked the wallpaper? And, how about some navigation? It looks like this site was created over the weekend, sometime after a long and successful "happy hour." Back to the drawing board.						
Williams & Connolly	0	0	0	0	1	1
It is 2002. Unbelievable. I'll give you one point for at least having the domain name registered.						
Day Berry	0	0	0	0	0	0
The Web site was down on each day checked. Although, I know that has changed by now. Next year!						

THE NIFTY FIFTY from InternetMarketingAttorney.com

Law Firm Web Site Components that go beyond bios, practice areas, offices and news. Raising the Bar in online business development. Introduced for the first time in January 2001, "Micah's Nifty 50" was used by many law firms and Web developers as a tool to monitor the progress of originality and commitment to successful Web sites in the law firm market. Over the last year, many firms have sent in nominations for this year's edition. It is never too early to nominate firms for 2003!

Last year's Nifty 50 only provided the general URLs for the named firm. Many people asked that I provide the exact link to the nifty component. Please recognize that many of these links may change during the course of the year. If the link proves dead, please visit the site's home page and search for the category. And, if you are counting, there are actually sixty this year. Narrowing down over 100 nominations was too tough a task. The Original Nifty Fifty 2001 are available on InternetMarketingAttorney.com.

Miller Nash
http://www.millernash.com

When the IMA Awards expand beyond the largest 250 firms in the nation, the Miller Nash will rate as one of the best, if not the best law firm Web site in the USA. I could practically do an entire Nifty 50 with this site alone. Start with the ability to personalize the site. Then, chat live with someone at the firm. There is the ability to save, e-mail or print each page. Check out the "Briefcase" and "Jump Start" features under "Utilities". And what you can not see is the client-only extranet area, and the online proposal center. Spend some time here before developing your next site! This is assignment one for any firm in redevelopment!!!

McGuire Woods
http://www.mcguirewoods.com/services/leo/

The "Legal Ethics Opinion Summaries" is another example of establishing a unique database offering content well beyond the basics. Thomas Spahn is one of the nation's leading ethics attorneys and an outstanding presenter.

Siskind Susser
http://www.visalaw.com

The Granddaddy of Law Firm Web Sites continues to grow and improve. The best-known immigration law site on the Web features live chats, excellent online form capabilities and its newsletter is now available on your Palm. The Jeopardy answer to the question, "What law firm best built its practice by wisely using the Internet?"

Perkins Coie
http://www.perkinscoie.com/casedigest/default.cfm

The "Internet Case Digest" offers yet another example of a legal resource that would bring users back to the site, time and again. A "bookmark" for anyone in the industry.

Howrey Simon
http://www.howreybootcamp.com/

Yet, another different approach to the recruiting wars.

Hale and Dorr

http://www.haledorr.com/practices/email_alerts.asp?areaID=17

They take the use of e-mail to a higher plane, with numerous offerings and subscription options. Not enough firms take advantage of this component of Web site development.

Osler Hoskin

http://www.osler.com

This very strong site starts by asking which language you are interested in. French or English? A necessity for Canadian firms.

Jenkens & Gilchrist

http://www.jenkens.com/seminars.htm

The firm offers interactive, on-line seminars, which includes video, power point, and the ability to even ask questions!

Epstein Becker

http://www.ebglaw.com/news_type_7.htm

The "Reporter's Resource" in the firm's strong "Newsstand" is a database of media coverage, complete with links to the practice area and relevant attorney.

Steptoe & Johnson

http://www.steptoe.com/Webdoc.nsf/lawnet-others/Archive

The "Law and the Net" section offers a free subscription to the weekly E-Commerce Law Week, with good content, and a reason for interested parties to visit the site 52 times a year, minimum.

Lord Bissell

http://www.lordbissell.com/events_current.cfm

Another take on a creative events section, with a month by month timeline, and links to additional information for each.

Michael Best

http://www.mbf-law.com/

See that "Archive" button throughout the site. It seems so intuitive, yet so many sites continue to display old, old, old stuff throughout a site, instead of archiving. You do not need to get rid of the content, just archive it! And the home page "Daily Feature" does change daily—something I wondered about when reviewing the site for the IMA Reviews.

Jackson Lewis

http://www.jacksonlewis.com/about/

"Bookmark This Page" offers the ability to quickly add to your Favorites. There is certainly no harm in asking, and getting added to the bookmark list is always an accomplishment for any site.

Stoel Rives

http://www.stoel.com/edefault.shtm

At the bottom of the home page, "We Support" shows examples of both pro bono work and firm sponsorships, complete with logos and appropriate links. Yet another good way to cross-reference.

Davis Wright

http://www.dwt.com/books.htm

This IMA award-winning site offers a "Bookstore" for purchasing firm materials, such as publications and CD-ROMS. And, YES, you can buy right there, using Visa or Mastercard!

Thompson Hine

http://www.thompsonhine.com/firm/clients.asp

I never get tired of seeing representative clients, with that link off to the client Web site. I'm still amazed that more firms have not used this component properly. Another nifty hurrah to the "Resources" section of the site. Good organization with good searching.

Milberg Weiss

http://www.milberg.com/frames_contact.html

Good use of online forms, for reporting fraud, joining a class action or simply requesting more info. Just keepin' it interactive.

Long Aldridge

http://www.lanlaw.com/ourPeople/alumniMap.cfm

The Alumni Map. Not as in alumni of the firm, but law school alums. Click on the flash map of the USA, pick a state, then pick a law school, to see the bios of firm attorneys. One strange thing I found was that it is listed under "Our People", but not also listed under "Your Career", where it is equally appropriate.

Hughes Luce

http://www.cafepress.com/cp/store/store.aspx?storeid=commerceby

Talk about eCommerce. The firm's outstanding www.commercebynet.com site links over to a store for buying branded firm clothing and paraphernalia. Likewise, the www.lawyerware.com site offers all kinds of products for purchase.

Flowers Law Firm

http://www.flowerslawfirm.com

"A different kind of firm" is what it says at the top of the home page. Is there another law firm that offers "Daily Sex News"? I don't think so! A place that combines some of our favorite things—lawyering, sex and the Internet—beat that!!!

Robinson & Cole

http://www.rc.com/BioSELLAY.htm#

I just picked William's bio as an example, but each attorney profile offers a print version, but the nifty piece is the "contact card" use of the vCard electronic business cards, which can be downloaded onto the visitor's computer (with permission, of course).

Bradley Arant

http://legalspan.com/barw/

Another excellent use of outsourcing a piece of technology to improve the firm's Web site offerings. Similar to online CLE offerings, a visitor can register and watch a presentation at no charge. The catalog of offerings is broken down by practice category.

Pennie & Edmonds

http://www.pennie.com/index.ihtml

A slightly different touch to the attorney listings on the home page. The quick-finder offers a drop-down box of attorneys, with the option of viewing the bio, or going straight to sending him or her e-mail. Helpful to someone who knows the firm and the attorney, but is unsure of the e-mail address for the individual.

Taft Stettinius

http://www.taftlaw.com/news/alumninews.html#o

Taft is one of many sites to now offer alumni sections. This is one of the stronger approaches, allowing people to contact former firm members, with a directory that not only includes e-mail and phone numbers, but gives the alum a chance to say a few words.

Brown Rudnick

http://www.brownrudnick.com/html/inhouse.htm

*A double-dose of niftiness to Brown Rudnick. One of the few firms to dedicate a section to in-house counsel...only one of the most important audiences for a corporate law firm to be concerned about! Duh. Many should take a lesson here. Also, the public interest, **www.brownrudnickcenter.com**, is a pro bono masterpiece.*

Thacher Proffitt

http://www.thacherproffitt.com/

Excuses, excuses. There is too much going on at law firms to worry about the Web site. Yet, sometimes harsh realities of life remind us what an important element of business and society it is today. On September 11th, I thought about TPW. The building was gone, but the site was still up and running. It would become a key information source for family, friends, clients and interested observers.

Jones Walker

http://www.joneswalker.com/news/ezine.asp

Publications like USA Today started it, with cable and the Web making it more so. Keep it short and sweet. The E*Zine Center offers subscriptions to many practice area tip sheets—short, informal, breaking news. This is a site with a wealth of valuable content.

Butzel Long

http://www.butzel.com/resource/rescoll.htm

If you've got kids, you will want to spend some time in the Butzel resource section on College Savings Plans. Articles, summaries and helpful links make this an added-value resource for all types of end-users. This is a section that can hit home for many, and endear a firm to a client, or create a bond with a prospect. I hope the firm has marketed this well.

Lowenstein Sandler

http://www.insurance-lowenstein.com/home.html

The "Insurance Outpost" specialty site offers a unique view of the insurance law practice, on the Web. Once again, it makes it clear to visitors that this is truly an area of firm focus.

Brobeck

http://www.brobeck.com/news_events/ads.asp

Not many firms run television ads, but if you do, make sure they also run on your Web site. Some people have knocked their aggressive, entrepreneurial style. I say, keep it up.

Mayer Brown

http://www.mayerbrown.com/

The first thing to do when you get to the home page is see if there is a specialty site for your area of interest. To my knowledge, no other firm has put together the staffing and resources to offer this many different Web sites for one firm. If you've never checked it out, you are really missing something.

Morrison & Foerster

http://www.mofotalkradio.com/

Mofo returns to the Nifty 50 for a second year in a row. Last year, it was the Mofonics garage band. This year, it is talk radio, offering an archive of audio clips on numerous subjects.

Akin Gump

http://www.akingumpcases.com/

Sort of law firm Web site meets A&E or Court TV. Painstaking detail of an Akin Gump case study, featuring video, articles, transcripts and a complete overview of the inner workings of the firm on a matter. This is an extremely impressive effort that deserves much greater play off the Akin Gump main home page. It would be a crime to visit this firm's site and not spend some time here.

Shearman & Sterling

http://www.shearman.com/history/history_index.html

If you are a history buff, Shearman's history exhibit offers a lesson in legal from 1865 through 2000, with a tie-in to the firm and a practice area with each trip through the past. A somewhat hidden gem on the site.

Testa Hurwitz

http://www.tht.com/thtvideo.htm

Ah, the video section. As connectivity increases, the value in such sections does as well. I look at my home connection as an example. In the last three years, I've gone from the phone, at 28 and 56k, to high-speed cable. Only now would I click on a video. Many others are doing the same.

Pepper Hamilton

http://www.pepperlaw.com/practice_areas.htm

Another simple but smart, low-tech interactive device. At the top of each practice area description is an e-mail address for that practice. For example, **antitrust@pepperlaw.com** *or* **sports@pepperlaw.com**. *This just makes it that much easier for an interested party to just zip off a note for more information, rather than send either a generic info@ e-mail or pick an attorney, and hope for the best. These also could be set up to send dual e-mails, one to marketing and one to the practice group, for tracking purposes.*

Womble Carlyle

http://wcsr.yellowbrix.com/pages/wcsr/Headlines.nsp?type=newsbites

A handful of firms go the extra mile in trying to keep people coming back constantly and consistently. With a deal for syndicated content from Yellowbrix, the site offers up to the minute breaking news, as well as industry news for key practice groups.

Covington & Burling

http://www.cov.com/publications/pdfhtml.asp

*Sometimes it is the little things that make a site more user-friendly. **Cov.com** asks if you know the difference between html, pdf and ppt. If not, click over for a little instruction and learning for the tech-impaired (which is the majority).*

Gray Cary

http://www.gcwf.com/journal/index.html

Many firms have debated giving away journals and publications on the Web. Gray Cary's Journal of Internet Law gets it half-way right, by offering a taste of each issue, along with an 800 number for subscribing to the journal. Now, if they really wanted to do it right, you would offer the ability to sign up and pay online, right then and there! After all, it is an internet journal.

Milbank Tweed

http://www.milbank.com/knowledgecenter.html

The flashy, bell and whistle-rich Web site also offers a separate research portal for those interested in a research tool. Flash for the flashy; knowledge for the learned.

Troutman Sanders

http://www.troutmansanders.com/off/dc.asp

*A nice little "touch" that a few firms took advantage of is providing a weather box from **weather.com** as part of each office location. It is free, it is content, it is presently a cool 32 degrees in Washington, DC; 43 degrees in the London, England office.*

McKenna & Cuneo

http://www.mckennaevents.com/

For some firms and sites, the ability to expand upon event promotion, posting and registration makes it easier to create a specialty site simply for events. It can also be more cost-effective, depending on the site and developer.

Palmer & Dodge

http://www.palmerdodge.com/frmFindEvents.cfm

With the conversion of most firms to database-driven Web sites, many such sites have almost become db-cookie-cutter in nature. P&D's cold fusion site offers a little different look, display and search functionality than many.

Fish & Richardson

http://www.fr.com/practice/patent.cfm?child=patent

Sometimes the most powerful stuff on your site is not even at your site at all. Click on the "Search USPTO" button to open a second browser, taking you directly to a list of patents secured by FR for clients. Why reinvent the wheel? And the section really continues to update itself, so long as the firm is concerned.

Crowell Moring

http://www.crowell.com/Template.cfm?Section=Events&template=Calendar/CalendarEventList.cfm

The "events" calendar is just that, a searchable calendar of various firm events. A little better look, and detail than simply providing a scrolling list.

Nelson Mullins

http://www.nelsonmullins.com/locations/default.asp?location=Atlanta&area=atty

Another "simple but powerful" section is "Locations". However, Nelson Mullins makes each office location a mini-site, with everything from food choices to attorney selections.

Finnegan Henderson

http://www.finnegan.com/fr_fed.htm

Looking for recent decisions handed down by the U.S. Court of Appeals for the Federal Circuit? Right here. Updated several times a week by the D.C. based IP firm. For interested parties and clients, a definite bookmark destination. Quality content, added-value, updated often.

Schulte Roth

http://www.srz.com/tour.asp

So many firms are moving locations nowadays. Why not show off your new digs to clients with an interactive tour of the facilities?

Arent Fox

http://www.arentfox.com/quickGuide/discussions/discussions.html

It is not new to the Arent Fox site, but few firms take advantage of the interactivity of moderated discussion forums to promote a practice, or create a reason to come back and interact on an ongoing basis.

Dickstein Shapiro

http://www.legalinnovators.com/Puzzle.asp?Menu=Advertisements

Besides the clever marketing URL of "legal innovators," is the tie-in with the firm's print media campaign offering an array of puzzles, where the Web site

offers the solutions. Excellent tie-in between print and online, with the draw to the firm site.

Winstead Sechrest

http://www.winstead.com/pressroom/mediainfo/mediakit.html
Few firms maximize the use of the Web as a resource for media relations. An interested party can download the Winstead media kit, as well as access a number other of journalist-friendly resources.

Holland & Knight

http://www.hklaw.com/Webcasts.asp
Real Media Web casts available in a number of practice categories.

Bryan Cave

http://www.bryancave.com/join/trivia.asp
Not quite as much fun as an arcade, but "Cave Trivia" does offer an interactive Q&A on the firm history and fun facts.

Baker Botts

http://www.bakerbotts.com/careers/student/break.asp
The "Break Zone" in the "Student Center" offers up on-line arcade games. For me, Yahtzee was the game of choice.

Cooley Godward

http://www.cooley.com/practice_and_people.ixe?section=Client+Profile
The "Client Profile", promoted on the home page, offers a chance to not only show off clients with a detailed accounting, but provide the client with some nice, complimentary pub from its' law firm.

Rene Larson

http://www.renelarson.com
Another one of my historical favorites, Rene's site continues to grow and improve. Click on the Web Cam, and see how the weather is in Thunder Bay, Ontario.

O'Melveny & Myers

http://www.omelveny.com/Webcode/navigate.asp?nodehandle=519
Many sites offer a keyword search (which really is a must today), but often the search results are jumbled and difficult to make good use of. Not the case with OMM, where the results are broken down by category, and include details such as whether it is in a pdf or an html format.

Hunton & Williams

http://www.hunton.com/cwrhunton/index.htm

A number of firms have developed home-grown extranet programs for clients and prospects. If you are a client, log-in; if interested, see the demo.

Kirkland & Ellis

http://www.kirkland.com/client/client.asp

You have to look for it, but Kirkland offers the chance to participate in on-line opinion polls throughout their site (from www.opinionlab.com). This interactive approach to finding out what the end-user likes and dislikes helps the firm spend (time and money) effectively in further on-line development.

Greenberg Traurig

http://www.gtamericas.com/

"One point of contact for the Americas" is the mantra of this specialty site. A powerful presence that puts the "world wide" into the World Wide Web.

About the Internet Marketing Attorney

In 2002, Micah Buchdahl founded HTMLawyers, Inc. (High-Tech Marketing for Lawyers), an independent, full-service marketing consulting business for attorneys, law firms and companies doing business in the legal industry. Micah can be reached through the company Web site, at **www.HTMLawyers.com** or e-mail **micah@HTMLawyers.com**.

Index

 THE SECTION OF
LAW PRACTICE
MANAGEMENT

CUSTOMER COMMENT FORM

Title of Book:_____

We've tried to make this publication as useful, accurate, and readable as possible. Please take 5 minutes to tell us if we succeeded. Your comments and suggestions will help us improve our publications. Thank you!

1. How did you acquire this publication:

☐ by mail order ☐ at a meeting/convention ☐ as a gift

☐ by phone order ☐ at a bookstore ☐ don't know

☐ other: (describe) _____
_____

Please rate this publication as follows:

	Excellent	Good	Fair	Poor	Not Applicable
Readability: Was the book easy to read and understand?	☐	☐	☐	☐	☐
Examples/Cases: Were they helpful, practical? Were there enough?	☐	☐	☐	☐	☐
Content: Did the book meet your expectations? Did it cover the subject adequately?	☐	☐	☐	☐	☐
Organization and clarity: Was the sequence of text logical? Was it easy to find what you wanted to know?	☐	☐	☐	☐	☐
Illustrations/forms/checklists: Were they clear and useful? Were there enough?	☐	☐	☐	☐	☐
Physical attractiveness: What did you think of the appearance of the publication (typesetting, printing, etc.)?	☐	☐	☐	☐	☐

Would you recommend this book to another attorney/administrator? ☐ Yes ☐ No

How could this publication be improved? What else would you like to see in it?

_____
_____
_____
_____

Do you have other comments or suggestions? _____
_____
_____

Name _____

Firm/Company _____

Address _____

City/State/Zip _____

Phone _____

Firm Size: _____ Area of specialization: _____

We appreciate your time and help.

Fold

NO POSTAGE
NECESSARY
IF MAILED
IN THE
UNITED STATES

BUSINESS REPLY MAIL
FIRST CLASS   PERMIT NO. 16471   CHICAGO, ILLINOIS

POSTAGE WILL BE PAID BY ADDRESSEE

AMERICAN BAR ASSOCIATION
PPM, 8th FLOOR
750 N. LAKE SHORE DRIVE
CHICAGO, ILLINOIS 60611–9851

Fold here first

Membership Application

Access to all these information resources and discounts – for just $3.33 a month!

Membership dues are just $40 a year – just $3.33 a month.
You probably spend more on your general business magazines and newspapers.
But they can't help you succeed in building and managing your practice
like a membership in the ABA Law Practice Management Section.
Make a small investment in success. Join today!

☑ **Yes!** **I want to join the ABA Section of Law Practice Management Section** and gain access to information helping me add more clients, retain and expand business with current clients, and run my law practice more efficiently and competitively!

Check the dues that apply to you:

❏ $40 for ABA members   ❏ $5 for ABA Law Student Division members

Choose your method of payment:

❏ Check enclosed (make payable to American Bar Association)
❏ Bill me
❏ Charge to my: ❏ VISA®   ❏ MASTERCARD®   ❏ AMEX®

Card No.: _____   Exp. Date: _____

Signature: _____   Date: _____

ABA I.D.*: _____
(∗ *Please note: Membership in ABA is a prerequisite to enroll in ABA Sections.*)

Name: _____

Firm/Organization: _____

Address: _____

City/State/ZIP: _____

Telephone No.: _____   Fax No.: _____

Primary Email Address: _____

Save time by Faxing or Phoning!

Get Ahead. 🏃

/BA Law Practice Management Section
AMERICAN BAR ASSOCIATION

750 N. LAKE SHORE DRIVE
CHICAGO, IL 60611
PHONE: (312) 988-5619
FAX: (312) 988-5820
Email: lpm@abanet.org

▶ Fax your application to: (312) 988-5820
▶ Join by phone if using a credit card: (800) 285-2221 (ABA1)
▶ Email us for more information at: lpm@abanet.org
▶ Check us out on the Internet: http://www.abanet.org/lpm

I understand that Section dues include a $24 basic subscription to Law Practice Management; this subscription charge is not deductible from the dues and additional subscriptions are not available at this rate. Membership dues in the American Bar Association are not deductible as charitable contributions for income tax purposes. However, such dues may be deductible as a business expense.